INTEGRITY AND CONSCIENCE

NOMOS

XL

NOMOS

Harvard University Press
I   *Authority* 1958, reissued in 1982 by Greenwood Press

The Liberal Arts Press
II   *Community* 1959
III   *Responsibility* 1960

Atherton Press
IV   *Liberty* 1962
V   *The Public Interest* 1962
VI   *Justice* 1963, reissued in 1974
VII   *Rational Decision* 1964
VIII   *Revolution* 1966
IX   *Equality* 1967
X   *Representation* 1968
XI   *Voluntary Associations* 1969
XII   *Political and Legal Obligation* 1970
XIII   *Privacy* 1971

Aldine-Atherton Press
XIV   *Coercion* 1972

Lieber-Atherton Press
XV   *The Limits of Law* 1974
XVI   *Participation in Politics* 1975

New York University Press
XVII   *Human Nature in Politics* 1977
XVIII   *Due Process* 1977
XIX   *Anarchism* 1978
XX   *Constitutionalism* 1979
XXI   *Compromise in Ethics, Law, and Politics* 1979
XXII   *Property* 1980
XXIII   *Human Rights* 1981
XXIV   *Ethics, Economics, and the Law* 1982
XXV   *Liberal Democracy* 1983
XXVI   *Marxism* 1983

NOMOS XL

Yearbook of the American Society for Political and Legal Philosophy

INTEGRITY AND CONSCIENCE

Edited by

Ian Shapiro, *Yale University*
and
Robert Adams, *Yale University*

NEW YORK UNIVERSITY PRESS • *New York and London*

NEW YORK UNIVERSITY PRESS
New York and London

© 1998 by New York University

Library of Congress Cataloging-in-Publication Data
Integrity and conscience / edited by Ian Shapiro and Robert Adams.
p.   cm. — (Nomos ; 40)
Includes bibliographical references and index.
ISBN 0-8147-8097-0 (alk. paper)
1. Integrity. 2. Conscience. I. Shapiro, Ian. II. Adams,
Robert Merrihew. III. Series.
BJ1533.I58I58   1998
170—dc21   97-33867
                    CIP

New York University Press books are printed on acid-free paper,
and their binding materials are chosen for strength and durability.

Manufactured in the United States of America

10 9 8 7 6 5 4 3 2 1

CONTENTS

PREFACE

Many of the chapters in this volume began life at the annual meeting of the American Society for Political and Legal Philosophy, held in conjunction with the Eastern Division of the American Philosophical Association in New York City, in December 1995. The society's membership selected the topic "Integrity and Conscience" by ballot, and I count myself fortunate to have persuaded my colleague Robert Adams to serve as the program chair and associate editor. His choices, suggestions, and assistance were greatly appreciated in putting together both the program and the book.

As usual, great gratitude is due to the NOMOS production team. Our managing editor, Kathryn McDermott, and the New York University Press team, Niko Pfund and Despina Papazoglou Gimbel, worked with characteristic efficacy in guiding the book into print. Thanking them has become a ritual, even though their work is anything but routine. Every volume presents varying demands, and I am continually impressed by the quiet creativity with which they are met. I must also thank our authors for keeping to a demanding schedule while responding, with admirable doses of good humor, to editorial suggestions that may not always have been entirely welcome.

With this fortieth volume of NOMOS, the society has reached middle age. It therefore is a propitious time to take appreciative note of the multiple contributions from the officers, editors, publishers, members, and—of course—authors that have made the Society the unique institution that it has become over the past four decades. Middle age is also a good time to think about renewal. The next volume of NOMOS, entitled *Global Justice,* will be my last as editor before passing the baton to Stephen Macedo of Syracuse University. We will edit *Designing Democratic Institutions* together, after which Macedo will work with the program chairs in conformity with recent practice.

Ken Winston is also stepping down as secretary-treasurer, and Judith Wagner DeCew of Clark University has been persuaded to take his place. Thanks are due to Ken for his service and Judy in anticipation of hers. It has been gratifying for me to play a role in this ongoing collaboration among the dead, the living, and those who are yet to be born. We leave the society, along with its annual volume, in excellent new hands. I look forward to the results in the years ahead.

I.S.   December 1997

CONTRIBUTORS

DAVID DYZENHAUS
Law and Philosophy, University of Toronto

MARK A. GRABER
Government and Politics, University of Maryland

KENT GREENAWALT
Law, Columbia University

THOMAS E. HILL JR.
Philosophy, University of North Carolina, Chapel Hill

KAREN JONES
Philosophy, Cornell University

JOHN KANE
Politics and Public Policy, Griffith University

GEORGE KATEB
Politics, Princeton University

ELIZABETH KISS
Kenan Ethics Program, Duke University

MICHAEL W. MCCONNELL
Law, University of Utah

ROGERS M. SMITH
Political Science, Yale University

NOMI MAYA STOLZENBERG
Law, University of Southern California

CATHARINE PIERCE WELLS
Law, Boston College

KENNETH I. WINSTON
Philosophy, Wheaton College and Kennedy School of Government, Harvard University

1

INTRODUCTION

IAN SHAPIRO AND ROBERT ADAMS

It is difficult to think of someone believing that he is acting with integrity yet disobeying the dictates of his conscience. By the same token, one is hard-pressed to imagine a person feeling compelled to ignore her sense of what integrity requires to remain faithful to her conscience. Even though these observations might appear to suggest that integrity and conscience are closely related ideas, perhaps even different aspects of a single idea, the chapters in this book support a rather different and more complicated generalization. Acting with integrity and obeying one's conscience might be mutually reinforcing in some settings, but in others they can manifest varying degrees of mutual tension.

Conscience is intensely, perhaps inherently, personal, and in some contexts, so is what we mean by "integrity." But integrity also has a more public meaning when it is identified with professional, political, and legal codes. Professional integrity, public integrity, and integrity in the law are at least partly interpersonal standards that can coexist more or less felicitously with a person's sense of what conscience requires. This is not to deny that conscience often, perhaps typically, exhibits an other-regarding dimension. When we describe someone who lacks a conscience as a sociopath, we invoke this dimension implicitly. But the conscience seems necessarily linked to a person's experienced sense of right and wrong in ways that do not always accompany public integrity. This difference, among others, creates the possibility of conflict

1

between integrity and conscience. It prompts the sustained examination of these two ideas, and of the relations between them, that is undertaken here.

We have divided the chapters in this book into three parts. The first is principally concerned with conceptual issues. In it, Thomas Hill, Nomi Stolzenberg, Elizabeth Kiss, and George Kateb explore various understandings of integrity and conscience in light of different readings of ruminations about them advanced by Plato, Hume, Kant, and others. In part II, John Kane, Karen Jones, and Kenneth Winston look at integrity and conscience in the realms of professionalism and professional ethics, with particular attention to the conduct of science and proprietary access to public officials. The focus in part III is on integrity and conscience in the law, in which David Dyzenhaus, Rogers Smith, Kent Greenawalt, Catherine Wells, Michael McConnell, and Mark Graber consider different dimensions of the complex relationship between the law and personal morality. Some see the tensions between the two as both profound and inescapable; others examine ways in which they may be mutually constraining. All are ultimately concerned with how the law's legitimacy is linked to conscientious appraisals of the system's operation by litigants, lawyers, judges, and legal commentators.

I. CONCEPTUAL ISSUES

In chapter 2, Hill explores four different understandings of the general idea of conscience: a popular religious conception, a deflationary social relativist idea, Joseph Butler's teleological account, and Immanuel Kant's metaphorical view of conscience as an "inner judge." Hill examines and compares these different accounts of the importance of conscience in ethics and of the circumstances in which conscience should be respected. He looks at the Kantian conception in greater depth, with particular attention to the ways in which this conception differs from the others and why Kant gave conscience so limited a role in his ethics.

In chapter 3, Stolzenberg takes issue with Hill's delineation of four differing conceptions of conscience. She disagrees with his contention that each represents a different view of conscience, arguing instead that each of the four conceptions offers a different perspective on the same subject. In her account, it is the perspective that differs from conception to conception, not the object of understanding—the faculty of the conscience—itself. Features that Hill attributes to the so-called relativist conception of conscience—such as awareness of the subjectivity, cultural variability, and potential fallibility of conscientious judgment—are also present in the other three conceptions, not least the Kantian one that he favors.

In chapter 4, Kiss focuses on what Hill concedes are troubling aspects of Kant's austere view of the conscience. Taking issue with the moral psychology that she discerns behind the Kantian view, Kiss advances in its stead the claim that conscience is first and foremost the emotional capacity to empathize with others. Alluding to the arguments of Hume, Adam Smith, and such contemporary philosophers as Annette Baier and Lawrence Blum, Kiss argues that when we detect a failure of conscience, the problem is not a lack of self-scrutiny in Kant's sense. Rather, it is a cramped or shattered capacity for emotional identification with others. Although this alternative understanding of the voice of conscience need not contradict the claims of a Kantian ethics, it does suggest a distinct understanding of the moral life in which affect plays a comparatively larger role. According to Kiss, Hill's critique of "deflationary" understandings of the conscience discounts too much the resources they can offer for moral self-scrutiny.

In chapter 5, Kateb shifts from conscience to integrity, drawing inspiration from readings of Plato's *Apology* and *Crito*. For Kateb, Socrates personified integrity in both public and personal realms. Socratic moral integrity involves an attitude of self-sacrifice, among whose constituent parts are relentless questioning, unwillingness to be an instrument of injustice, and what might be described as a nonretaliatory stance toward the world. Kateb makes the case that Socratic integrity involves shunning positive conclusions or ideals and instead consists of negatives such as abstention, dissent, noncompliance, and dissatisfaction. There is one positive, however: a compound of affection and compassion for others. Without devotion to this, Kateb argues, Socratic integrity could not exist. For Kateb, supporting integrity involves promoting fidelity to this outlook.

II. INTEGRITY, CONSCIENCE, AND PROFESSIONALISM

Kane takes a more minimal view of integrity in chapter 6 when describing its place in science. The integrity demanded of practitioners by science's professional ethic is an instrumental matter tied to the conditions required to generate reliable knowledge claims. By contrast, Kane argues, the most important matters of conscience that arise in science concern its products: the knowledge it produces and the uses, good and bad, to which this knowledge may be put. The two issues can be related, however, via the question of trust. Scientific integrity concerns scientists' trust in one another and the public's trust in apparently authoritative scientific opinion, as well as the mistrust of lay interference and a faltering of public trust in science's freedom to pursue whatever knowledge it chooses. Kane looks at both what the public might learn from a greater understanding of scientific practice and what science as an enterprise might gain from inviting increased public appraisal of its processes and products. With respect to the public, Kane argues that it is beneficial for the pronouncements of scientific experts to be met with less deference and a better-informed public skepticism. With respect to science, a better-informed appraisal by outsiders should enhance the wide public trust on which the scientific project depends.

Jones takes issue with this argument in chapter 7. Given the need for a cognitive division of labor, she contends that we must often trust experts and defer to their cognitive authority. The real question, in her view, is how to be responsible in our deference to experts. Drawing on a discussion of the concept of autonomy in moral and political contexts, she maintains that when properly understood, cognitive autonomy is compatible with such deference, provided that the experts meet certain burdens of persuasion. In most instances, Jones believes, we should approach expert opinion from a default position of distrust. This consists of a rebuttable presumption against accepting expert opinion, about which it is wise to be especially vigilant in four circumstances: when the stakes are high, when we have a past history of too ready a trust, when science as an institution fails to create a confluence of motives for trustworthiness, and when the subject matter of the testimony invites ideological distortion. In such circumstances, defeating the presumption against acceptance should follow a thorough investigation into the trustworthiness of the alleged expert. Deference to experts, whether arrived at following the rebuttal of default distrust or from a default position of trust or neutrality (when the burden-shifting circumstances are absent) can be compatible with cognitive autonomy, provided that we refrain from seeing autonomy as requiring independence. Jones encourages us thus to refrain and instead to understand autonomy as involving a reflective endorsement of our cognitive dependencies.

In chapter 8, Winston takes up the issue of whether violations of professional integrity might in certain circumstances be justifiable. He does this by using an actual instance of moral opportunism, which leads to an exploration of principled reasons that might be adduced in its defense. Winston's case concerns a lawyer in the solicitor general's office who was able to exploit his access to a Supreme Court justice so as to have a decisive influence on the decision in *Brown v. Board of Education*. Following a description of the solicitor general's office and its operative norms, Winston examines the decisive interactions between the lawyer and the justice, and the lawyer's willful violation of the norm known as the ex parte rule. By investigating the considerations that should figure in any moral assessment of the violation, Winston reveals the issue to be considerably more complex than our unexamined intuitions might lead us to suppose.

III. Integrity and Conscience in the Law

At least since Ronald Dworkin singled out integrity as the sine qua non of a principled jurisprudence in *Law's Empire*,[1] integrity's role in legitimating a legal order has been extensively debated. Attended to less is the role of conscience. Dyzenhaus argues in chapter 9 that in a secular and pluralistic age, the scope for exercising conscience in legal interpretation is essential to the law's legitimacy. Dyzenhaus distinguishes liberal perspectives on this matter—which tend to focus on the conscience of judges— from a democratic one that he advocates, in which the emphasis is on the conscience of the citizen. Drawing on Jürgen Habermas's arguments against positivism and in support of democracy, Dyzen-

haus makes the case that the Habermasian institutional account
can be detached from its contentious philosophical moorings and
usefully modified in the service of a democratic account of law's
legitimacy.

Whereas Dyzenhaus is skeptical of trusting the law's indeterminacies to the moralities of individual judges, Rogers Smith goes
further and indicts U.S. lawyers and especially legal commentators
for their propensity to attempt forced marriages between the
U.S. Constitution's meaning and the results they seek to achieve
through its application. In chapter 10, Smith contends that this
promotes a state of affairs in which constitutional arguments become unnecessarily deceptive and confusing. Too often, interpreters feel impelled to argue simultaneously that their preferred
outcomes reflect the original intent of the Constitution's framers
and that they constitute the best overall outcome. Almost inevitably, he argues, this interpretation creates pressure to conflate what
is constitutional with what is good. Smith identifies the sources
and costs of sitting judges' failure to distinguish constitutionality
from beneficiality, and he illustrates how contemporary scholars
themselves have evaded the distinction between the good and the
constitutional. Smith also puts forward the majority opinion in
Brown v. Board of Education—specifically, the claim that racially
"separate but equal" schools are inherently unconstitutional—as
an example of a ruling that produced good results despite resting
on what is at best an exceedingly shaky constitutional foundation.
In Smith's view, because constitutionalism is an instrument of,
rather than a synonym for, good government, he contends that
decisions that conflict with the original intent behind the Constitution (and so undermine some of the goods that constitutionalism promotes) may nonetheless produce the best result. Given
this fact and the overwhelming public support for the substance
of the *Brown* decision, Smith concludes that scholars will not be
able to describe accurately the function of the judiciary until they
acknowledge that jurists serve not merely as arbiters of original
intent but also as executors of Locke's "prerogative power."

In chapter 11, in response to this argument, Greenawalt contends that although Smith's basic distinction between constitutionality and goodness is sound, his reduction of the criteria
for constitutional rulings to a single dichotomy is misleading.

Greenawalt supplements Smith's account with observations concerning the relationship between truth and scholarship, the stages at which constitutionality may conflict with goodness, the diminished value of constitutionality under consequentialist (as distinct from deontological) value systems, and the pervasiveness of problems of self-consciousness and candor in the American legal system. He observes that Smith adopts, without defense, a narrow standard for original intent that excludes the framers' own view of the principles underlying the constitutional provisions. Greenawalt also chastises Smith for his misstatement of the role of accumulated case law in constitutional discourse. Smith, he notes, appears to suggest that when judges adhere to precedent, they are basing their ruling on a consideration of the best outcome rather than the constitutional soundness of a given position. But since Smith believes that continuity is one of the chief virtues of constitutionality, then adherence to precedent must be an indispensable component of any inquiry into the constitutionality of a measure (if constitutionalism is to produce the benefits that Smith associates with it). Greenawalt concludes that although valuable, the dichotomy between goodness and constitutionality is an insufficient guide to the broad range of factors that influence judges and scholars.

In chapter 12, Wells offers a different critique of Smith's emphasis on a sharp distinction between goodness and constitutionality, by advancing three related claims. First, she points out that an insistence on a strict distinction between goodness and constitutionality is subject to many of the same objections that can be advanced against the version of originalism that Smith endorses. Second, she argues that Smith's distinction is overly simple in that it obscures an important aspect of constitutional decision making. Third, she contends that Smith's argument about integrity is circular. That is, on one hand, Smith argues that we should distinguish goodness from constitutionality on the grounds it promotes judicial integrity. On the other hand, he employs a notion of judicial integrity that takes for granted a particular theory about what judges should do when deciding constitutional cases. As a consequence, Wells concludes that Smith's notion of judicial integrity presupposes a particular jurisprudence and that it cannot be used as a separate endorsement of this same conclusion.

In chapter 13, Michael McConnell argues that Smith is mistaken in attempting to trace deceptiveness in constitutional discourse to the mixture of positive and normative arguments. In McConnell's view, the problem is, instead, the enduring lack of agreement across ideological lines concerning the norms of legitimacy for constitutional interpretation. The result is an asymmetrical, and therefore unstable, system in which one side is constrained by what Smith describes as "constitutionality" and the other is not. This state of affairs is fueled, in McConnell's view, by the myth that Smith perpetuates: that *Brown v. Board of Education* is historically insupportable. McConnell thinks that it is time to reconsider this myth and that even in this instance, goodness can be reconciled with constitutionality.

In the last chapter, from a different perspective, Graber takes up the significance—for constitutional interpretation—of pervasive disagreements about good and evil. He argues that recent explorations of the gap between constitutionality and the requirements of morality often fail to appreciate the profundity of moral disagreements. Through either the examples they choose (slavery or Jim Crow segregation) or their reference to "stupidities," modern constitutional critics too often assume that intelligent people agree on just what these contemporary constitutional imperfections are. In practice, however, alleged constitutional stupidities or evils exist only when a substantial part of the population regards these practices as wise or good. Given the disagreements that exist in any heterogeneous society on what policies are deemed desirable, Graber contends that a constitutional union can be maintained only if most citizens are sometimes willing to sacrifice both integrity and conscience to accommodate persons whose vision of the best society is different from theirs. Constitutional commentators and citizens would do better to recognize this state of affairs more often than they now do. One way to advance toward this goal would be to conceptualize and respond to possible gaps between constitutional law and political morality by exploring examples that highlight the mediating role of constitutions and constitutional adjudication in societies that lack consensus on broad political principles. Although to some people this "institutional" solution may seem like an unsatisfying abdication of jurisprudential aspiration, Graber is surely persuasive that more ambitious ventures have not been, to date, fully successful.

NOTES

1. Ronald Dworkin. *Law's Empire* (Cambridge, Mass.: Harvard University Press, 1986).

PART I

CONCEPTUAL ISSUES

2

FOUR CONCEPTIONS
OF CONSCIENCE

THOMAS E. HILL JR.

Controversies about the nature, reliability, and importance of conscience have a long history. Diverse opinions reflect not only differences in theological beliefs and political context but also deep divisions in moral theory. Some scholars hold that relying on conscience is a sure path to morally correct, or at least blameless, conduct and that the imperative to follow one's conscience is unconditional, taking precedence over all other authorities. Making moral decisions conscientiously and sticking by them are widely thought to be essential ingredients of integrity, and some would add that they also affirm one's autonomy and individuality.

This sanguine view of individual conscience has not been shared by all, however. Many traditional moralists place more confidence in church and state authority than in private conscience, arguing that those authorities have better access to moral truth or that, practically, giving precedence to individual conscience is a recipe for anarchy. Observing that those people who rely on conscience often approve of radically different practices, including some that may seem outrageous, many reflective people understandably come to doubt that conscience is each individual's unerring access to moral truth. Recalling how often cruel and destructive conduct has been excused in the name of conscience, they naturally question as well even the more modest doctrine that following one's conscience guarantees a *blameless* life.

These controversies provide the background for my discussion, although I shall not address them directly. My more modest aim is to highlight, as a preliminary aid to understanding the larger issues, some of the similarities and differences among four important conceptions of conscience. In particular, I want to call attention to the various ways in which these conceptions interpret the origin, function, and reliability of conscience. How one conceives conscience makes a significant difference regarding one's attitude toward one's own conscience and the (alleged) conscientious judgments of others. So, in contrasting the four conceptions of conscience, I also call attention to the implications of each conception regarding whether and (if so) why one should respect conscience in oneself and in others. More specifically, for each conception, I address the following question: If one conceives conscience in this way, and confidently so, then to what extent and why should one (1) treat the apparent promptings of one's own conscience as one's authoritative guide and (2) respectfully tolerate the conduct of others when they are apparently guided by conscience?[1]

Here I differentiate between various particular "conceptions" of conscience and a general "concept" of conscience in a way analogous to John Rawls's distinction between the general concept of justice and various particular conceptions of justice.[2] That is, the several *conceptions* of conscience are specific interpretations, or more detailed understandings, of a general *concept,* or core idea, of conscience. The core idea that they have in common is, roughly, the idea of a capacity, commonly attributed to most human beings, to sense or immediately discern that what he or she has done, is doing, or is about to do (or not do) is wrong, bad, and worthy of disapproval.[3] Moreover, the general concept, I assume, includes the idea that a person's conscience, whatever else it may be, is something that apparently influences (but rarely, if ever, completely controls) that person's conduct. It also is something that, when disregarded, tends to result in mental discomfort and lowered self-esteem.

This general idea leaves open further questions about how conscience is acquired and developed, how it operates, what it purports to "say," how trustworthy it is as a moral guide, whether it is universal or found only in certain cultures, what purposes it serves individuals and society, and even whether saying "her conscience tells her to" is a purely descriptive statement or one that also expresses the speaker's attitudes or moral beliefs. These particular conceptions of conscience are the various ways in which questions such as these are addressed in moral theories, in systems of theology, and also in less articulated, popular ways of thinking that extend (and sometimes distort) religious and scientific ideas prevalent in a culture.

Although it will become evident where my sympathies lie, it is not my aim to argue that one or another of these conceptions is correct or even—all things considered—superior to the others. I do not pretend to be neutral regarding the merits of the various conceptions under discussion, but my primary purpose here is merely to sketch the different conceptions, note significant variations, and draw out some of their practical implications.

Besides this, I have another aim that leads me to make some more explicitly evaluative remarks. The context is my ongoing project to develop a moral theory in the Kantian tradition that is as plausible as possible. This gives me a reason to examine and call attention to the merits and weaknesses of various conceptions of conscience from this perspective. The point is to consider how a reasonable, modified Kantian ethics should interpret conscience and why it should reject other interpretations.[4] Although Kant's own account of conscience is one of the four conceptions to be considered, it is not necessarily the best conception, even for my purposes, simply because Kant proposed it. The reason is that developing a plausible "Kantian" moral theory requires selectively endorsing some of Kant's claims and rejecting others, according to one's best judgment as to what is both sustainable and most fundamental to the theory. Since a full exposition and defense of such a theory is obviously impossible here, my evaluative remarks should be understood for now as tentative and hypothetical, suggesting reasons that if one adopts certain basic features of a Kantian ethics, it is preferable to interpret conscience in a certain way and not in others.

The four conceptions of conscience, briefly described, are the following: first, a popular religious view that bases a strong confidence in an instinctual conscience on theological beliefs about its origin and purpose; second, a deflationary cultural relativism that regards conscience as nothing but an unreflective response to the socially instilled values of one's culture, no matter what these happen to be; third, Joseph Butler's idea of conscience as reason, making moral judgments by reflecting "in a cool hour" on what conduct is morally appropriate, given human nature and the facts of one's situation; and fourth, Kant's narrower, metaphorical conception of conscience as "an inner judge" that condemns (or acquits) one for inadequate (or adequate) effort to live according to one's best possible, though fallible, judgments about what (objectively) one ought to do.[5]

My comments on the relations of the first three conceptions are too diverse to summarize briefly, but my main suggestions regarding the Kantian perspective are the following: First, Kant's conception of conscience makes room for some central ideas in each of the other conceptions while avoiding aspects of them that, at least from the basic Kantian perspective, are problematic. Furthermore, Kant's own account of conscience does fit coherently with the basic features of his moral theory, even though it might seem at first that "conscience" should have no place in rationalistic moral theories such as Kant's.

In the Kantian view, we must treat basic moral beliefs as known, or to be determined, through *reason.*[6] When we deliberately try to apply general principles to particular kinds of problems, we use *judgment,* and whether we act on our moral beliefs depends on the strength and goodness of our *wills. Conscience,* however, is not the same as reason, judgment, or will. In fact, Kant assigns conscience a limited role in his moral theory. It is not a moral expert with an intuition of moral truth or a moral legislator that makes moral laws or a moral arbitrator that settles perplexing cases. Rather, the role of conscience is restricted to that of an "inner judge" who scrutinizes our conduct and then imposes sentence on us as guilty or else acquits us of either of two charges: (1) that we contravened our own (reason-based) judgment about what is morally right or (2) that we failed to exercise due care and diligence in forming the particular moral opinions on which we acted. Presupposing rather than providing our basic understanding of morality, conscience brings into focus a sometimes painful awareness, not that our action is "objectively" wrong but that we are not even making a proper effort to guide ourselves by our own deepest moral beliefs.

For general moral guidance, especially in perplexing cases, Kant agrees with Butler that we should not rely on instinct but on reason in deliberate reflection. Kant granted that conscience (narrowly construed) should be considered authoritative within its limited sphere, but he also believed a further point that others (such as Butler) might describe as "respecting the authority of conscience" because they work with a broader conception of conscience. That is, Kant's moral theory holds that each of us must, in the end, treat our own (final) moral judgments as authoritative, even though they are fallible. When others disagree, we must listen to them and take into account their reasons; and when civil authorities demand conformity, we must give due regard to the moral reasons for obeying such authorities. Having taken all this into account, however, each of us must carefully make and rigorously follow our own best moral judgment.[7] To do so, in Kant's view, enables us to live with a clear conscience, but it does not guarantee that our acts are objectively right (since our moral judgment may be misguided).

I.

Let us begin with a popular religious conception—conscience as God-given instinctual access to moral truth. There are many variations, but for contrast, I shall describe an extreme version. Here are the main themes.

1. Each human being is born with a latent conscience, which (barring certain tragic interferences) emerges into its full working capacity in youth or young adulthood. It is a capacity to identify, among one's own acts, motives, intentions, and aims, those that are morally wrong and those that are permissible (i.e., not wrong). Conscience, however, does not identify acts and motives as morally admirable and praiseworthy. At best, conscience is "clear" or "clean," not self-congratulating.

2. That certain acts, such as murder and adultery, are morally wrong is a matter of objective fact, independent of our consciences. That is, what makes such acts wrong is not just that they

are, or would be, disapproved by the agent's conscience or even the consciences of everyone. However, once our conscience has persuaded us that to perform a certain act would be wrong, there arises the possibility of doing a second wrong, namely, violating our conscience. Since this is intentionally doing what we believe to be morally wrong, it is generally regarded as wrong, independently of whether our initial moral belief is correct.[8]

3. In acknowledging the wrongness of an act, our conscience gives us a sense that we cannot comfortably view that act as something that was, is, or will be optional, to be pursued or not according to our interests. It imposes painful feelings of self-disapproval when it recognizes the wrongs of our past or ongoing activities, and it threatens the same when we entertain future plans that it would condemn.

4. Conscience originates as God's gift to human beings, a special access to moral truth that can work independently of church authority and rational reflection.[9] Its authority, moreover, stems from the fact that its content is part of God's own knowledge and/or will. That is, it stems from the part that God chose to make accessible to us, for our guidance, in this special way.[10]

5. Appealing to conscience is not the same as using rational, reflective judgment to resolve moral questions. Conscience may be partly shaped and informed by such judgments, as well as by public debates, religious education, and the like, but it is pictured as operating not so much like an intellectual moral adviser as like an instinct-governed, internal "voice" or sign that "tells" us what we must or must not do, warns us when tempted, and prods us to reform when guilty.[11]

6. Once we have correctly identified and heard its "voice," conscience is a reliable source of knowledge of our own moral responsibilities in particular contexts. The story is that God gave each of us a conscience as a guide for our own conduct, not for judging or goading others. Each of us is commanded to follow our conscience and is directly accountable to God for having done so or not. Judging that an act is wrong for us means that it is wrong for everyone unless there is a relevant difference between the cases, but others' cases may differ in so many ways that we have no practical license to make extensive generalizations from what we "learn" from our own conscience.

A more modest thesis might say that following our conscience is a reliable guide to living a blameless life and not necessarily a guarantee that we will do what is morally correct in every instance. The popular conception I have in mind, however, holds the stronger thesis that the voice of our conscience coincides with what is objectively right or wrong for us to do, that is, what it is correct, on the basis of the known facts, to judge as right or wrong.

Even this strong thesis, however, inevitably leaves a loophole for error. Whether or not we believe that conscience itself is infallible, we must still acknowledge that we can make mistakes about whether what we take to be dictates of conscience are authentic. Wishful thinking, fear, childhood prejudices, and indoctrination in false ideologies can imitate or distort the voice of conscience, especially if we have dulled that voice by frequently disregarding it. So in effect, the doctrine that conscience is very reliable, even infallible, with regard to objective right and wrong is subject to practical qualifications. As with some marvelous technologies thought to be virtually 100 percent reliable if used properly by flawless operators under ideal conditions, errors of application occur but are blamed on the user, not the equipment.

What are the implications of this popular conception of conscience with regard to how we should treat it? First, what should our attitude be toward our own conscience? Since by hypothesis, conscience provides reliable access to both moral truth and subjective rightness, we would have good (moral) reason to avoid "dulling" our conscience, to "listen" carefully for its signals, and in general to be cautiously guided by what apparently it tells us to do. Several factors, however, can combine to recommend caution even to the firm believer in the popular conception. For example, although conscience is supposed to be a reliable signal of moral truth, it is not necessarily the only, or the most direct, means of determining what we ought to do. When secular and religious authorities, together with the professed conscientious judgments of others, all stand opposed to what we initially took to be the voice of conscience, then these facts should raise doubts. Even assuming that genuine pronouncements of conscience are infallible, we may not be infallible in distinguishing these from our wishes or fears or the echoes of past mentors. In effect, we may need to check our supposed instinctual access to moral truth by reviewing more directly the relevant evidence and arguments, for example, concerning intended benefits and harms, promises fulfilled or broken, and the responsibilities of our social role. To confirm that our instinctive response is a reflection of "true conscience" rather than a morally irrelevant feeling, we would need to consult other sources, for example, to see whether the response coincides with reflective moral judgment, based on a careful review of pertinent facts in consultation with others.

Without such a check, there is no way to be confident that the instinct on which we are about to rely is "conscience" rather than some baser instinct. By analogy, suppose that we believe we have an intuitive sense that somehow regularly signals dishonesty in job applicants when this "sense" is properly identified and used under ideal conditions. Although the suspicions we formed by consulting this intuitive sense might serve as useful warning signs, they would not be a substitute for investigating the candidates' records and seeking direct evidence of dishonest conduct. Only an examination of the relevant facts could ascertain whether what we suppose is an accurate intuitive signal really is so.

Second, how should we regard the consciences of others? Here, again, it is clear that the popular conception, if true, would give us some reason to encourage others to develop and listen to their consciences and to tolerate their conscientious acts within limits. However, we should be cautious in trusting the appearance of conscience, for others are presumably just as subject as we are to self-deception in identifying conscience, and besides, they may intentionally deceive us about what they really believe. Again, when opinions differ, a check seems needed, for how can we reasonably believe another's claim that what he or she is following is really an instinctual "sense" of moral right and wrong, rather than an instinct of another kind, unless the person can give plausible moral reasons for thinking that what "the voice" recommends is right?

From a Kantian perspective, the popular religious conception is untenable for several reasons. First, it draws conclusions about ethics from theology, whereas Kant insisted that whatever reasonable beliefs we can have about God must be based on prior moral knowledge, not the reverse. Second, the popular view of conscience as instinctual access to God's mind or will omits (what the Kantian takes to be) the prior and indispensable roles of reason and judgment in determining what we ought to do. For Kantians, what is morally required is ultimately a matter of what free and reasonable people, with a proper respect for one another, would agree to accept as a constraint on the pursuit of self-interest and other goals. That is not the sort of thing that we could claim to know directly "by instinct." Once we have a basic grasp of the reasons for moral principles and acknowledge their authority because of this, our respect for the principles may be signaled by unbidden "pangs" and "proddings" that feel like instinctual responses. But from the Kantian perspective, what should make us count these as signs of conscience is the plausibility of seeing the feelings as due to the agent's internal acceptance what of he or she judges to be reasonable moral principles.

Third, the popular religious conception regards the voice of conscience—when it has been identified as authentic—to be a completely reliable, even infallible, reflection of moral truth, but Kantian ethics (rightly, I think) rejects the idea that there is any way we can infallibly judge the morality of particular acts. Although Kant himself had confidence that reason could provide certainty regarding basic principles and many substantive duties, the basic Kantian view of moral deliberation and judgment, as I understand it, leaves more room for uncertainty and error than Kant allowed regarding specific moral questions. The reason is that in the Kantian view, moral deliberation and judgment are processes by which we try to identify choices that we could justify to all other reasonable persons, and the processes require subtle application of fundamental moral principles to empirical circumstances that are often uncertain and only partially understood.[12]

II.

Those who cannot accept theological accounts of the origin and function of conscience often adopt an extreme cultural relativist conception, perhaps because they assume this to be the only secular alternative.[13] The term *relativism* is, of course, used loosely to refer to many different ideas, but what I mean by "an extreme cultural relativist conception" of conscience (or ECR, for short) sees the promptings of conscience as nothing but feelings (1) that reflect our internalization of whatever choice-guiding, cultural norms we have internalized and (2) that serve to promote social cohesion by disposing individuals to conform to group standards. This conception replaces the theological story about the origin and function of conscience with a contemporary sociological hypothesis, but more radically, it goes beyond this empirical hypothesis by claiming that conscience reflects "nothing but" whatever cultural choice-guiding norms we have internalized. That is, ECR is actually a combination of (1) a widely accepted causal explanation of the genesis and social function of the feelings ascribed to "conscience" and (2) the controversial philosophical thesis that what is called *conscience* is not, even in the best case, a mode of access to moral truth, knowledge, or objectively justifiable moral beliefs.

What I call *conceptions* of conscience are complexes of beliefs about how feelings of conscience come about, what purpose they serve, and how reliable they are as a guide to moral truth or well-justified moral belief. Accordingly, what I call ECR is not merely a view of the origin of conscience but also a view of its social function and reliability as a moral guide. Regarding origin, ECR explains the "conscientious" person's feelings of constraint as due to a learning process by which he inwardly accepts local cultural norms as his standard of self-approval. Regarding function, ECR sees the development of conscience as a way by which social groups secure a measure of conformity to their standards without relying entirely on external rewards and punishments. Regarding reliability, ECR holds that although conscience reliably reflects the local norms that we have taken up from our environment, there is no objective standard by which we can ever determine that some cultural norms, but not others, are morally "true" or "justified."

To avoid misunderstanding, I must stress that this second conception of conscience, the ECR, is not merely the scientist's refusal, as a matter of methodology, to include moral judgments and metaethical doctrines as a part of scientific theory. That attitude, in fact, is one that advocates of other conceptions of conscience may well applaud. Also, ECR is much more than an empirical hypothesis about the origin and social function of feelings attributed to conscience. If it were just that, it would be compatible with a variety of theories about moral justification and truth, including contemporary Kantian theories that disassociate themselves from certain aspects of Kant's metaphysics.[14]

Moral theory is not science, of course, but any moral theory that is worthy of contemporary support should, in my opinion, at least be compatible with empirical explanations regarded as well established in the current scientific community. What especially distinguishes ECR from the other three conceptions reviewed here is its deflationary stance regarding the nature and justifiability of moral beliefs, which is a position reached only by a giant step beyond empirical explanation into an area of perennial philosophical controversy.

Returning now to the main task of describing the ECR and its implications, I should note that like my first (theological) conception, the ECR also treats conscience as something experienced as an instinctual feeling rather than as a deliberate judgment about how basic moral principles apply to particular circumstances.[15] Briefly, the picture is something like the following: The origin of conscience is largely early socialization, resulting in cultural norms being so deeply internalized that we respond to them for the most part without thinking about them. The "voice" of conscience is a felt discomfort, analogous to "cognitive dissonance," generated by a conflict between our (perhaps unarticulated) awareness of what we are doing and a cultural norm that we have internalized.[16] The discomfort is a signal not that an objectively true moral principle has been violated or threatened but merely that we are about to step across some line that early influences have deeply etched on our personality. As cultures differ, then, we expect variations in what consciences disapprove. And even when we find uniformities, we regard them merely as signs that different cultures have some common social needs and processes, not that we have discovered universal moral truths.[17]

What are the implications of ECR regarding the attitude we should take toward our own conscience? If ECR is true, virtually everyone will spontaneously feel that certain acts are "bad" and "worthy of disapproval," but how should an informed and reflective person who accepts ECR regard these feelings and respond to them? Clearly, these feelings should be seen for just what they are (according to ECR), namely, a fairly reliable sign that some past, present, or anticipated action of our own violates some cultural norm that we have internalized. The result is that we can expect to experience further internal discomfort and to incur the disapproval of others if we continue acting as before (or as planned). These expectations give a prudent person a self-interested reason to "heed conscience." And if a person's culture's norms serve socially useful purposes, that person would have some altruistic reason to obey the promptings of "conscience." On the other side, however, those who accept ECR also have reason to try to "see through," dispel, or discount the feeling that to violate conscience would be "wrong," "immoral," or "unreasonable" by any objective, culturally independent standard. Moreover, when the rewards of acting against conscience outweigh the unpleasantness of residual guilt feelings and predictable social disapproval, then the smart thing to do, believing ECR, would presumably be to stifle conscience or, if need be, simply tolerate the discomfort it causes in order to gain the greater rewards.

If we accept ECR, how are we to view the consciences of others? Since a person with a conscience is liable to suffer inwardly when contravening it and this normally serves as a deterrent, we have a self-interested reason to be pleased when others' consciences discourage behavior that we dislike. Moreover, insofar as we are concerned for the others, we should be glad when their consciences prompt social conformity that is useful to them, but otherwise we should merely pity them for their unnecessary inhibitions and needless suffering.[18]

Kantians obviously reject some features of ECR, but not necessarily all. It is important not to mislocate the major disagreement. Despite what some might suppose, it is arguable that the ECR's empirical hypothesis about the development of conscience, or some similar empirical account, should pose no special problem for the Kantian perspective.[19] The main deep point of disagreement concerns ECR's denial of objective standards of moral reasoning and judgment. This denial is often mistakenly thought to be a logical consequence of the empirical hypothesis, but as the philosophical literature on relativism repeatedly points out, the empirical observations that cultural standards differ and that people tend to internalize their local standards do not, by themselves, prove anything about objectivity in morals or any other field. Objectivity, whether in normative or descriptive matters, is not constituted simply by de facto agreement. By the same token, objectivity is not necessarily undermined by de facto disagreement.[20] The issues are more complicated than that and obviously cannot be resolved here, one way or the other. The point of mentioning the issue now is just to stress that although there remains an unresolved disagreement between ECR and the Kantian perspective, the main point at issue is a long-standing, many-sided controversy about moral objectivity (truth, justification, etc.). It is not a debate about whether the feelings attributed to conscience are empirically explicable and tend to reflect social influences that vary from culture to culture.

There is another, more minor difference between ECR and the other conceptions of conscience, including Kant's. This has to do with terminology. ECR, as presented here, treats "conscience" as a broad descriptive term, covering felt responses to any action-guiding standard internalized in a culture. Having such a broad, evaluatively neutral term to refer to similar phenomena in different cultures is probably useful, for example, as a term of art in comparative anthropological studies. However, I suspect that the term *conscience* is commonly used more narrowly than this. At least the cultural norms attributed to conscience are usually assumed to be "moral" norms, in a broad sense of "moral" that contrasts with the norms attributed only to a society's laws, customs, religious rites, or code of etiquette or to specific club rules, gang taboos, prudential maxims, and the like.[21] This point could be accommodated in a more sophisticated cultural relativist (SCR) conception of conscience simply by stipulating that "conscience" refers to our felt responses to the moral (as opposed to merely legal, customary, etc.) norms that we have internalized from our culture. To call norms "moral" in this (weak) sense does not imply that the norms are "true," "correct," or "objectively justifiable," and so a kind of neutrality would be maintained, even though the cases attributed to "conscience" would be somewhat limited.

I conjecture, however, that even this broad, neutral sense of "conscience" (SCR) differs in another respect from the narrower, more normative senses of conscience found in ordinary discourse and the other conceptions. If so, this is not in itself an objection to SCR, but to avoid confusion, the difference should be noted. What I suspect is that apart from social science, the term *conscience* is typically used in a partially laudatory sense or tone, implying or expressing the speaker's limited endorsement of the source, if not the content, of the beliefs he or she attributes to conscience. My speculation here can be put in either cognitivist or expressivist terms. That is, when we attribute a person's reluctance to act in a certain way to that person's "conscience," then typically either (1) we express an (endorsing) belief about the source of that person's reluctance—that is, that it is generally a reliable sign of what is objectively wrong for that person to do—or (2) we express an (endorsing) attitude toward the source—that is, approval of treating it as a guide generally to be followed. If so, the partial approval (commonly) expressed when we speak of a person's "conscience" would explain why it sounds a bit odd (or not intended literally) when someone, outside anthropology class, says that Himmler's conscience told him to keep gassing Jews despite his momentary sympathy for them. If, as I suspect, Himmler's norms were fundamentally vicious, self-serving, and subversive of morality, then any bad feelings he may have had when thinking about violating them do not deserve to be called *pangs of conscience* in the usual (partially laudatory) sense.

Similarly, I suspect that Mark Twain had his tongue in his cheek when he attributed to "conscience" Huck Finn's "guilty" feelings about helping the slave, Jim, to escape. If it seems odd to say that Huck's conscience made him feel guilty for helping Jim, this may be because we suppose Huck was moved by a genuine (but not articulated) moral reason for helping him. By contrast, we suppose that Huck's reluctance to help Jim reflected no comparable moral commitment, only his having been socialized in an evil system.[22] Given the ways the word *conscience* commonly expresses approval, the description of Huck seems paradoxical: it is as if we are told that the "good" source of moral feelings in Huck is condemning him for doing what his (genuinely good) sense of humanity impels him to do. The oddity reflects the fact that we take the feelings we attribute to conscience as more worthy of attention than the feelings we would describe as merely responses to social upbringing. As perhaps the author intended, the paradox reminds us that far from being a sure sign of wrongdoing, the discomfort experienced in violating cultural norms may be nothing but an unfortunate side effect of doing what is really only decent and humane.

The endorsing function of the word *conscience* should not be exaggerated, however, for in many cases we acknowledge that others' "consciences" prompt them to do what they think is morally right but what we consider extremely wrong. For example, I might say this of the Inquisitors who ordered heretics burned at the stake if their reasons and motives were convincingly "moral" ones (e.g., saving the heretics from eternal torture) but applied in conjunction with false empirical and theological beliefs (e.g., burning them was necessary to that end). Alan Donagan believed that utilitarianism was deeply misguided, but he did not deny that people could sincerely follow consciences shaped ("corrupted") by utilitarian standards. Generally, given the common core concept of conscience, those who accept any of our four particular conceptions of conscience should be able to understand much of what others are saying when they speak of conscience.

Still, those who accept a particular normative conception of conscience tend to hold back the usual endorsing connotations of the term, or to cancel them partially, when describing others whom they suspect are making grave moral mistakes. That is, when we suppose that others are sincerely following their moral beliefs but doing what (we believe) is grossly immoral, we are inclined to say "it was false (corrupt, not genuine) conscience that told him to do that." Alternatively, we may say, "You might describe them as conscientious in a sense, but those crimes couldn't have been prompted by conscience as I understand it." [23]

III.

In his *Fifteen Sermons* (1651) Joseph Butler articulated a conception of conscience as reflective moral judgment. Although as an Anglican bishop, Butler had theological beliefs that he thought supported his conception of conscience, in the *Sermons* he explicitly set himself the task of developing ethics from an empirical understanding of human nature.[24] Human nature, he argued, consists of several faculties, which have an organizing "constitution" that determines their proper functions and relations.[25] The main aspects of human nature are particular passions, self-love, benevolence, and conscience. *Particular passions* are desires and aversions, loves and hates, for particular objects or events.[26] *Self-love* is a more sophisticated, higher-order desire for the satisfaction of a set of other desires, conceived as our "happiness." *Benevolence,* too, involves the desire to satisfy other desires, for it is the disposition to care about the happiness of others.[27]

The supervisory faculty, Butler says, is *conscience.*[28] He refers here to our capacity to deliberate reasonably before acting and taking proper account of our nature, circumstances, options, estimated consequences, and certain (supposedly obvious) deontological constraints. Such deliberation requires a time of "calm," "cool" reflection, and the result—our deliberative judgment—is neither purely intellectual nor purely sentimental but, rather, "a sentiment of the understanding" and "a perception of the heart."[29] Conscience has a limited motivational power, but its authority is unchallenged.[30] The reason is that its verdicts are conceived as, all things considered, deliberative judgments of our own reason, a faculty whose natural role is to supervise our conduct and direct us to a life that gives appropriate expression to all our basic natural dispositions. Based on this assumption, Butler argued that the recommendations of conscience, reasonable self-love, and reasonable benevolence coincide, even though they are conceptually distinct.[31]

In sum, Butler holds the following: (1) Conscience is in fact God-given but is recognizable as authoritative without its theological backing. (2) The voice of conscience is not a mysterious signal passively received ("heard") but, rather, is the verdict of our own active, reason-guided judgment, accompanied by corresponding feeling. (3) Conscience does not simply deduce its conclusions from given determinate principles but, rather, is guided by the vague standard of whether our acts are "fitting" or "appropriate" to the situation, given our human nature as rational, desiring, self-loving, and yet also benevolent persons. (4) Conscience often motivates us and ought never to be contravened, but at times particular passions, self-love, and even love of others overpower it. (5) Because even small variations in the capacities and specific situations of individuals can matter, what conscience rightly tells one person may differ from what it rightly tells another who seems similarly situated. (6) Each person's conscience is a highly reliable, if not perfect, guide to what is morally required of him or her.[32] (7) Finally, conscience's approval or disapproval is not what makes acts objectively right or wrong, but it provides the agent with an (internally acknowledged) reason, as well as a motive, to do what he or she thinks right, and this is an important part of his or her sense of moral obligation.[33]

If we were to accept this Butlerian conception, what should our attitude be toward our own conscience? Obviously, we would have good reason to cultivate, inform, and guide our conduct by conscience, for conscience would be accepted as a reliable access to moral requirements, a reflection of our own best, reasonable judgment, and a liability to self-loathing if we flouted it. It represents our own reflective conviction about what is "fitting" to do in the light of a realistic view of our situation and our nature as human beings.

The preceding two conceptions, seeing conscience as an instinctual or conditioned response, left their advocates room for doubts that called for independent, reasoned moral reflection. But in Butler's account, the voice of conscience is already the conclusion of our best, reasoned reflection. If other individuals or state or church authorities disagree with our initial judgment, then this is new information that may call for new reflection; but it remains information to be conscientiously reflected on, not a verdict that any person of conscience can blindly accept. From the point of view of a deliberating conscientious agent, the knowledge that others disagree with our initial moral judgments then becomes part of the description of the next problem we face, and the question is what we should do now. Others' disagreement may be a sign that our initial judgment was based on a self-deceptive picture of the facts or that we were too hasty or emotionally distracted in our initial deliberation. In either case, however, the check is a new use of conscience, not a decision to accept the authority of someone else's judgment over our own.

Perhaps certain public officials do have legitimate authority, in a sense, over an area of our conduct. In Butler's view, however, for us to have grounds to acknowledge their authority, we would have to conclude, in our own conscientious reflection, that given the particular situation (including their social role and their particular pronouncements), it is right for us to do what they command. Far from being a limitation on the moral authority of our conscience, this amounts to treating individual conscience as the ultimate source of the right of public authorities to expect obedience.

What, then, does Butler's account prescribe as a proper attitude toward the consciences of others? Insofar as we want others to conduct themselves morally, we should, other things being equal, favor whatever promotes the cultivation, protection, and employment of informed conscience by others. Although Butler does not discuss political matters, the point does have obvious political implications. He concedes, however, that anyone who claims to make a conscientious judgment may be self-deceived, and obviously others may try to deceive us by claiming to follow their consciences when they know this is not so. Therefore, we can find ourselves in situations in which our best conscientious judgment is that we must hinder, even by force, what another claims to be a conscientious act.[34] Each case of this sort must be judged in its own context.[35]

From the Kantian perspective, a good feature of Butler's conception of conscience, compared with the previous ones, is that Butler's account promises to preserve the good name of conscience even among those who reject its theological supports.[36] It does so, however, primarily by identifying conscience with a natural capacity to determine our moral responsibilities in a reason-governed, reflective manner and to guide our conduct by these judgments. Conceiving of conscience in this way broadens its secular appeal, but it abandons some of the connotations that Kant and others accept as associated with conscience and as expressed in the familiar metaphors used to describe it.

What I have in mind is the notion that conscience is, in some ways, more like an immediate, instinctive response than the product of a long, careful, process of rational deliberation.[37] We are "struck" by pangs of conscience; we "find" ourselves suffering from a guilty conscience; and even when we are reluctant to engage in a moral assessment of our acts, it "speaks," "demands," "warns," "prods," "forbids," "rebels," and at times "is revolted." Explicit reflection and judgment seem neither necessary nor sufficient for us to experience the promptings of conscience. Often, it seems, we simply feel its inner demands or reprimands. In stressing this familiar aspect of conscience, Kant's conception, the popular religious conception, and the cultural relativist conception all seem more in line with common thinking than Butler's is.[38]

From a contemporary (modified) Kantian perspective, there are other problems with Butler's account. For example, it rests on the foundational assumption that as a matter of natural teleology, our particular passions, self-love, benevolence, and reason are structured in a normative hierarchy that assigns to each a place and a function.[39] Again, like Plato and Aristotle, Butler is more inspiring than convincing in his teleological argument that human nature is so constituted that reasonable self-love never recommends injustice. Few would dispute Butler's ideas that moral judgment, at its best, requires the use of reason in wide-ranging, honest reflection "in a cool hour" and that it should take into account human nature, our individual capacities, and the facts of our situation. But to distinguish moral from other forms of deliberation and perhaps to reach any definite conclusions at all, we need a fuller account of what we are deliberating about, what we are looking for, and what criteria or constraints in such deliberation make its outcome morally binding.

IV.

Let us turn now to Kant's idea of conscience as judicial self-appraisal.[40] Butler identified *conscience* as the faculty by which we make moral judgments, but what Kant calls *conscience* is something distinct that can come into play only after one has made, or accepted, a moral judgment.[41] Moral judgments are simply applications of basic moral requirements (the "moral law") to more specific circumstances. These basic requirements, articulated in the forms of the Categorical Imperative, are supposed to be part of the rational knowledge of all ordinary moral agents, even though nonphilosophers may not be able to articulate them in their pure abstract form.[42]

According to Kant, ordinary people normally judge quite well whether their acts are right or wrong, and they do so without much conscious, explicit reflection. However, if subject to strong temptations and confused by philosophical sophistries, they are apt to try make self-serving exceptions to rules that they generally acknowledge as universal.[43] The result is that although every moral agent is presumed to have an adequate grasp of the fundamentals of the moral point of view, errors of judgment are possible. Obviously, errors of fact, culpable or not, can lead us to a judgment that we would not make if we had a correct, realistic view of our circumstances. But this is not the only source of mistake. Inattention, wishful thinking, and self-deceptive special pleading all can result in misapplications of moral principles that in the abstract, we know well enough. Presumably, too, we might come to have unjustifiable moral opinions without making any direct judgments of our own, for example, by simply accepting the prevailing standards in our culture or placing complete reliance on the moral judgment of some other person.[44]

These errors of moral judgment, however, do not amount to an erring conscience. In fact, conscience has yet to enter the picture. What, then, is conscience? There are puzzling features about Kant's remarks on conscience, and there seem to be some changes among Kant's several works, but we can summarize the main points as follows:[45]

1. All moral agents have consciences. The belief that this is so is not based simply, or mainly, on observation. Rather, that someone has a conscience is a presupposition of his or her being a moral agent. Moral agency also presupposes practical reason, but practical reason is a broader concept. It includes our capacity and disposition to acknowledge the moral law and to apply the moral law through "judgment." But neither of these is identical with conscience.

2. Conscience is mostly described in metaphorical terms, but the metaphors can be unpacked. Conscience is "an inner judge" that issues verdicts of acquittal or condemnation. Like a trial judge, who is not legislating or merely informing others about the law, conscience "imputes," "reproaches," and passes "sentence." If it judges us to be guilty, we are made to suffer, and at times the result can be torment. The verdict of acquittal brings relief but not happiness. Although the inner "forum" of conscience is not a real court, we must think of ourselves as playing several roles: that of accuser, defender, and finally a judge who yields a verdict and

passes sentence. The metaphor requires that we think of ourselves from different perspectives, but it is important that it also be the same person who accuses and who stands accused. We can also think of conscience as demanding accountability to God, but this a "subjective" construal rather than an essential feature of conscience.[46]

3. Although the metaphors suggest that the moral agent is active in the operations of conscience, Kant also describes conscience as like an "instinct," as something that we "find" in ourselves, something that we "hear" even when we try to run away, and something that "speaks involuntarily and inevitably."[47] The point, I think, is to distinguish conscience—as the often painful self-accusation, guilty verdict, and consequent suffering—from the general activities of moral deliberation, reasoning, and judgment. Conscience presupposes and makes use of these activities and thus is not (as in the popular conception) a mere felt clue or symptom that we have done wrong or are about to.

Like a well-grounded judicial verdict and sentence, the "voice" of conscience imposes a painful awareness of two distinguishable things: (1) that what we have done (or intend to do) is at odds with what, even in our own judgment, is wrong in the circumstances and (2) that the act is fully imputable to ourselves as a free agent.[48]

In effect, conscience presupposes and uses the results of our general reasoning and judgment in answer to the question "What sorts of acts, in what circumstances, are morally permissible, and what sorts are morally forbidden?" When we "compare" or "hold up" our past (or projected) acts (as we perceive these) to these answers (our general judgments about what is permissible and what is forbidden) and also realize that those acts are (or will be) imputable to ourselves as their "free cause" (without excuse), then conscience imposes (or threatens) "sentence," that is, makes us (as the guilty party) feel bad and yet (as the sentencing judge) feel that the pain is warranted. Here we see that conscience, although working more like an instinct than a capacity for reasoned moral judgment, is not a mere instinct because it depends crucially on that basic capacity.

In *Religion within the Limits of Reason Alone,* when discussing "the guide of conscience in matters of religious faith," Kant introduces what seems to be a slight variation on this main theme. He first states a strict "postulate of conscience" about prospective acts, namely, "concerning the act I propose to perform I must not only judge and form an opinion, but I must be sure that it is not wrong." This is a special, but quite broad, duty of due care; that is, we must undertake and diligently carry out a moral appraisal of our projected acts (presumably unless we are already sure, from previous appraisals, that the acts are permissible). Metaphorically speaking, "judgment$_1$" (one sense of "judgment") is what is responsible for appraising the act diligently, and "conscience" then "passes judgment$_2$" (a second sense of "judgment") on judgment$_1$ as to whether it has fulfilled that responsibility. Paradoxically, then, conscience is "judgment passing judgment on itself." [49] Thus the particular offense of which conscience accuses us is the failure to undertake seriously and carry out diligently a moral appraisal of our acts, a violation of the special duty of due care in making sure that one "hazard[s] nothing that may be wrong." [50]

The Metaphysics of Morals also includes something like this duty of due care, a duty to try to "know (scrutinize, fathom) yourself." This "First Command of All Duties to oneself," Kant says, requires impartiality in appraising ourselves "in comparison with the law" and sincerity in acknowledging our "inner worth" or lack thereof.[51]

In the light of this, we can perhaps put the two accounts of conscience together as follows: Conscience is an involuntary response to the recognition that what we have done, are doing, or are about to do is contrary to the moral judgments that we have made (by applying moral law to different types of circumstances). Prominent among the many moral judgments that persons of conscience will have made is that they have the special, second-order duty to submit their acts to the "inner court" of conscience, scrutinizing them diligently, impartially, and sincerely. Once they submit their acts to appraisal, conscience gives its verdict and "passes sentence" automatically, for this is just a metaphor for the painful awareness of wrongdoing that such sincere appraisal causes in a person with the basic dispositions of "practical reason." Combining Kant's two accounts, we can say that conscience can acquit or condemn with regard to accusations of both violations of first-order duties (e.g., truth telling) and failures to fulfill the second-order duty of due care in scrutinizing and appraising our acts diligently (by "holding them up" to our judgment of the first-order duties). In both cases, conscience presupposes but is not the same as "moral judgment" in the sense of "drawing from the moral law a more determinate specification of our duties."[52]

4. Our judgment about whether certain acts are "really" right or wrong can be mistaken, and so presumably our consciences may at times be working from mistaken premises regarding this. However, Kant claims that in a sense, conscience itself does not err.[53] Why he thinks this is not entirely clear, but perhaps the basic thought was that conscience is not liable to common "external" sources of error that may infect ordinary moral judgment. For example, mistakes about the facts of our situation can lead us to make mistakes about what is objectively permissible, but they cannot cause us to err in regard to whether our act as we conceived it was contrary to our judgment about what is right. Mistaking a lost hiker for a moving target on a firing range can lead to the erroneous judgment that shooting at what we see is permissible, but this same misidentification does not mean that the act as intended (e.g., shooting at the target here) was contrary to our moral judgment about it (e.g., that shooting at the target here is permissible). Errors of conscience, if there were any, would have to be a matter of failing, even after we raised the question, to recognize either the fact that what we intentionally did was (or was not) against our best moral judgment or the fact that we had (or had not) exercised due care to determine whether our act was right. Perhaps, despite Kant, errors are possible even in these "subjective" judgments, but the important point remains that in Kant's sense, even an unerring conscience is in no way a guarantee that what we believe is right is really so.

The implications of the Kantian conception regarding our attitude toward our own conscience should now be clear. Conscience is no substitute for moral reasoning and judgment but in fact presupposes these. A clear conscience is no guarantee that we acted in an objectively right way, and so it is no ground for self-righteous pride or presumption that our moral judgment is superior to that of those who conscientiously disagree. However, insofar as the warnings and pangs of conscience actually reflect our diligent efforts to hold our acts up to our best moral judgments, conscience is as reliable a subjective guide as we can get. Conformity to conscience is necessary and sufficient for morally blameless conduct, in Kant's view, even though it cannot ensure correctness.[54] Thus as Kant says, conscience ought to be "cultivated" and "sharpened" as well as heeded. Our impartial moral judgments (about what anyone in various situations should do) will not affect our conduct unless they are applied to our own case and the acts in question are imaginatively "imputed" to ourselves, which is a function of conscience. Again, past misdeeds often call for restorative acts in the present (apology, compensation, etc.), but it is conscience that makes us feel the force of our wrongdoing and thus presumably aids in the recognition of these duties.

How, then, should we view the consciences of others? Many of the same points apply, but there are some asymmetries. Although in moral debate, my appeal to conscience weighs no more than anyone else's, in the end I must heed my own conscience, not that of others. This is not to deny that the conscientious disagreement of others gives us grounds for questioning, listening to their reasons, consulting more widely, and rethinking our initial moral judgment. Also, knowing that others conscientiously disagree may itself be a reason for altering our judgment about what, all things considered, we should do, even if we are fully convinced that these others are mistaken. Here the fact of disagreement serves as new relevant information rather than grounds to suspect our earlier process of judgment. The same would apply if our initial moral judgment turned out to be contrary to legal authority. But in all these cases, our final responsibility is to heed our own consciences, which are based on our diligent effort to judge, all things considered, what is right.

Another asymmetry follows from Kant's view that the basic ends of a virtuous person are his own perfection and the happiness of others. Practical concern for others' happiness, not worries about their souls, should motivate us to avoid tempting others into activities that would cause them to suffer agonies of conscience. But concern for making ourselves morally more perfect, not concern for our own happiness, is what should move us to keep our own consciences clean.[55]

So far I have avoided discussing the content of Kant's moral law, but given more time, I would argue that Kant's idea of the moral law itself gives deep and compelling reasons for taking seriously the moral judgments of others, especially those who use their "consciences" in sincere and diligent self-appraisal. The main idea here is that Kant's basic moral point of view, expressed by the combination of forms of the Categorical Imperative, holds that moral standards are found by analyzing (rational) human willing. They are not perceived in Plato's heaven of Forms or derived from God's will or identifiable with any empirical facts (e.g., about human sympathies). Rather, they are constituted by what reasonable, autonomous persons ideally would "legislate" for themselves, subject to certain constraints (conceptually) built into the idea of moral reflection. A crucial constraint is that all legislation must respect the value of humanity as an end in itself. This places a priority on our concerns as rational beings, forbids our thinking of human beings as exchangeable commodities, and, especially, puts forward an ideal that policies should be morally justifiable to all.

Kant, I think, had too much confidence that all who take up the moral perspective would reach agreement on moral principles. But in the face of disagreement about matters of vital moral importance, it is clear that his theory implies that the best each of us can do is, first, to make our own moral judgments about what we can sincerely recommend as reasonable to others who will take up the moral legislative point of view and, then, after duly consulting with others and giving due weight to their concerns, to act according to these judgments faithfully but with humility. Universal agreement would be a regulative ideal, perhaps constituting "correctness" about what is "objectively" right, but in practice this would only be an aim and a hope.

Given even this brief sketch, it should now be clear that consulting with others and taking into account their reasons for the moral judgments must be an important part of the Kantian process of moral deliberation. This speaks in favor of treating the moral judgments of others respectfully and also of creating the social conditions in which sincere and diligent efforts to make and apply moral judgments are encouraged. It does not support an absolute ban on coercing someone against his or her conscience, but it does urge respect for conscientious resistance even when we believe it is mistaken.

It was no accident, apparently, that Kant developed his special conception of conscience rather than simply incorporating one of the previous conceptions into his moral theory. To review, Kant's special conception fits his basic moral theory in several respects better than other conceptions would.

First, the Kantian conception, unlike the popular religious conception, is not based on theology, and so it is compatible with Kant's doctrine that ethics must precede religion. Moreover, the Kantian conscience reflects Kant's idea that only the use of reason can determine what is moral, for it denies the (popular) view that conscience is a mysterious, instinct-like access to truth about what is morally forbidden.

Second, as opposed to the relativistic conceptions, ECR and SCR, Kant's conception does not deny, but in fact presupposes, the possibility of objective moral judgments, which is a central tenet of Kant's moral theory. Also, ECR and SCR treat *conscience* as a descriptive, or evaluatively neutral, term, but Kantian moral theory would encourage the common practice of speaking of conscience in a partially laudatory way. The reason is that in the Kantian conception, pangs of conscience, unlike most pains, stem from a morally respect-worthy source, a deeply rooted disposition of moral agents to hold up their own conduct to the same moral judgments that they make for others in comparable situations.

Third, as opposed to Butler, Kant clearly avoids making natural teleology foundational for ethics and so avoids making what Kant regarded the mistake of founding morals on "heteronomy." Arguably, too, Kant has a more plausible and determinate idea of the standards that should guide reasonable moral reflection. Butler sees conscience as making rational, reflective judgments, but he gives very little hint of the premises from which we are to reason. In addition, Kant's conception of conscience is closer to common sense and ordinary language than Butler's, in that Kant treats conscience not as our general capacity to reflect morally regarding our acts but, rather, as a special disposition to "find" ourselves involuntarily warning, accusing, and judging ourselves when we compare our acts (as we conceived them) with our moral judgments about the sorts of acts that are right and wrong.

Finally, the special Kantian conception of conscience promises to highlight and give a deep sense to the idea that a person who consistently follows her conscience is a person of integrity. Integrity has been viewed in different ways, of course, but in an sense, I suggest, persons who follow their conscience as understood in the previous conceptions may nonetheless lack a kind of integrity. For example, a person who followed the popular religious conception of conscience would, given his premises, be wise and prudent to do so because conscience is a sign of divinely sanctioned standards, but this seems no guarantee of genuine integrity. The latter presupposes not simply reliable, responsible public behavior but also self-governance by principles that one knowingly affirms for good reasons. One who regularly follows the mysterious "inner voice" of popular conscience may do so from fear and with little understanding.

Similarly, those who follow conscience in the ECR or SCR sense would reveal a steady disposition to be governed by cultural norms internalized early in life, and this might lead to many of the patterns of public behavior and the freedom from inner conflict that we associate with persons of integrity. But unless they are to some degree critically reflective and selective regarding the local norms they endorse as adults, something important would be missing. They may rest content with cultural norms that encourage deception and manipulation of a sort incompatible with integrity, as commonly understood. And even if their internalized principles happen to be morally decent, they continue to hold them as blind conformists, with too little appreciation of the principles' grounds to qualify them for the virtue of integrity.

Finally, Butler's account of conscience relies so heavily on the alleged facts of natural teleology that even though Butler claims that a person following conscience is "a law to himself," one might argue that his or her ultimate guide is the given "constitution of human nature," whose normativity seems to be accepted as a given natural fact, independently of the person's reflective, reasonable endorsement of it. Although this is sufficient for some sorts of integrity, arguably there is a deeper notion of integrity attributable to persons faithful to the Kantian conscience. The latter not only strive to make good moral judgments and govern themselves by their best moral judgments, but they also are supposed to follow a moral law that is itself a reflection of their own autonomous, rational will, not an acceptance of standards found "in nature." These notions obviously need interpretation and are subject to doubt, but they are suggestive. Insofar as "integrity" has to do with being a principled, self-governed person, Kant's account of the conscientious person tries to carry this a step further than even Butler does.

A last caveat may help forestall misunderstanding. Although I have compared different conceptions of conscience partly to show the merits from a broadly Kantian perspective of the special conception that Kant adopted, I do not mean to deny or minimize the many problems with Kant's ethics that are not addressed here. Kant's conception of conscience is a part of his larger moral theory and so is not immune to familiar doubts about, for example, the adequacy of his formulas of the moral law, their alleged status as universal rational principles, and their apparent neglect of animals. Moreover, there are special doubts that one may raise about Kant's account of conscience. For example, even if Kant's metaphors of the accuser, defender, and judge reflect the phenomenology of moral experience for many of us, we may question whether the images stem from excessive preoccupation with legal models that are not essential to, or best for, understanding morality.

In our age we can hardly help but doubt Kant's faith in the universality of conscience. His best defense might be that analysis of "common rational knowledge of morality" reveals possession of conscience (as Kant conceives it) as a precondition of full moral agency, that is, of being subject to duties conceived as categorical imperatives. But this analytic claim, too, may be doubted. Finally, Kant's ethics is most plausible when seen as a less comprehensive account of morality than he thought. Despite Kant's later work on virtue, his main focus from the beginning is on duty, or what one morally must do, and its presuppositions of freedom, respect for humanity, and the like. However, there are moral values and ideals not readily expressible in this framework, and so it seems there must be more to ethics than Kant acknowledged. Whether these values and ideals are incompatible with the basic Kantian theory has yet, in my opinion, to be worked out.

NOTES

1. What do the various conceptions imply, for example, about whether we should endorse and protect other people's reliance on conscience? Which conceptions, if any, imply that the voices of conscience in others are relevant data for our own moral decision making? Do they imply that we must tolerate the conscientious acts of others even when we are convinced that their judgments are mistaken and harmful and, if so, within what limits?

2. See John Rawls, *A Theory of Justice* (Cambridge, Mass.: Harvard University Press, 1971), 5ff. The concept of justice, according to Rawls, is specified by the role that different particular conceptions are supposed to have in common. It is, roughly, the idea of publicly affirmed principles that assign basic rights and duties and determine a proper distribution of benefits and burdens in a cooperative scheme. By contrast, the particular "conceptions of justice" characterized by justice as fairness, utilitarianism, and perfectionism are different ways of specifying what the principles are that should play the general social role of a concept of justice.

3. Roughly, to say that conscience is a capacity to "sense or immediately discern" is to say that it is a way of arriving at the relevant moral beliefs about our acts by means of feeling, instinct, or personal judgment. Becoming convinced by conscience that our conduct is immoral is supposed to be distinct from reaching that conclusion by explicitly appealing to external authorities or by engaging in discussion with others, although perhaps most people would grant that public opinion and authoritative pronouncements tend to influence the development of consciences and so may indirectly affect what conscience "says" on particular occasions.

4. I describe features of a Kantian ethical theory that I regard as most plausible—as distinct from aspects of Kant's own views that I regard as untenable—in my previous essays, some of which are collected in Thomas E. Hill Jr., *Dignity and Practical Reason in Kant's Moral Theory* (Ithaca, N.Y.: Cornell University Press, 1992). Others include "Kantian Pluralism," *Ethics* 102 (1992): 743–62; "A Kantian Perspective on Moral Rules," *Philosophical Perspectives* 6 (1992): 285–304; "Beneficence and Self-Love: A Kantian Perspective," *Social Philosophy and Policy* 10 (1992): 1–23; "Donagan's Kant," *Ethics* 104 (1993): 22–52; and "Moral Dilemmas, Gaps, and Residues: A Kantian Perspective," in H. E. Mason, ed., *Moral Dilemmas and Moral Theory* (New York: Oxford University Press, 1996), 167–98.

5. "Adequate effort" here is meant to cover "due care" in forming judgments about what one ought to do as well as firmness of will in

following those judgments. It is intended to cover both of Kant's some-what different accounts of conscience, which I describe later. The first account is in Immanuel Kant, *The Metaphysics of Morals* (hereafter abbre-viated *MM*), trans. Mary Gregor (Cambridge: Cambridge University Press, 1991), 59–60, 59–60, 197, 233–35. The second is in Immanuel Kant, *Religion within the Limits of Reason Alone* (hereafter abbreviated *Religion*), trans. T. M. Greene and H. H. Hudson (New York: Harper & Brothers, 1960), 173–74.

6. It is important to note that from the Kantian point of view, reason is not regarded as a faculty of intuition by which we can "see" certain moral norms as "self-evident." However, to say something is determined by reason also does not mean that it is provable in any formal way. Practical reason is not simply instrumental, determining efficient means to our ends. Rather, it is supposed to be a shared capacity of moral agents to think from a common point of view that respects and takes into account the interests of all.

7. It is significant that despite Kant's rigorous condemnation of participating in revolutionary activities, he granted that one must refuse to obey state orders to do what one judges wrong in itself. See Kant, *MM*, 133, 176; also Hans Reiss, "Postscript," in Hans Reiss, ed., *Kant: Political Writings* (Cambridge: Cambridge University Press, 1991), 267–68; and Kant, *Religion*, 142, n.

8. The possibility of this second wrong, in regard to our moral beliefs, is the source of a number of traditional puzzles and controversies about conscience. For example, if we "conscientiously" believe an act to be a duty when it is "objectively wrong," then it seems, paradoxically, that we must inevitably do wrong, no matter what we do: either we (unknowingly) do what is objectively wrong or else (intentionally) do what we believe is wrong, which is a wrong of another kind. Philosophers have responded to this puzzle in various ways, depending on whether they grant that conscience can "err," whether they believe that there are "objective wrongs" defined independently of the agent's intention, and whether they judge the source of moral error to be culpable or inculpable in origin. See Alan Donagan, "Conscience," in Lawrence and Charlotte Becker, eds., *Encyclopedia of Ethics* (New York: Garland Press, 1992).

9. Note that the "natural law" tradition in Western religious ethics, unlike the popular conception, emphasizes individuals' reason as their mode of access to moral truth. This makes the view more similar to Kant's, which is why, for starker contrast, I selected the "popular" view.

10. According to some, conformity or nonconformity to God's com-mands is what constitutes objective right and wrong. According to others, objective features of the acts are what make them wrong. But either way,

all who accept the popular religious conception agree that God in fact forbids and disapproves of wrong acts while commanding and approving conformity to duty. All agree that it is generally wrong to act contrary to conscience, but this is not because it is thought that the objective wrongness of acts in general consists simply of its being against the agent's conscience. Rather, acts against conscience are typically wrong because, given that conscience is our God-given means of access to the truth about what is objectively right and wrong, the acts that conscience warns us against are truly wrong (independently of that warning).

When I say that the wrongness of acts against conscience is not in general constituted by their being against conscience, the qualification is important. In those special cases in which due to error of conscience, the acts (described independently of the agents' beliefs and conscience) are not in fact wrong (even though the agents think they are), the agents still would be doing something wrong (namely, "intentionally doing what they believe wrong") by acting against conscience. In this special case, the wrongness does consist entirely of the acts being violations of conscience.

11. Typically our conscience is pictured not as judging the moral quality of particular acts from first principles but, rather, as identifying a limited class of (our own) wrong acts by means of the characteristic painful feelings aroused in contemplating them. This is a feature of several conceptions of conscience that fits well the metaphor of conscience as a warning, nagging, and reprimanding Jiminy Cricket or a tiny angel that follows us through tempting times. Butler's view is a partial exception.

12. Kant, as we shall see, does at one point claim conscience to be infallible, but there is a catch. It is not an infallible guide to objective moral truth, but only an (allegedly) infallible judgment that we violated our own principles or failed to exercise due care and diligence in moral judgment.

13. Types of relativism are usefully distinguished in Richard Brandt, *Ethical Theory* (Englewood Cliffs, N.J.: Prentice-Hall, 1959), chap. 11, 271–94; William Frankena, *Ethics* (Englewood Cliffs, N.J.: Prentice-Hall, 1973), chap. 6, esp. 109–10; and James Rachels, *The Elements of Moral Philosophy* (New York: Random House, 1986), 12–24. See also John Ladd, ed., *Relativism* (Belmont, Calif.: Wadsworth, 1973); and David Wong, *Moral Relativity* (Berkeley and Los Angeles: University of California Press, 1984).

14. It is not obvious whether Kant himself could have consistently accepted the particular empirical account that I attribute to ECR, although it is clear that he rejected its "nothing but" thesis. Kant was

deeply committed to the idea that all "phenomena," including those associated with human thought and action, are in principle subject to empirical causal explanations when viewed as natural occurrences from a scientific point of view. He also insisted that the same, or corresponding, phenomena related to human action can be "thought" under practical "ideas" of free will, rational justification, and so forth when one considers them from a irreducibly different perspective needed to make sense of morality. Many, if not most, contemporary Kantian moral theorists, I think, accept the validity of both the empirical and the practical perspectives but want to reconcile them without Kant's "transcendental idealism."

15. It shows itself in a "sense," often painful, that something that one has done, is doing, or is about to do is wrong and blameworthy; it has motivational force; and people are inclined, at least initially, to treat their own consciences as authoritative, a reliable sign of something deeper and more important than mere customs or personal preferences.

16. See Gilbert Ryle, "Conscience," *Analysis,* vol. 7 (1940). This is reprinted with other discussions of conscience in John Donnelly and Leonard Lyons, eds., *Conscience* (New York: Alba House, 1973), 25–34.

17. Virtually all complex societies consist of various subcultures, which may instill somewhat different norms in their participants. This accounts for variations and conflicts of conscience, but it does not alter the fundamental story.

18. If obedience to conscience is essential to our sense of integrity and self-respect, then, other things being equal, we should no doubt want to encourage them to act conscientiously. But according to ECR, conscience is not something to be especially treasured, protected, and tolerated, at least not for the reasons suggested by the popular conception—that conscience is God given, that it signals moral truth and motivates moral conduct, and that even if mistaken, those who try to follow it are obeying a divine/moral imperative (to follow their conscience to the best of their ability).

19. Contemporary Kantians who reject certain aspects of Kant's metaphysics should expect that the development of conscience can be explained empirically, and in my opinion, there is no need to deny that conscience requires certain cultural contexts in which to develop.

20. It should be noted, to avoid misunderstanding, that the Kantian perspective that I sketch is concerned not with actual, or de facto, agreement in the moral opinions of people across the world and history but, rather, with the regulative ideal of what free, reasonable, and mutually respectful people (defined in a certain way) would agree to if they were "legislating" moral principles (under certain ideal conditions). This

theory is subject to many objections, but not that it reduces objectivity to actual contingent agreement in people's moral opinions.

21. For example, see the distinctions drawn by H. L. A. Hart, *Concept of Law* (Oxford: Clarendon Press, 1961), 163–80; and Kurt Baier, *The Moral Point of View* (Ithaca, N.Y.: Cornell University Press, 1958). To say that the concepts of a group's "custom," "law," and so on differ from the concept of the group's "moral" beliefs is not, of course, to deny either that the same prohibitions may belong to several categories or that the borders between categories are often fuzzy.

22. It is important to distinguish Huck Finn from others who may have had sophisticated, though gravely misguided, moral defenses of the slave system. Huck is described as going through the motions of considering "reasons" and feeling (painfully) that the reasons would show that he "should" in some sense not help Jim escape, but I still see it as more plausible to suppose that young Huck internalized his culture's attitudes without much thought and that his more humane, moral sense was awakening through his friendship with Jim. Huck had to lie and cross the wishes of his elders to help Jim, but his history did not reveal him as someone with a deep commitment to moral ideals of truth telling and obedience to adult rules.

For a different view of the "consciences" of both Huck Finn and Heinrich Himmler, see Jonathan Bennett's challenging essay, "The Conscience of Huckleberry Finn," *Philosophy* 49 (1974): 123–34.

23. These remarks about how those who have a particular normative conception of "conscience" may speak of those who do not share their conception are in response to the worry expressed by my commentators that, by my initial account, Kantians would have to say that only Kantians can have consciences. To say this would be a mistake. Clearly, using the broad core concept, we can be quite inclusive in attributing conscience, and those who hold one conception (e.g., Kantian) can acknowledge that anyone who lacks a conscience as Kantians conceive it may still have "a conscience" as conceived in some other way. As long as we specify what we mean to attribute, we can understand one another, and there is no profit for moral theorists to haggle over who has exclusive title to the honorific term.

24. From this perspective, he argued that observation of human conduct, properly described in plain English, was in conflict with the cynical views of human motivation expressed by Thomas Hobbes and Bernard Mandeville. Self-love is not, and indeed conceptually could not be, the only concern that moves us. Benevolence, conscience, and particular passions influence and sometimes override self-love. Other British moralists, Butler thought, underestimated the moral significance of self-love

and too readily concluded that moral concern is simply concern for the general welfare. See Joseph Butler, *Five Sermons,* ed. Stephen L. Darwall (Indianapolis: Hackett, 1983).

25. Butler did not pretend to describe human nature in evaluatively neutral terms. More like Plato than Hume, he freely speaks of the purposes for which faculties are "designed," always with the assumption that we thrive better as individuals and as a community when each faculty serves its function in a way judged by reason to be appropriate to the whole.

26. Some are intrinsic, such as to solve a puzzle, to taste a cookie, or to help an injured bird, and some derivative, such as desires for tools, money, or medicine. Particular passions may be good or bad, inner directed or outer directed.

27. These basic dispositions exist in different people to different degrees, Butler thought. How to express them suitably may, to some extent, differ according to this and other contextual features. Although all our basic dispositions are good, unless properly supervised they may pull us in different directions and result in immoral and destructive behavior.

28. This is also described as "the principle of reflection," "the moral faculty," and "reason."

29. Butler, *Five Sermons,* 69.

30. That is, human nature is so constituted that anyone with a conscience is disposed to follow it, although sometimes we let other motives overpower it, and human beings with conscience take its judgments to reflect what they ought to do, all things considered, even when its demands are to give up some immediately pressing concern.

31. More important to my present purposes, in arguing for this conclusion, Butler treats conscience as neither a power of pure "rational intuition" nor the ability to deduce particular moral conclusions from abstract necessary "principles of reason." Admittedly, Butler does suggest that we have an unexplained (intuition-like?) grasp of deontological principles against deception, injustice, and unprovoked violence (*Five Sermons,* 70). But unlike those who identify moral judgment with rational intuition regarding particular cases, Butler seems to think that for the most part with conscience, we make reasoned judgments from a basic moral standard derived from natural teleology. The standard, admittedly vague but not empty, is that we should always do what is appropriate to the constitution of our human nature. That is, we must do what is "fitting" for human beings, whose (empirically discerned) basic faculties have natural purposes and are related to one another in a structure that, if properly respected, leads to individual happiness and social harmony. Rationalistic natural law theorists agree with Butler that in moral judg-

ment, reason applies general standards, but Butler's position also differs from theirs. For unlike classic natural lawyers, Butler is skeptical about the project of articulating necessary rational first principles of morals so that individuals need only apply them, more or less deductively, to their particular circumstances. When he keeps his theology to the side, Butler offers his basic moral standard as empirical, and he is under no illusion that it can be applied merely by subsuming particular cases under fully determinative general principles. Although Butler articulated this conception of conscience more thoroughly than anyone else I know of, certain main features of his idea, I think, are still widely shared.

32. Butler typically writes as if conscience is perfectly reliable, although he warns that his methodology is to describe the predominant tendencies of human nature, suggesting that allowing a few exceptions would not be incompatible with his main claims (*Five Sermons*, 32). He allows that we can corrupt our nature and then perhaps might live with vice without "real self-dislike" (18). We might take this to mean that conscience can lose its power to motivate, rather than its ability to distinguish right and wrong correctly. Whether conscience is a "reliable guide" may also depend on how determined we are to consult it, for Butler often stresses our liability to self-deception, a tendency to "avert the eyes of the mind" from what we could see if we were willing to look. What is clear is that Butler thought that at least for all practical purposes, we can and should treat our conscience, if consulted honestly and diligently, as a reliable guide to moral requirements.

33. See Stephen Darwall, *The British Moralists and the Internal "Ought"* (Cambridge: Cambridge University Press, 1995), 244–83, esp. 282–83.

34. In theory it could even be that one person's conscience tells her to thwart another's opportunity to follow his conscience, even though the second person *correctly* judged his instructions of conscience. Since what we ought to do, all things considered, can depend, among other things, on our social role and past commitments, there is no guarantee that two people, each acting correctly by conscience, will not oppose each other, even after each adequately understands the position of the other. In Butler's view, contrary to what some philosophers have maintained, "A has a duty to X" does not entail for all others "it is wrong to prevent A from X-ing."

35. Again, as suggested earlier, the fact that the conscientious judgments of other sincere and honest people sharply differ from our own should be grounds for self-doubt and reconsideration. Such conflicts call for review of the relevant facts, for self-scrutiny to identify bias, for effort to counteract self-deception and wishful thinking; but in the end, after due reflection, we must rely on our own best judgment. Others may

continue to disagree and may punish us for our conscientious act, but acting conscientiously, and only this, in Butler's view, is acting "according to our nature" and in a way that warrants self-approval.

36. I am not arguing here that a theory that "preserves the good name of conscience" independently of theology is necessarily better than one that does not, for I have not attempted to refute ECR, SCR, or the alleged theological underpinnings of the religious conception. Some may accept the various implications I have noted and yet hold that the claims of conscience should be deflated or, alternatively, that they should be retained in a religious context; and I have not argued otherwise.

37. I am reminded of a story once related by Gilbert Ryle. A professor of mathematics was laying out a proof and, moving from one step to another, remarked, "It's obvious that this follows." A student put his hand up and asked, "Excuse me, sir, but is it obvious?" The professor then set about to check his move and in the process covered two more boards with an elaborate proof and then at the end remarked, "Yes, see, it is obvious." In some ways, "my conscience tells me" is like "it is obvious"; it makes a claim to justifiability but is not itself the product of a process of deliberate justification. (If the story is funny, it is because although the professor established the truth of the proposition that he had said was obvious, his elaborate proof could not show that "it is obvious." Similarly, by means of moral argument, one can back up a claim regarding the voice of conscience, but the argument does not show that "conscience said so.")

38. Reflecting the ordinary sense of our moral terms, I take it, is a prima facie, but by no means decisive, consideration for including a particular conception (e.g., of conscience) in our moral theory. An entirely revisionary moral theory is unlikely even to get a hearing, but there are many possible considerations for not automatically adopting current (or even persistent) "common sense." For example, it may presuppose what is contrary to (not just beyond) our best scientific knowledge.

39. Readers will recall that Kant, too, often appeals to (dubious) teleological claims in applying his fundamental principles, but the basic argument for the Categorical Imperative does not rest on these assumptions. It would be contrary to his idea of autonomy to suppose that at the basic level, one might argue for morality from natural teleology.

40. I assume some basic points, including the following: The principal elements of human nature relevant to moral judgment are *sensuous inclinations, reason,* and *will.* The first category includes all ordinary desires and aversions, second order (e.g., the desire for happiness) as well as first order ("particular passions"), self-regarding (self-love) as well as other regarding (benevolence), cultivated desires for pleasures of the mind as

well as instinctual cravings for pleasures of the body. Such inclinations are passive, given facts, not the sort of thing we can control at will, and so in themselves are neither good nor bad. Their value neutrality, I think, is Kant's dominant view, despite some unfortunate passages, reminiscent of Plato, about how rational beings wish to be rid of them. Viewed from a practical standpoint, they are presumed to incline but not determine our behavior. *Will*, in one sense, is a power of choice, enabling us to deliberate and "freely" choose which inclinations, if any, to incorporate into our maxims. *Will* in another sense is the same as *practical reason*. This includes our capacity and disposition to set ourselves ends, to follow hypothetical imperatives in taking means to our ends, and to recognize and follow categorical imperatives in morally significant situations. Practical reason is a broad term that apparently includes the functions of conscience, namely, passing judgment on ourselves for having acting against our judgment as to what is right (or without sufficient effort to determine what was right) or "acquitting" ourselves from self-accusations of such guilt.

Kant treats practical reason not merely as a source of abstract truths but as a set of dispositions to govern ourselves in accord with certain norms of decision making. To have practical reason is to be predisposed to deliberate and choose our courses of action in accord with the rational norms expressed in the Categorical Imperative (various forms) and the Hypothetical Imperative (the general principle behind reasoning to particular hypothetical imperatives, namely, "If one wills an end and finds certain means to that end necessary and available, then one ought to take [will] those means or abandon the end.") I discuss this general principle in *Dignity and Practical Reason,* chaps. 1 and 7.

This is not a stipulative definition of "practical reason" for Kant, nor does he think it is "analytic" that practically rational wills accept the forms of the Categorical Imperative. Nonetheless he thinks the point can be argued, at least that it can be shown to be a presupposition of our belief that we have moral duties that we are committed to the Categorical Imperative (in all its forms) and to viewing this as a "command of reason." These basic "rational" dispositions are unavoidable, demanding, and sometimes painful to live by. They are not seen as something unfortunate, alien, or to be resisted but, rather, as basic self-defining norms and so, as it were, imposed on ourselves by ourselves (our "better self" perhaps). Although not an empirically attributed desire or set of inclinations, practical reason (like these) is a constant and potentially effective element of human motivation. It is attributed to moral agents a priori because analysis (supposedly) reveals it to be a necessary precondition of having duties and obligations, and even of making moral judgments.

Moral feelings, such as respect for moral law, are analyzed as the consequences of recognition of how this basic moral/rational disposition can
conflict with our inclinations. We can, of course, question Kant's claim
that the norms expressed in the Categorical Imperative are necessary
principles of reason, but the fact that we are committed to them as
authoritative is the essential background assumption that enables us to
think of conscience and conscientious judgment as having motivating
force.

41. "Judgment" is ambiguous in many of the passages on conscience.
In one sense it refers simply to drawing more specific conclusions from
general moral principles, that is, "applying" them as when we conclude
that "one mustn't spit in another's face" from "one ought to respect every
person." In *Lectures on Ethics,* trans. Louis Infield (New York: Harper &
Row, 1963), 129, Kant refers to this as "the logical sense," as opposed to
the "judicial sense." The latter is the sort of judgment made by a legal
judge who "condemns or acquits," sentences, and "gives legal effect to his
judgment." See also Kant, *Religion,* 173–74.

42. Intermediate-level principles, articulated in Kant's *The Metaphysics
of Morals,* are supposed to be derivable from the basic requirements,
together with some general empirical facts about the human condition.
The rational capacity to apply the Categorical Imperative and intermedi-
ate principles to specific cases, which is judgment (in one sense), is not
some mysterious special access to moral truth but simply an ability to
interpret the principles, perceive relevant features of one's particular
circumstances, and arrive at a specific directive by subsuming the case at
hand under the principles.

See Immanuel Kant, *Groundwork of the Metaphysic of Morals,* trans. H.
J. Paton (New York: Harper & Row, 1956), 71–72. Kant here treats "judgment" in moral matters as analogous to judgment regarding science and
ordinary matters of fact, that is, as the capacity to apply general principles
and concepts to more specific circumstances. In writing about conscience
as the inner "judge," however, the sense is different, the model being a
legal judge passing sentence on an accused or acquitting him or her.

43. Ibid.

44. We can distinguish, then, these possible sources of mistaken moral
beliefs: (a) one makes no moral judgments for oneself but blindly takes
on the mistakes of one's adviser or one's culture; (b) one judges badly, or
misjudges, what follows from the basic moral law because one is inatten-
tive, careless, and/or self-serving in the process of judgment (implicit or
explicit); and (c) one misperceives, or fails to consider as relevant, facts
about one's situation that are in fact morally important. Like most moral
philosophers in his tradition, Kant did not acknowledge radical igno-

rance or misunderstanding of the basic moral law as a further source of mistaken moral belief. The errors here are presumably failures to exercise due care in self-scrutiny. Consider, for example, *MM*, 236. His theory can allow (even if Kant himself did not) that there might be adult, functioning members of our species who do not know or understand what Kant calls the moral law, but then their norms, if any, would be amoral and their applications of them not erroneous moral judgments but, rather, judgments of some other kind.

45. Notably there are shifts from Kant's *Lectures on Ethics*, to *The Metaphysics of Morals*, to *Religion within the Limits of Reason Alone*. See *MM*, 202, 233–35; and *Religion*, 173–74. There are places where Kant seems to use "conscience" broadly, like Butler, for our capacity to determine whether our acts are right or wrong by applying the basic moral law to them. See, for example, Kant's *Groundwork*, 79, 89–90.

46. Carrying the metaphor to an extreme, Kant writes, "Only the descent into the hell of self-knowledge can prepare the way for godliness." *MM*, 236, 233.

47. See Kant, *Lectures*, 129; *MM*, 100–1, 59–60.

48. Also Immanuel Kant, *Critique of Practical Reason*, trans. Lewis White Beck (New York: Macmillan, 1956), 101–3.

See also Kant on imputation, *MM*, 50, 53. In German law, apparently, the two phases of determining whether an agent's act is a legal offense ("objective" guilt) and determining whether the act is "imputable" to the agent (culpability) are more separate than in our legal system. See Joachim Hruschka, "Imputation," *Brigham Young University Law Review* (1986): 669–710. A series of articles on imputation, particularly in Kant and in German law, appeared in *Jahrbuch für Recht und Ethik*, band 2 (1994), ed. B. Sharon Byrd, Joachim Hruschka, and Jan C. Joerden (Berlin: Duncker & Humblot, 1994).

49. Kant, *Religion*, 174.

50. A puzzling passage in *The Metaphysics of Morals* also suggests that what conscience judges is simply "whether I have submitted [my act] to my practical reason (here in its role as judge) for such a judgment" (*MM*, 202). My best efforts to untangle what Kant means there is that the relevance of "whether I have submitted" is not literally that this is what conscience judges but that it is a background fact that one knows unmistakably and that is part of the suggested argument that conscience cannot err.

Roughly, that argument might be reconstructed as follows: If on the one hand, we did scrutinize our act by our moral standards, we would have known this easily by introspection, and if so, conscience would have "involuntarily" reached its verdict and (if appropriate) imposed its sentence. Mistakes here are apparently assumed to be impossible because what we compare is all "internal": our conception of our act and our moral judgment regarding its rightness or wrongness. But if we did not submit our act to our moral standards, we did not make any prior moral judgment on the particular act, and so our conscience (which presupposes such judgments) never operated and so cannot have yielded a false verdict. Mistakes due to bad memory of our past acts and/or deliberations, misjudgment of objective duty, self-deceived conceptions of our acts, and the like are not counted as errors of conscience but as failures antecedent to its operation.

51. *MM*, 236.

52. Presumably it is rare that we have a clean conscience with respect to due care but a guilty conscience with respect to first-order duties, for that would mean that despite the most diligent effort to ensure that our projected acts are not wrong, we nevertheless acted in a way that was wrong even in our own judgment. In other words, we weakly or perversely ignored the conclusion of our diligent search. Assuming this to be rare, we can suppose that satisfying conscience in the *Religion* sense (due care) typically leads us to satisfy it in the prior sense of *The Metaphysics of Morals* (imputation and judicial judgment of first-order duty violations).

53. Kant's remarks on this are puzzling. One crucial passage denying "erring conscience" is *MM* 59–60 [401]. But in the much earlier *Lectures on Ethics*, 132–33, Kant acknowledges "errors of conscience," based on errors of fact or errors of law, some culpable, some not. Conscience can be "natural" or "instructed" (and apparently at times "misinstructed"); the natural conscience takes precedence in cases that conflict. Again, however, Kant reaffirms that there can be no nonculpable errors about the basic moral law, that one can mistake something else (e.g., prudence) for conscience but cannot "deceive" or "escape" it.

54. "But when a man is aware of having acted according to his conscience, then as far as guilt or innocence is concerned, nothing more can be demanded" (*MM*, 202).

55. See *MM*, 192–93.

3

JIMINY CRICKET: A COMMENTARY ON PROFESSOR HILL'S FOUR CONCEPTIONS OF CONSCIENCE

NOMI MAYA STOLZENBERG

Professor Hill's delineation of four seemingly different conceptions of conscience draws attention to the major conceptual contrasts that inform the concept of conscience in the tradition of Western philosophy: reason versus faith, judgment versus instinct, calm cool reflection versus the heat of passion and the warm rush of interest, subjective versus objective, and self versus other. Hill also turns our attention to practical and political questions: "To what extent and why should one (1) treat the apparent promptings of one's own conscience as one's authoritative guide and (2) respectfully tolerate the conduct of others when they are apparently guided by conscience?" [1]

In this chapter, I argue that these are not really two separate questions but, rather, two ways of articulating one central conundrum that arises out of the fact that moral judgments are ultimately subjective and inevitably subject to disagreement yet, by their very nature, claim the "objective" authority to be imposed on others. By the same token, on inspection, the four conceptions of conscience that Hill differentiates turn out to be not different conceptions but the same conception—conscience as the faculty of subjective moral judgment—viewed from different perspectives. The fact that we adopt these different perspectives—and that we sometimes do so without even realizing it and mistakenly confuse our shift in perspective with a change in the conception of conscience itself—reflects the basic conundrum of moral disagreement and subjectivity, as I will explain.

Hill identifies four conceptions of conscience: (1) the "popular–religious" conception, (2) the "deflationary cultural relativist" or "extreme cultural relativist" conception, (3) the "Butlerian" conception of conscience as reflective judgment, and (4) the Kantian conception of conscience as judgment passing judgment on itself. As the main focus of his chapter, Hill tries to determine which of these four conceptions best fits Kantian moral theory and concludes that it is Kant's own account of conscience. This conclusion is perhaps more surprising and significant than it sounds, since as Hill points out, "it might seem at first that 'conscience' should have no place in rationalistic moral theories such as Kant's."[2] My concern, however, lies elsewhere. I take (and challenge) no position on whether Kantian moral theory is consistent with any concept of conscience, let alone whether the "Kantian conception" of that concept is the most suitable one from a Kantian perspective. Instead, my concern is whether the four conceptions of conscience that Hill delineates do differ from one another in the ways that he suggests.[3]

According to Hill, each of the four conceptions has different implications for the reliability of our own conscience and for the advisability of tolerating, encouraging, or respecting the right of other people to be guided by theirs. The popular–religious view of the conscience as a sort of internal oracle, a God-given instinctive capacity to discern what is objectively right or wrong for us to do, offers strong support for relying on our conscience and encouraging others to do the same. Butler's view of the conscience as residing in our capacity to deliberate rationally the moral "fittingness" of our actions as human conduct also is a good reason to rely on our consciences. Indeed, Hill sees the Butlerian view as providing even better support for the authority of conscience than does the popular–religious conception. The reason is that in the popular view, conscience operates through mere intuition and not rational reflective judgment. Since there will always be (both religious and nonreligious) grounds for doubting that each individual's intuitions unerringly identify wrong acts, moral doubts are generated that call for checking by independent reasoned moral reflection.

Hill thinks that "reflective moral judgment, based on a careful review of pertinent facts in consultation with others," is required because "without such a check, there is no way to be confident that the instinct on which we are about to rely is 'conscience' rather than some baser instinct."[4] In other words, precisely because the instinct posited by the popular view of conscience is not rational deliberation, it needs to be supplemented by rational deliberation in order to avoid moral error. The problem, in short, is that the popular view of conscience as an instinct "omits (what the Kantian takes to be) the prior and indispensable roles of reason and judgment in determining what we ought to do."[5]

By contrast, Hill informs us, Joseph Butler expounded a conception of conscience as reflective, deliberative moral judgment. Because Butler equates conscience with "our own best, reasonable judgment" after due reflection (i.e., " 'calm' 'cool' reflection," or "reasoned reflection") about the best course of action to take, his view creates even less "room for moral doubts" about the reliability of conscience than does the popular conception.[6]

If Butler fortifies the case for the authority of conscience by integrating moral reasoning into the concept, Kant, according to Hill, perfects it by supplying a "more plausible and determinate idea of the standards that should guide reasonable moral reflection" and, furthermore, by distinguishing the special role of conscience from the process of making moral judgments, the latter of which is necessary to, but separate from, the faculty of conscience itself. (The superego, discriminating between the self-serving and the morally creditable rationalizations of the ego, might be an apt analogy to this view of the conscience as an inner judge of judgments, which Hill ascribes to Kant.)

For our purposes, the crucial point is that in the Kantian view, as Hill explains it, "I must heed my own conscience" because it is "as reliable a subjective guide as we can get." Implicit in this pronouncement is the view that subjective guidance is as good as it gets—that subjective judgment is, in the final analysis, the only guidance that we have. As Hill explains, "A clear conscience is no guarantee that we acted in an objectively right way," although it is both "necessary and sufficient for morally blameless conduct."

Because the conscience is not equated with objectively true moral principles, the Kantian view "does not support an absolute ban on coercing someone against his or her conscience" (his or her conscientious judgment could be wrong). It nonetheless urges "respect for conscientious resistance even when we believe it is mistaken."[7]

Hill thus presents the popular, Butlerian, and Kantian views sequentially as providing strong, stronger, and finally the strongest possible support for relying on conscience as a guide to moral decisions, albeit not an objectively authoritative or infallible guide. The only view that he regards as generating little respect for conscience—one's own or others'—is what he calls the "extreme cultural relativist" view of the conscience as "nothing but" feelings symptomatic of internalized, local, cultural norms. This is also the view for which Hill evinces the most disdain. (He is respectful of all the other three accounts, although he singles out the Kantian one as the most plausible and commendable.)

Hill makes it clear that he has no quarrel with the "relativist" position insofar as it is limited to providing a naturalistic "causal explanation of the genesis and social function of the feelings ascribed to 'conscience.' " As an empirical, anthropological thesis, relativism is all well and good (even undeniable). The problem arises when "relativism" ventures "outside the anthropology class" and takes "a giant step beyond empirical explanation into an area of perennial philosophical controversy." Specifically, the "deep point of disagreement" is with relativism's "denial of objective standards of moral reasoning and judgment." With the issue thus joined, Hill allows that "the issues are more complicated" than he has space to elaborate and simply moves on.[8]

Soft spoken as they are, these are fighting words, and Hill rounds up the usual suspects. Himmler's Nazi norms, Hill charges, amount, in the "relativist" view, to conscience because that view reduces the conscience to internalized local, cultural norms, whatever they happen to be. Such a view is problematical, according to Hill, because it does not require that conscience express true, correct, or "objectively justifiable moral beliefs."[9] In other words, it is too subjective, or so Hill argues.

This is powerful rhetoric. But when we examine more closely the argument against the relativist conception, we find that it is not fully supported. Furthermore, and perhaps more important, we find that the relativist conception does not really differ in its essentials from any of the others. In the final analysis, the other three ways of understanding the conscience all appear to be variations of the so-called relativist or, what I prefer to call, the *subjectivist* view. To see this, though, we must determine what the basic features of that view are.

Hill and I do not disagree over what the content and perspective of the subjectivist (relativist) view are—indeed, I will draw on his excellent description. Rather, we disagree over its practical and political implications regarding the reliability of our and others' consciences. We also disagree over how and whether the conception of the conscience that is the object of the subjectivist view differs from the others.

The subjectivist view of conscience certainly bespeaks a perspective on the matter different from that of the other views. The popular view is rooted in a religious perspective, in a belief in God and a faith that God would not play such a cruel joke as to instill in human beings a mistaken yet strongly felt sense of right and wrong. The Butlerian view shares this earnest belief in the existence of a human faculty, whose natural purpose is to correctly discern moral obligations and requirements. Even though Butler based his ideas on empirical observation, rather than on religious faith, his view of human nature, and of nature generally, as being "designed" to fulfil benevolent, moral purposes resists moral cynicism. Like Kant, he sees morality as morality, rather than as some sort of illusory belief structure or myth, as the more cynical naturalists might have it.

By contrast, the perspective of the subjectivist, typified by Hill's armchair anthropologist, is quintessentially detached, external, academic—in a word, "objective." It is a perspective that neither affirms nor denies the truth or the validity of the beliefs under examination; it simply documents their existence as such, as beliefs (i.e., subjective beliefs) characteristic of a certain time and place and set of individuals. From this standpoint, which aims to be not a moral but a neutral point of view, the content of what we call the conscience consists of social norms that have been internalized through diffuse cultural processes of moral education and socialization.

In this account, conscience is experienced subjectively, much along the lines described by the popular conception—as an instinctual response to transgressions rather than as a conscious deliberative or reasoned judgment about how basic moral principles apply to particular circumstances. Instead of our making fresh independent deductive judgments about what is right and wrong in each case, the subjectivist perspective views us as having deeply internalized norms, which cause us to respond to our own actual or anticipated transgressions with a feeling of discomfort. These feelings are produced "for the most part without thinking about them," as automatic effects of value inculcation.[10] They signal "not that an objectively true moral principle has been violated or threatened but merely that we are about to step across some line that early influences have deeply etched on our personality."[11] From the external point of view, values are thus subjective. Moreover, since cultures differ and since values are simply internalized cultural norms, values are seen to differ among and within the ever-changing and proliferating cultures and subcultures of the world.

So here we have the two essential features of what I earlier maintained is the basic conundrum to which a single conception of the conscience responds. First, there is disagreement, both across cultures and among individuals, over what is moral or immoral. Second, morality is subjective, in the sense that it is culturally specific and that it is ultimately a matter of personal, individual opinion or belief. The idea of conscience represents the concrete embodiment of morality as a subjective judgment, feeling, opinion, or belief that resides in the individual. The subjectivist, or "relativist"—or, better yet, external—perspective simply throws into relief the inherent subjectivity and variability of morality.

But is Hill correct in concluding that it thereby offers little reason to rely on or protect the right of others to act on conscientious beliefs? And more to the point, is he correct in maintaining that the other views are more successful in avoiding what he regards as these pitfalls of relativism? Are they really any different from the subjectivist view? Hill believes that relativism leads to a devaluation of conscience, to a diminution if not an outright denial of its moral authority. Since the conscience reflects "noth-

ing but" internalized cultural norms and since it is always possible
that a culture's norms are unjust, needlessly self-constraining, and
no longer socially productive, the claims of conscience are always
"defeasible"—and this applies to the claims of one's own conscience as well as those of others.

The subjectivist perspective reveals that "we have a self-interested reason to be pleased when others' consciences discourage
behavior that we dislike." But when their consciences lead them
to take positions with which we disagree, the subjectivist account
suggests that "we should merely pity them for their unnecessary
inhibitions and needless suffering." [12] Once we adopt the neutral,
external point of view with regard to other people's conscientious
beliefs, there is no reason to suppose that our own consciences
are any less immune to such potential defects or that our own
feelings of guilt or shame are any less "unnecessary." (Witness
the popularity of the many contemporary therapeutic movements
designed to cure us of such unnecessary feelings.)

My question is how this conception of conscience differs from
the popular, Butlerian, and Kantian views and in what respect it
is not only different but inferior—for Hill is making both a
comparative and a normative claim. According to him, the subjectivist account makes a stronger case for the defeasibility of the
claims of conscience. (Presumably, then, if Himmler had adopted
the subjectivist view, he would have been inclined to question
the validity of Hitler's and his own moral beliefs.) The greater
defeasibility of conscientious beliefs is supposed (by Hill) to result
from the absence of a role for moral reasoning in the formation
of conscientious beliefs. As a culturally induced "gut feeling,"
the faculty of conscience is supposedly disconnected from moral
reasoning.

The disconnection of conscience from rational judgment and
moral reasoning is precisely what is supposed to distinguish the
subjectivist from the Butlerian and Kantian views of conscience.
Regarded from a subjectivist perspective, the claims of conscience
are more defeasible (i.e., they carry less authority) because they
are not generated by moral judgments or indeed by any kind of
individual judgment (i.e., the rational process of deliberation) at
all.

The argument, as I have said, is a comparative one. It goes

hand in hand with Hill's assertion that conscience, understood along Butlerian and Kantian lines, is less defeasible—commands more authority and warrants more respect—because these accounts incorporate a mental process of moral judgment exercised by individuals as either an adjunct to or the essence of the faculty of conscience. Even the popular conception of conscience—though lacking the essential ingredient of moral reasoning or rational judgment and hence needing such a mental process as a supplement or "check"—is superior to the relativist account and lends more authority to the claims of conscience because it relies on a notion of access to a distinctively moral class of values.

Hill makes no bones about the fact that his view of what is lacking in the inferior conceptions and what they require as necessary supplements, reflects his own commitment to (his understanding of) Kantianism. The very idea that the absence of individual deductive reasoning is a deficiency—the assumption that instinctive or "gut" responses to injustice are less reliable than individual applications of general moral principles to the particular case at hand—presupposes a belief in the separability of nonrational beliefs from rational knowledge and in the priority of the latter over the former.

To many of us, this is not an obviously correct view—we may be disinclined to agree with the proposition that Hill attributes to Kant and seemingly endorses: "that whatever reasonable beliefs we can have about God [or, we might add, about secular principles of right and wrong] must be based on prior moral knowledge, not the reverse." [13] Hill does not supply an argument for the priority of knowledge over faith or nonrationally supported beliefs—in particular, the ability to know what moral values are without subscribing first to any articles of faith. But such a position stands as the chapter's indispensable foundation, and it accounts for Hill's comparative judgment that moral instincts are inferior to moral reasoning and that individual engagement in moral reasoning is required to certify the authority of conscience.

But is there really a process of moral reasoning that individuals can engage in that adequately certifies the authority of conscience so that its claims are rendered any less defeasible than on the "deflationary" subjectivist account? Is there any view of the conscience that needs no supplement or check, and is there any possible supplement or check that itself requires no further supplement or check? Such an argument is needed to support the inferiority of the subjectivist view, yet Hill himself casts doubt on the proposition.

The question boils down to whether the proposed cure for the moral doubts that haunt the claims based on gut moral instincts delivers what it promises—whether the "medicine" (judgment or rational deliberation) carries any more immunity to the "disease" (moral doubts) than does the original patient (divinely or culturally instilled nonrational moral instincts). Can the exercise of individual moral judgment eliminate doubts about the moral correctness of a person's moral views? Can it guarantee that one's own or another person's views and actions really are moral? Is it an adequate license to act in ways that others disapprove? Does another person's claim to have made a conscientious moral judgment necessarily warrant deference?

Hill, correctly in my view, makes it clear that the answers to all these questions must be no. He effectively argues that there is no guarantee that anybody's judgments are correct, even if they are based on conscious, explicit reflection, cool deliberation, and diligent attempts to interpret and apply sound moral principles to the relevant features of a person's particular circumstances. The best we can do—and it is here that Hill sees Kant as improving Butler's endorsement of engaging in deliberative judgment—is to submit (and resubmit) our own judgments to further self-scrutiny for possible errors. Was I really applying a sound moral principle to my actions, or was I making a self-serving exception? Did I correctly perceive the morally relevant features of my circumstances, or was I engaging in wishful thinking or some other form of self-deception? Was I adequately attentive and diligent in my moral accounting? Was I blindly influenced by others or by the culture at large? It is this kind of self-criticism, the retrospective criticism of our own prior moral reasoning that, Hill says, Kant sees as the precondition of conscience. Here conscience is not the original act of rational reflection about the morality of our actions or even the subsequent reflection about the moral quality of our earlier moral reflections. It is, rather, an involuntary response—

the voice of our "inner judge" passing judgment on our judgments after we have reviewed the relevant evidence and considered the arguments in our own favor and against it.

Thus conceived, the "voice" of conscience can never ensure correctness. Every encounter with differing views is a fresh occasion for self-questioning and renewed rational deliberation. It is true that "in the end I must heed my own conscience, not that of others," but this is a sort of endless end, in which I am continually obliged to diligently reconsider what the voice of my own conscience says, informed by the views of others. My conscience always requires a supplement or a check. But the only check ever available is yet another inherently subjective and fallible application of individual human judgment.

Thus, even in the Kantian view, which improves on Butler's by supplementing original acts of moral judgment with self-critical judgments about one's judgment, the claims of conscience are always defeasible. Moreover, the causes of—and the usual occasions for—their defeasibility are (1) their inherent subjectivity and (2) the differing moral views of others—precisely the conditions highlighted by the subjectivist view and regarded by Hill as "deflating" the authority of the voice of conscience.

Hill himself makes clear that none of the supposedly differing conceptions of conscience—not the popular or the Butlerian or the Kantian view—escapes subjectivity. He makes it equally clear that each view, no matter how strong its arguments for the authority of conscience, leaves open a "loophole" for the possibility of error, moral fallibility—for the continual possibility of our being wrong and others being right, or vice versa. Moral disagreement in every account generates a need for checking conscience and then checking it again, and so on and so on, without end. And the only ways of checking it—recommended in each view—are using our head, consulting with others, listening (though not genuflecting) to external authorities, and sensing our gut instincts. Although none of these processes can be finally authoritative over the others, any one can serve as a check on the others, and, taken together and repeated over and over, they comprise our "best judgment" after "due reflection." In the end, as Hill says himself, they are the best that we can do.

Conscience, as understood by each of the four views that Hill identifies, thus exhibits the same basic, recognizable features. It is, according to all accounts, fallible and susceptible to error, hence defeasible. Moreover, the fallibility of conscience is traced in all accounts to its inherent subjectivity. Conscience resides in each of us and can never transcend our opinions or beliefs, although it may transcend our baser whims and preferences and although opinions and beliefs may evolve, in significant part through our contact with others. In all accounts, the existence of moral disagreement is singled out as an occasion that should trigger the reconsideration of our original conscientious judgments. Still, in all accounts, the "voice" of conscience (and interestingly enough, it is imagined by all four accounts as a voice) commands a certain amount of authority and respect—as much authority and respect as any human feature possibly can. It preserves a contrast between our purely self-interested whims and preferences and altruistic desires, and it represents our best efforts to heed the needs and the viewpoints of others while giving due (but no more than due) weight to our needs and interests. This is no less true in the subjectivist account than in the other views. To hold otherwise is to confuse the moral content of the *perspective* of the subjectivist view with the content of the object that is viewed from this perspective—the phenomenology of the conscience itself.

The subjectivist perspective itself is not distinctively moral; indeed, it is supposed to be scrupulously amoral, value neutral, and, in this sense, "objective." It does not determine the validity of the great variety of conflicting conscientious judgments and beliefs, which it observes from the outside. Nonetheless, what it describes—the phenomenology of conscientious beliefs—includes judgments about the moral validity of competing beliefs. It observes such judgments as being informed by the distinctions between selfish and altruistic acts, between "mere" whims and preferences, on the one hand, and other-regarding decisions, on the other, that characteristically define distinctively moral norms. Recognizing that the surrounding culture is the source of the content of these norms does nothing to flatten out these distinctions as they operate in the minds of the individuals observed— the example of Himmler notwithstanding.[14]

If I have not yet persuaded you that the same image of con-

science animates all four "conceptions"—which I would rede-
scribe as four different perspectives on one and the same conception—perhaps the similarity of all four to a ubiquitous popular
image of the conscience will. Walt Disney's recreation of Pinocchio gave to us the image of Jiminy Cricket, deputized by the Blue
Fairy to serve Pinocchio as his conscience as he undertook to earn
the right to become a real boy by proving himself to be brave,
truthful, and unselfish and to learn to choose between right and
wrong. As the physical embodiment of Pinocchio's conscience,
Jiminy Cricket is above all a voice—the same admonitory voice
that appears in each of Hill's four accounts.

Consider this Jiminy Cricket–like description of how conscience is pictured in the popular–religious view—in Hill's words,
"not so much like an intellectual moral adviser as like an instinct-
governed, internal 'voice' or sign that 'tells' us what we must do
or must not do, warns us when tempted, and prods us to reform
when guilty." The same basic image reappears in Hill's description
of the relativist view in which " 'the voice of conscience' " is still
experienced as a voice and is still "experienced as an instinctual
feeling rather than as a deliberate judgment about how basic
moral principles apply to particular circumstances." [15]

Jiminy Cricket perfectly exemplifies the inchoate quality of the
moral principles that animate the popular–religious and relativist–subjectivist views. He has a voice, but a singularly inarticulate
one. When Pinocchio asks the Blue Fairy how he will know the
difference between right and wrong—and after all, how could he
know?—the Blue Fairy tells him, "Your conscience will tell you."
Jiminy Cricket earns his chance to serve as Pinocchio's conscience
when he explains that a conscience is "that still small voice that
people won't listen to," but when Pinocchio asks Jiminy Cricket to
explain what temptations are—the avoidance of temptation having been decreed by the Blue Fairy as the hallmark of acting in
good conscience—Jiminy Cricket can only stammer, "They're the
wrong things that seem right at the time—but, uh, even—even
though the right things may seem wrong sometimes, sometimes
the wrong things may be right at the wrong time or, or vice
versa—understand?" The joke, of course, is that Jiminy Cricket is
blathering incomprehensibly, and we all share his relief when he

is allowed to lapse into the catchy jingle "give a little whistle" in lieu of having to articulate principles distinguishing right from wrong.

The inchoate nature of the moral principles that Pinocchio is supposed to follow and his obvious inability as a puppet to act as a free agent deliberately choosing between right and wrong (as the Kantian Blue Fairy prescribes) surely have bothered many children before me. Jiminy Cricket, unable to articulate general moral principles, strongly resembles the "instinct-governed, internal" nag that Hill ascribes to both the popular and the relativist conceptions of conscience. His description of Butler's view of conscience is not notably different in this respect; like Jiminy Cricket, Butler's conscience can provide only the vaguest specification of the standards that it is supposed to be applying when engaging in moral deliberation.

Butler's moral "judgments" hardly differ from moral intuitions insofar as they remain inchoate. And if Butler's conception of conscience resembles Jiminy Cricket (and the popular and relativist views) in this respect, Hill finds fault with Butler's conception of the conscience insofar as it departs from the Jiminy Cricket–like imagery of a voice that " 'speaks,' 'demands,' 'warns,' 'prods,' 'forbids,' 'rebels,' and at times 'is revolted.' "[16] Like the Blue Fairy, Butler's conception just assumes that individuals somehow have access to the standards of right and wrong, which are to "guide" their conscience. As in the popular–religious and subjectivist–relativist conceptions, some articles of faith—for example, that certain acts, such as murder and adultery, are morally wrong—are required to get the thing going. Reason is not used to establish what is in the class of wrong acts; the existence of a class of wrong acts and the knowledge of what it contains are simply assumed. Butler apparently expects us, like Pinocchio, to "know" them by virtue of some nonrational process.

Kant's conception of the conscience bears an even closer resemblance to the image of Jiminy Cricket. Kant imagines the conscience as "an inner judge" that "reproaches" us.[17] As Hill approvingly notes, "Although [Kant's] metaphors suggest that the moral agent is active in the operations of conscience, Kant also describes conscience as like an 'instinct,' as something that we 'find' in ourselves, something that we 'hear' even when we try to run away"—just as Pinocchio "ran away from Jiminy Cricket and Gepetto.[18] Hill approves of Kant's image of conscience as "something that 'speaks involuntarily and inevitably,' " apparently because that metaphor more accurately describes the felt experience of having a conscience.[19]

The same image of conscience as inner, admonitory voice—an inner judge that relies on instinctive as well as on strictly rational judgments—animates all four of the supposedly different conceptions that Hill delineates. Imagining the conscience as residing in each individual, speaking to each individual alone, the metaphor of an inner voice of an inner judge represents the ultimate subjectivity of conscience, which, far from undermining its authority, makes it as "reliable a guide as we can get."

In pointing up the subjectivity and the cultural variability of conscience, the subjectivist perspective is no more or less skeptical and relativistic than any of the other conceptions; it is no more or less skeptical and relativistic than is warranted. It simply represents a perspective on conscience external to the voice of conscience itself and external to the individual whose conscience it is. That is, it represents the perspective that each of us assumes with regard to the conscience of others and, likewise, the perspective that others assume with regard to our own. This is why Hill's two questions—how much authority each of us should give to our own conscience and how much authority each of us should give to the consciences of others—devolve into the same basic question: how should we manage our moral disagreements, given that none of us can ever be certain of being right? It is impossible and undesirable to always refrain from imposing our moral judgments on one another. From the internal perspective of the individual, modeled by Butler, Kant, and the popular–religious view, our conscience makes claims to moral correctness that feel authoritative, even "objective." But when we switch to the external perspective and regard the consciences of others or, with a little detachment, self-critically regard our own conscientious views, we see them for nothing more or less than what they are: culturally influenced, personally generated, subjectively held moral opinions—the very stuff of morality.

NOTES

1. Thomas E. Hill Jr., "Four Conceptions of Conscience," this volume, 14.

2. Ibid., 15–16.

3. To avoid confusion, let me emphasize that I am not arguing that there are no differences among the accounts at all; rather, I am arguing only against the specific distinction that Hill makes. It is possible, for example, that the Kantian conception of the conscience succeeds in building a stronger case for deferring to conscientious beliefs insofar as it, alone, insists on the necessity of double- (and triple-, indeed endless re-) checking one's moral judgments. The process of continual reconsideration, prescribed by the Kantian account (as Hill describes), can be seen as minimizing the risk of moral error and thus resting its claim for the authority of conscience on that risk minimization, rather than on some unattainable ideal of moral "objectivity." The fact that none of the various accounts can claim "objectivity" does not imply that they are equally good at minimizing the risks of moral error. My gratitude to Professor Jody Armour for helping me see this point.

4. Hill, "Four Conceptions of Conscience," 20.

5. Ibid., 20–21.

6. Ibid., 29.

7. Ibid., 35–36, 37.

8. Ibid., 21–22.

9. Ibid., 26.

10. Ibid., 23.

11. Ibid., 23.

12. Ibid., 24.

13. Ibid., 20.

14. Although I do not have the evidence to prove this essentially empirical point, I find it unlikely that Himmler experienced the rationalizations in his head as the promptings of his conscience. It seems far more likely that he—or at least others who participated in the Nazis' crimes—had internalized certain cultural norms that created some sense of moral discomfort regarding those crimes but that they let other (non-conscientious) desires overcome those pangs of conscience. It is also conceivable that some Nazis were socialized in a way that lacked the distinctively moral concerns that properly merit the label of *conscience.* The possibility that the Nazis felt the impulse to exterminate Jews and others *as the voice of the conscience* is only one possibility among others.

15. Hill, "Four Conceptions of Conscience," 18, 23.

16. Ibid., 30.

17. Ibid., 32.

18. Kantian notions of free agency ought to be disturbed by the fact that in the Disney movie, Pinocchio is abducted yet is held to account as if he had run away. A psychoanalytic explanation of Pinocchio's guilt may be more convincing than a Kantian one here.

19. Hill, "Four Conceptions of Conscience," 33.

4

CONSCIENCE AND MORAL PSYCHOLOGY: REFLECTIONS ON THOMAS HILL'S "FOUR CONCEPTIONS OF CONSCIENCE"

ELIZABETH KISS

Thomas Hill's characteristically lucid, careful, and fair-minded essay provides a richly textured account of four interpretations of conscience and its proper role in moral life. In evaluating these four conceptions, Hill focuses on two criteria. The first is the extent to which a conception of conscience accords with what he calls our "core idea" of conscience, which he defines as "a capacity, commonly attributed to most human beings, to sense or immediately discern that what he or she has done, is doing, or is about to do (or not do) is wrong, bad, and worthy of disapproval." Hill argues that two of the four conceptions he discusses fall short because they veer too far from this core idea. Joseph Butler's seventeenth-century understanding of conscience as reflective moral judgment packs too much into the notion of conscience and thus fails to capture the way that conscience is commonly perceived as "an immediate, instinctive response," a sudden "demand or reprimand," rather than as "the product of a long, careful process of rational deliberation." And the deflationary sociological account of conscience that Hill terms "extreme cultural relativism" obscures the specifically moral force of pangs of conscience, since it fails to distinguish between the wide range of people's responses to cultural norms and the particular way in which conscience operates as a voice of moral admonition.[1]

Hill's second criterion for evaluating conceptions of conscience is whether or not they situate conscience in a coherent and defensible account of moral reasoning and moral life. The popular–religious view of conscience as God's voice, giving (some?) human beings direct intuitive access to moral truth, is problematic on this score because it leads to confusingly mixed conclusions about the infallibility of conscience and omits or underestimates the role of reflection and judgment in determining what we ought to do. Hill concludes that it is Kant's conception of conscience as "judicial self-appraisal" that best meets both these criteria for adequacy.

Kant's metaphorical description of conscience as an "inner judge" that condemns or acquits captures the immediacy and emotional force of the voice of conscience. At the same time, the Kantian conception stresses the limited role of conscience. It is "not a moral expert with an intuition of moral truth or a moral legislator that makes moral laws or a moral arbitrator that settles perplexing cases."[2] Rather, conscience presupposes and uses the results of moral reasoning and judgment; it is the voice of moral self-evaluation that prompts us to recognize when our conduct fails to accord with our moral judgments. More deeply, conscience compels us to engage in self-scrutiny to ensure that we are diligently and sincerely examining ourselves and our actions.

There is much to admire in the Kantian conception of conscience, and Hill offers a compelling argument for why the Kantian account is superior to the other three conceptions he discusses. Moreover, he acknowledges, rather disarmingly, that there may be some troubling aspects of Kant's account of conscience and that "there are moral values and ideals not readily expressible in this framework."[3] I want to elaborate on these qualifications and to suggest three ways in which the Kantian account of conscience is neither complete nor uniquely or unambiguously admirable. My point is not to reject the Kantian account but to point out that its moral psychology and phenomenology are different from, and to some extent in tension with, other visions of conscience and of moral life. More generally, I want to show that some approaches to conscience lie beyond Hill's four conceptions or intersect them in ways that illuminate points left obscured by Hill's analysis.

I.

Kant's metaphorical description of conscience is strikingly austere. Conscience is a stern judge that imposes verdicts of guilt or acquittal. A guilty judgment brings suffering, whereas "the verdict of acquittal brings relief but not happiness." Conscience never issues psychic rewards, nor is it conceived as a merciful or forgiving judge. As Hill acknowledges, although this account of conscience may reflect widely shared moral experience in our culture, we may wonder whether the legal models it employs are "essential to, or best for, understanding morality." The Kantian account appears to be highly culturally specific, reflecting Protestant assumptions about human nature and sin. Moreover, such psychic austerity is not entailed by a commitment to moral self-scrutiny. For instance, an account of the moral life may stress diligent self-scrutiny while endorsing feelings of joy and pride in doing the right thing. But in a Kantian account, such psychic rewards are illegitimate or at least problematic.[4]

The moral ideal implicit in Kant's account of conscience includes a highly intellectual emphasis on self-scrutiny and a rather austere sense of moral failure as our default position. This is, it seems to me, a noble kind of moral vision. But in other accounts of the moral life, self-scrutiny may be less punitive; good deeds may legitimately bring joy; and other moral virtues—responsiveness to others, for instance—may be given a more central role. The austerity of Kant's account may even pose moral dangers. Taken to extremes, a Kantian conscience could lead to a cramped and self-doubting or even self-paralyzing moral agency.

My first worry about the Kantian account of conscience, then, is that it invokes a highly specific vision of moral psychology and that this vision is neither uniquely nor unambiguously admirable. I am not suggesting that this vision is inherently pathological but, rather, that it is associated with the risk of certain pathologies. Other accounts of the moral life are linked to different dangers and pathologies.

The conclusion to be drawn is not that Kant's account of conscience is wrong but that it has the descriptive shortcoming of presenting a particular account of moral psychology as if it were universally human. Conscience probably plays some role in any morality, as Annette Baier suggested when she defined morality as "the culturally acquired art of selecting which harms to notice or worry about, where the worry takes the form of bad conscience or resentment.[5] Or at least conscience plays an important role in accounts of morality that focus on the internal life of moral agents. But these accounts may exhibit different assumptions about moral psychology. Kant's account of conscience also exhibits what might be called a normative shortcoming in that it suggests that commitment to the Categorical Imperative entails this particular model of conscience and moral psychology. Yet one can be committed to humanity as an end in itself, and to the importance of self-scrutiny, without embracing the more austere elements of Kant's account of conscience. In other words, Kant's account of conscience may be parochial in ways that Kant's conception of humanity as an end in itself is not.

II.

My second concern about the Kantian account of conscience also involves issues of moral psychology. In Kant's view, the project of developing one's conscience, and indeed of developing one's capacities as a moral agent, are primarily framed in intellectual terms. Yet there is another common understanding of conscience that views it as first and foremost an emotional capacity to empathize with others. The cruel side of conscience is that people may, and do, inflict harm on others in good conscience because they view these others as enemies or as beings without moral status. Torturers and terrorists are dramatic examples of this human capacity, which is more widely observable in the everyday callousness of which all of us are guilty. Cruelty to others takes another form, sometimes popularly described as being "without conscience": the condition of those who commit violence and abuse without any apparent remorse, often against randomly selected victims. These actions are not prompted by conscientious adherence to an exclusionary moral framework but appear to reflect a complete lack of moral connection to others. They are the stuff of tabloid headlines, and often the perpetrators turn out to have been themselves victims of abuse and neglect.

The Kantian Categorical Imperative provides a powerful response to both these instances of cruelty, for both are condemned from the standpoint of treating others as ends in themselves. But what goes wrong, especially in the case of "conscienceless" sociopaths, appears to involve a lack of empathy, a failure or perversion of sentimental education, more than an incapacity for reasoning. This suggests a view—associated with theorists like David Hume and Adam Smith and with contemporary philosophers like Annette Baier and Lawrence Blum—that a capacity for empathic connection with others—what Baier calls "a progress of sentiments"—underlies the urgings of conscience.[6] The core of the problem is not inadequate self-scrutiny but a cramped or shattered capacity for emotional identification with others.

This alternative account of conscience needs much more elaboration than I am providing here. But I hope to have said enough to suggest that the voice of conscience, at least in some instances, might be conceived as arising from empathy rather than from the process of judging one's proposed actions in the light of deliberative moral commitments. These promptings of conscience are certainly not incompatible with Kantian ethics but imply a distinct understanding of the moral life, one in which affect plays a much larger role and in which the primary catalyst for the voice of conscience is an attentiveness to others rather than an attentiveness to the maxims of one's own actions.

III.

To view the Kantian account of conscience as embodying a particular vision of moral psychology is to engage in a form of sociological or psychological analysis similar to the deflationary accounts that Hill discusses in his second conception of conscience. Although he examines these accounts in their connection to extreme cultural relativism, they can also play an important role in moral theorizing that rejects relativism as Hill formulates it. My third worry about Hill's chapter, then, is that it obscures alternative accounts of moral theorizing about conscience. To be sure,

Hill acknowledges that a deflationary account of the cultural origins of conscience is compatible with nonrelativistic moral commitments and even with some forms of Kantian ethics. But his discussion does not do justice to the ways in which the sociological or psychological turn may be deployed not only to better understand the origins of conscience but also to think critically and constructively about what forms moral education should take.

Deflationary accounts of the cultural origins of conscience encompass a broad field of attempts by sociologists, psychologists, psychoanalysts, and others (including philosophers influenced by these disciplines) to understand the promptings of conscience as internalized cultural norms, whether these be, for example, echoes of early moral education, subconscious reflections of parental or social criticism, or introjected aggression arising from such criticism.

Such deflationary arguments can and sometimes do undermine the project of moral reasoning, leading to uncritical forms of cultural relativism or to psychological theories that see all feelings of guilt or bad conscience as ills to be eradicated and that advocate a thoroughly amoral "I'm OK—you're OK" attitude. But there is no necessary connection between the empirical claim that conscience arises initially from internalized norms and a normative abdication of moral responsibility—just as there is no necessary connection between the descriptive claim that "conscience is the voice of God" and the normative claim that "I'm always right because I know the voice of God." Moral blindness or smugness can follow from deflationary accounts of conscience—but they can also accompany any of the other conceptions.

Deflationary accounts of conscience can lead to more, not less, moral reflection—to a thoughtful sense that the promptings of conscience need to be subjected to moral scrutiny and that we need to pay attention to the processes of conscience formation. The analyses offered by theorists like Nietzsche, Freud, Kohlberg, Piaget, Gilligan, and many others provide us with a set of arguments concerning the cultural or psychological mechanisms by which conscience arises. We may remain skeptical about some of the specific arguments these theorists offer—for example, about Nietzsche's account of the origins of slave morality or about

Freud's model of the superego—but taken together, accounts like these reveal something about the sources of conscience that deserves to be taken seriously. And if conscience can be culti-vated—if our inner nag changes in response to changes in our moral beliefs and patterns of moral reasoning—then the sociolog-ical account can prod us to reexamine and change our approach to moral education.

Deflationary accounts of conscience reveal how the interior experience of moral life takes different forms reflecting specific cultural and psychological conditions and processes. Applying these insights to Kant would prompt us to consider whether the austerity of his account of conscience is a vision of morality we want to embrace in ourselves and nurture in others. Thus the sociological turn in theories of conscience offers incentives and resources for moral self-scrutiny.

IV.

I have raised questions about whether Kant's account of con-science is a uniquely and unambiguously attractive moral ideal and whether the options that Hill describes represent a compre-hensive picture of conceptions of conscience. I do, however, find the Kantian call to reflection and self-scrutiny morally persuasive and inspiring. There is a vivid sense in Kant's account of the many ways in which we, as moral agents, can fall short—and this is surely valid and important. As the Polish poet Wislawa Szymborska put it in a wonderful poem entitled "In Praise of Feeling Bad about Yourself,"

> The buzzard never says it is to blame
> The panther wouldn't know what scruples mean
> When the piranha strikes, it feels no shame
> If snakes had hands, they'd claim their hands were clean
> . . .
> Though hearts of killer whales may weigh a ton
> in every other way they're light
>
> On this third planet of the Sun
> among the signs of bestiality
> a clear conscience is Number One.[7]

Like Szymborska, Kant casts a skeptical eye on conscience and calls for a morality of self-scrutiny. But a psychologically and culturally reflective reading of Kant's account of conscience should prompt us to question some of his assumptions about moral life and moral psychology. It should, I have argued, lead us to acknowledge the Kantian account as a powerful—but not a uniquely or unambiguously admirable—moral ideal and to consider alternative visions of the psychological economy of a diligent conscience.

NOTES

1. Thomas E. Hill Jr., "Four Conceptions of Conscience," this volume, 14, 30–31.

2. Ibid., 16.

3. Ibid., 46.

4. Ibid., 32.

5. Annette Baier, *Postures of the Mind* (Minneapolis: University of Minnesota Press, 1985), 263.

6. David Hume, *A Treatise of Human Nature,* 2d ed. (Oxford: Oxford University Press, 1978); Adam Smith, *The Theory of Moral Sentiments* (Oxford: Oxford University Press, 1976); Annette Baier, *A Progress of Sentiments* (Cambridge, Mass.: Harvard University Press, 1991); and Lawrence A. Blum, *Moral Perception and Particularity* (Cambridge: Cambridge University Press, 1994).

7. Wislawa Szymborska, "In Praise of Feeling Bad about Yourself," in *View with a Grain of Sand,* trans. Stanislaw Baranszak and Claire Cavanagh (New York: Harcourt Brace, 1995), cited in Stephen Dobyns's poetry column, "Washington Post Book World," *Washington Post,* July 20, 1995, 8.

5

SOCRATIC INTEGRITY

GEORGE KATEB

The word *integrity* is derived from the Latin word *integer,* which means whole or wholeness and hence entirety or completeness and, by implication or extension, being unimpaired, uncompromised, and uncorrupted and being blameless. Things and conditions as well as persons can have or lack integrity. We can say that a person has integrity, then, when he or she has a certain concentration or purity or consistency. We can spell out these meanings a bit by saying that one has or shows integrity when one is entirely present (episodically or over a whole life) in what one does; one is all there; and one has all one's force of character and resources of action at one's disposal and under one's control. Relatedly, one has or shows integrity when one acts as oneself only, rather than unconsciously or thoughtlessly mixing in with oneself the attitudes or habits of others, imitating others without a sense of self-loss. Yet another description of integrity emphasizes a person's ability to remain steadfast to a commitment through thick and thin, overcoming internal and external obstacles, and devoting his or her whole life to that commitment or defining one's identity by reference to it. Integrity may also include standing alone for the sake of some commitment or other and refusing to go along with others or be incorporated in their plans or deeds. Thus, one remains whole by refusing to be included in an objectionable larger whole.

These brief accounts of integrity are derived from common

usage, and they also seem to suit Socrates quite well. That we apply to Socrates descriptions of integrity that probably were derived in part from his words and acts in the first place is a harmless circularity. He has helped mold later ideas of integrity. And if returning to his words and deeds may revivify a sense of his integrity and his right, even, to help define integrity, the fact remains that integrity as Socrates practiced it shows some strange features. My purpose in this chapter is to explore some of these features. For the most part, I concentrate on Socrates as Plato presented him in the *Apology of Socrates*, with some attention to the *Crito*. Whether or not the Socrates of the *Apology*, especially, was the real Socrates in every main feature cannot be established. Let it suffice to say that if it were not for the *Apology* but also the *Crito,* Socrates would not have been as influential in helping define integrity as he has proved to be. The hold of Socrates on the imagination altogether, but certainly on the understanding of the meaning of integrity, would be much less without these two works.

The strangeness of Socrates is owing to his negativity. It is no revelation to say that Socrates wrote nothing and maintained that he knew nothing. These are among his most famous manifestations of negativity. But his negativity is comprehensive and calls for an accounting that makes it constitutive of his integrity. That is, he may be a model of integrity because he is so extensively negative.

I use the word *negativity* to include more than the two manifestations just mentioned. Socrates practices negativity also in the sense that he says no to the doctrines of others without producing one of his own; his inner voice never says yes, but only no; he works on the hypothesis that the content of his wisdom is nothing, is ignorance; he knows what injustice is, not what virtuous excellence is; he knows how to act by abstention, avoidance, self-denial, and noncompliance; and he is prepared to contemplate eternal nothingness after death. There are other manifestations of negativity as well. Socrates' unforgettable presence is thus put together from elements that seem to lack any fullness, any positive definition. His integrity is nevertheless perfectly full; as a personage, he is most positively defined. But his fullness and definition arise from negativity. (At the end of this chapter, I will qualify this assertion.)

Thinking about Socrates may lead us to decide that any kind of integrity that takes him as a model must follow him in accentuating the negative (to negate an old song). To put it more strongly: there may not likely be a *secular* integrity unless negativity is, so to speak, affirmed. This is not to say that every feature of Socrates' integrity must be incorporated into all versions of secular integrity. Thoreau, for example, is powerfully inspired by Socrates and is equally negative. Yet he may be even more secular than Socrates, and he certainly introduces creative changes in the theory and practice of secular integrity.

On a theoretical level, perhaps the starkest contrast to Socratic integrity is found in the Aristotelian ideal system: a picture of full virtuous excellence authenticated by reference to a confident understanding of human nature and the human condition. Aristotelian integrity is integrity of a radically different kind, and to one who prizes the Socratic model, the Aristotelian kind can look both spurious and dangerous.

It may be useful to see in Socrates a model of two kinds of integrity, one intellectual and the other moral. He shows *intellectual* integrity by a single-minded intensity or concentration in pursuit of truth or of wisdom, but this pursuit issues in only a perpetual dissatisfaction. It is as if intellectual integrity must lead not so much to a strict skepticism as to a residual tentativeness or uncertainty about what one accepts as true. Some conclusions that others offer are clearly mistaken or confused. Socrates is prepared to say no to them, but to say no (even many times) does not automatically produce a yes (even after a long time), that is, a definite conclusion amenable to sustained elaboration. What his intensity or concentration earns him is the right to maintain that he has avoided common or prevalent errors. His truth or wisdom is negative: freedom from avoidable error on the most important matters.

Socrates shows *moral* integrity in his strict avoidance of injustice. He tries to demonstrate purity in his conduct toward others. He thinks he may be doing good to people by being continuously available for conversation and thus getting them to think. But when he engages in worldly action, in acts of citizenship, his whole concern is to avoid injustice. Depriving others of what is theirs, in accordance with their own understanding of what is properly theirs, is injustice; he will not ever act so to deprive them. His justice is abstention from the dispossession of others. In contrast, actively giving them or distributing to them some worldly good they lack but may deserve is not his moral aim as an actor in the world. He does not claim to know what anyone is positively owed. As for himself, after the Athenian jury finds him guilty, he can say that what he really deserves at the hands of Athens is "free meals at the prytaneum." [1] But it is only at the end that he estimates his own worth, and he does so only to throw irony on the requirement that he propose a counterpenalty to the death penalty proposed by his prosecutor, Meletus. Socrates does not have to know what anyone is worth because he does know what doing injustice amounts to. The avoidance of injustice lies within his power and places no exceptional demand on his knowledge.

The two kinds of integrity, which I have separated, exist, of course, in the same person. How are they connected? Do they have the same root in one commitment? Do they have equal worth, or is one kind an instrument of the other? Or are they only accidentally copresent? I am tempted to say that Socrates' intellectual integrity is at the service of his moral integrity and therefore does not exist for its own sake, for the sake of exact understanding. The fury that drives him to destroy the argumentative positions of others (as shown in some of Plato's inconclusive dialogues like the *Euthyphro*) is the conviction that assurance about one's rightness of opinion is rarely justified but that out of unearned assurance grows the strengthened proclivity to act unjustly. To purge himself and other people of substantive ideas is to induce greater hesitation in action.

Socrates' intellectual integrity is thus a weapon in his war on opinions that engender or nurture injustice. He would not be so relentless in examining others if he did not think that he could slow them down. He is not, however, offering a positive vision, for he has none to offer. His intellectual integrity does not prepare the way for correct substantive ideas about virtue or matters of any other kind. No clever intellection is needed to ascertain the nature of injustice. That is why I am tempted to think that for Socrates, intellectual integrity is a means to reducing the amount of injustice in the world—a purpose for which his life itself is a means. In regard to his own opinions, his intellectual integrity steadies his soul in his own determination to avoid doing injustice. At the same time, to promote the intellectual integrity of others by his relentless questioning— even though most people will not likely attain a high level—is to serve a moral cause. What I say here is naturally only a rough first statement about Socrates' intellectual integrity.

If we proceed with the assumption that the center of Socrates' integrity is moral integrity, we can look at some of its prominent features in their negativity. Then we will have reason to return to his intellectual integrity.

In the *Apology,* Socrates says that he is convinced that he has never wronged anyone deliberately.[2] This is a tremendous claim for a person to make about himself; the presumptuousness is considerable of entering a judgment about oneself and one's whole life heretofore. The majority of the jury finally does not agree with Socrates about himself. They thought that he has wronged the whole city, and quite deliberately. Now that he has been formally accused, they are ready to see as injurious the whole tendency of Socrates' life as a questioner, even though he thinks that his questioning is the greatest service that can be rendered to the city. The dispute cannot be settled amicably; the city has the last word. There is, however, nothing or very little that is speculative about doing wrong in the specific sense of acting unjustly toward another person. On this matter, Socrates makes a case that seems right, and none of the accusers tries to rebut it.

Socrates recounts in the *Apology* two political episodes in which he was involved. These episodes offer powerful support for the moral judgment that he makes of himself. In the first episode, he acts by being the only one to vote no; in the second, he acts by refusing to obey an order. Dissent and noncompliance constitute the salience of his active or direct citizenship, which is therefore negative. Moreover, in both cases, he is hardly a volunteer. When he dissents, he has to vote because it is the turn of his tribe to serve on the panel that prepares the agenda for the Assembly.

When he refuses to obey, he is picked by the Tyrants to carry out a mission. For the rest of the time, he refuses involvement; he does not give speeches in the agora;[3] and he explicitly refers to the fact that the public speech he gives to the jury, which is, as it were, wrung from him, is unique: the dire accusation against him occasions his first appearance (of any kind) in a law court.[4]

In the background is Socrates' general abstention, which derives from his wish not to implicate himself in the wrongdoing that the Assembly regularly sponsors. He says:

> There is no man who will preserve his life for long, either in Athens or elsewhere, if he firmly opposes the multitude, and tries to prevent the commission of much injustice and illegality in the state. He who would really fight for justice must do so as a private citizen, not as a political figure, if he is to preserve his life, even for a short time.[5]

The public voice of the leadership tends to corrupt any group of people. To answer that public voice with one's own voice in public would lead to nothing but the ruin or death of the person who made the effort and hence to the waste of an opportunity to do what one could do in one's everyday way to fight injustice. Socrates would wish to be the same person in public life as he is in private,[6] to speak in the same private voice about public matters, especially when injustice is urged. Although private interest regularly succeeds in cloaking itself in public purpose, a sincere private voice in a political place is not heard, or it is ridiculed or denounced as harmful. Socrates concerns himself with his own purity, but he conceives his purity as inseparable from avoiding injustice—that is, from not being an instrument of wronging others.

A principal negative element of Socrates' integrity is to abstain from hopelessly unjust active citizenship. Nevertheless, he does not absent himself from his duty in the panel of the Council of the Assembly when it is his tribe's turn. Thus, in the first episode, 406 B.C., ten victorious military leaders in a battle off the Arginusae Islands were severely criticized for neglecting to pick up the dead and rescue survivors. Pressure built to try the leaders as a group, rather than separately, and the panel succumbed; Socrates was the sole dissenter. The issue was, to use a modern term, due process of law: fairness dictated separate and unrushed trials and in a proper court. Seeming niceties of legal procedure provided Socrates the unwanted but accepted opportunity to stand up for principle. What is the principle? Avoiding injustice. Eventually six were tried together, condemned, and executed. The result was a foregone conclusion; injustice had to happen.[7]

Notice that in opposing public pressure in 406 B.C., and then seven years later at his own trial retrospectively explaining his dissent, Socrates does not appeal to any special, much less subjective, notion of injustice. Instead, he tries to hold Athens to its own principle of right conduct, which here involves not positive reward but deprivation: punishment in the form of death. The principle is that we should not harm—in the sense of wronging—the innocent; stated more narrowly, we should not harm—punish— those who have not been found guilty by means of a proper legal procedure.

The same conception of injustice covers the second episode. Socrates refuses the order by the Tyrants in 404 B.C. to apprehend Leon of Salamis and take him to Athens and certain death.[8] He does not say that the Thirty Tyrants had no legitimacy and hence could not validly order anyone to do anything; he does imply, however, that Leon was an innocent man who was the victim of official persecution. He includes the treatment of Leon as among the crimes of the Tyrants, who sought cynically and self-protectively to implicate as many people as possible in them.

If the principle that Socrates stands up for is part of Athenian life and not of his invention, he does adhere to that principle even to the point of self-sacrifice. He is willing to sacrifice himself, his life, rather than abandon the principle. He will adhere to his negative morality, cost what it may (to use Thoreau's phrase from "Civil Disobedience"). This is where the moral novelty of Socrates in the *Apology* is found. As he is well aware, many men risk death in battle.[9] Whatever any particular soldier's motivation may be— whether fear or interest or honor, or only conformity or habit— premature death or, perhaps just as bad, the threat of enslavement is a constant accompaniment. War is the central institution of citizenship.

Socrates likens himself, in his dissent and noncompliance, not only to a soldier who does his duty but also to Achilles.[10] But these comparisons obscure the main thing, which is that Socrates risks life and freedom in situations in which no one else does. He stands alone, as one person, as his naked moral self. He has only himself to fall back on. His courage is for the sake of refusing to be an instrument of injustice. The enemy he fights alone is his own city, when the city fails to be faithful to its own best principle, which is also his own: not to wrong or penalize the innocent (actual or putative). The city does not risk itself by avoiding injustice in the matter of the military leaders or of Leon. Morality on these occasions is free of cost to any licit interest. Socrates is not asking the city or anyone else for the kind of sacrifice he asks of himself.

Where is the precedent for Socrates' action, for his distinctive moral heroism? In the ordinary sense of self-sacrifice, Socrates is self-sacrificingly moral; his moral integrity is extreme. Moral integrity must cost something, but one can have some measure of it without practicing it, "cost what it may." We need not build extreme self-sacrifice into the very definition of moral integrity. To be sure, he is not hounded or put to death because of either of the two episodes; there is no indication that they played any role in the accusations against him or in the judgment of his guilt and the sentence of death. But when he acted, he did not know whether he would lose his life or liberty as a result. He took enormous chances, chances that no one else would have taken. That he was over sixty when he did so does not mean he would not have done so if the occasions had arisen when he was younger, even if it is true that for some people—whatever may hold for Socrates—to contemplate death is easier when older than when younger.

Let us also notice that just as there is nothing religious in Socrates' understanding of injustice, so neither does the answer of the priestess at Delphi nor the existence of Socrates' inner voice have anything to do with his moral heroism. There is probably a connection between Socrates' courage in the cause of avoiding injustice and a surmise he entertains about what it means to be dead. (I shall return to this point.) But that surmise is purely Socrates' own; it comes from no divine instruction; it promises no reward in the afterlife for moral heroism; it is purely secular.

That Socrates is also a hero of another kind as well—a hero in

the cause of truth in the negative sense of dispelling errors—
is undeniable. Here, there may be something religious in the
inspiration of his courage. The inner voice does not deter Socrates from appearing at his trial and speaking as he does.[11] The
answer given by the priestess—no one is wiser than Socrates[12]—
is construed by Socrates as a mandate to pursue wisdom, cost what
it may. He says that if the city were to offer to release him from
the charges against him on the condition that he henceforth
abstain from his inquiries, he would reject the proposal. "I should
reply: 'Athenians, I hold you in the highest regard and affection,
but I will be persuaded by the god rather than you.' "[13] Something
religious may fortify him here to be self-sacrificing, but it is not
anything conventionally religious. In any case, the motivation of
his dissent and noncompliance for the sake of avoiding injustice
has different grounds from his persistence in philosophical questioning, even though this persistence is finally also for moral
purposes, for the sake of enabling others to promote or lend
themselves to injustice less.

The question arises as to the importance of Socrates' dissent and
noncompliance. They were not followed by a subsequent deed or
gesture of protest, much less by resistance alone or with others (if
others could be found). Furthermore, Socrates fought in three
battles just before or during the Peloponnesian War and thus did
in fact lend himself to the systemic promotion or defense of
imperialism—that is, injustice on a great scale. Although Diogenes Laertius records that Socrates turned down Charmides' gift of
slaves,[14] there is no indication that Socrates criticized the institution of slavery—the capture of slaves in war and the codification
of their bondage in law. Isn't it the case, then, that in risking his
life in the two episodes, Socrates is courageous but for reasons
that show a lack of proportion: too much courage in small affairs
and none at all in large ones? And by doing nothing to try to
change the system, doesn't he strain at a gnat in each episode and
swallow a camel?

Certainly, by reformist and pragmatic standards, Socrates' negative citizenship had no political effect in his time, however one
may judge his later influence by example in the annals of conscientious and nonviolent politics. Perhaps, after all, he is interested

only in the future—in his subtle and long-term effects on the moral imagination. He has no illusions about his immediate efficacy: he says that he would have perished long before if he had been politically outspoken.[15] To the charge that he takes a heroic stand only in comparatively minor public situations, one can offer a reason that Socrates does not give. (Indeed, he does not indicate any awareness of the possibility of misplaced or disproportionate heroism.) The reason, however, is not foreign to Socrates' world. It is implicit, for example, in the successful effort of Diodotus, as recorded by Thucydides, to reverse the Athenian decision (428 B.C.) to kill the population of Mytilene, a rebellious confederate.[16] Certainly Socrates would not have given a speech like Diodotus's. Deliberately, even if transparently, Diodotus employs arguments that do not fully represent his own views. He clothes moral reasons in tough-minded calculations. He thinks he would not have been heard otherwise. He speaks to win. Morality needs him no less than it needs Socrates, even if Socrates' integrity is greater.

In any event, common to Socrates and Diodotus seems to be a hopeless resignation to the occurrence of large-scale tendencies of wrongdoing, especially toward other cities. The wrongdoing is systemic; it is almost unconscious, so ingrained and inveterate are the cultural causes of it. To be aggressive, predatory; to act to the limit of one's capacity and to attempt to act beyond it; to desire to possess more than one's share, as if true satisfaction exists beyond mere satisfaction; to see in one's power not so much a stake to defend as a precondition for transgressive adventure; and to thrive on risk, especially to one's continued existence—all this is the project of individual and group masculinity, the project of hubris and pleonexia, of rejecting the very idea of limits. This project is so driven that it cannot be withstood. But there is no excuse for base, small-minded horrors; people know better, or ought to; no imagination is required to see the wrong. People should not be carried away and in a real or manufactured passion initiate or sanction an atrocity or a profound evil of detail. That they do know better is proved by their repentance.

The Athenian Assembly rescinded the decree condemning the Mytelinians. But the Athenian ship carrying the decree made no haste to reach the city, so reluctant was the mission.[17] Likewise, Socrates says that the Athenians eventually realized that the decision to try the military leaders as a group was illegal.[18] (Later in the *Crito*, he says that the many who casually put men to death would as casually bring them back to life if they could.[19] Socrates' words do not imply that the people do villainy and then repent but, rather, that they are generally incontinent and their incontinence sometimes causes them to feel a vague disquiet. Their bad deeds are halfhearted, partly unmeant.)

The view that I have just sketched is only one possible way of making plausible the pattern of Socrates' political episodes against the background of his general abstention. There is no doubt that my rationalization has an affinity with the perverse notion that, say, a country can do anything it likes in the field of foreign affairs as long as it treats its prisoners of war correctly and follows other rules of war or that a system of slavery is tolerable as long as the slaves are not constantly brutalized. But the sense of things that I would like to attribute to Socrates contains no excuse for the large-scale tendency or system of wrongdoing in the midst of which a morally heroic episode suddenly appears, with the overall wrongdoing left untouched. Socrates excuses nothing: his general abstention is a general condemnation. When the Socrates of the *Gorgias* says that Pericles left the Athenians much wilder than they were when he took over,[20] the assertion is in keeping with the sentiments of the Socrates of the *Apology*.

I do not mean to suggest that the negative and episodic politics in which Socrates engages is the only politics compatible with some measure of integrity, whatever Socrates may have thought. One can imagine a tolerably good officeholder devoting himself or herself to doing only the lesser and necessary evil while also doing as much good as possible. But we have to strain hard to imagine someone like that. Those who are attracted to office are not attracted to a strict economy of wrongdoing. They are eager to do, to act, even if they are not devotees of the project of masculinity, cost what it may to morality, or even if they are not eager to pursue it precisely because it is immoral. The world cannot do without officeholders, but it has something to learn from pondering the nature of Socrates' citizenship. His episodes teach a lesson beyond themselves: the baseness of particular political decisions may direct attention to the larger tendency or system in its regular and cumulative wrongdoing. To the extraordinary excesses of politics-as-masculinity, ordinary moral resistance may be futile, whereas extraordinary gestures of independent and solitary self-sacrificial morality may alone have a countervailing grandeur. These gestures have the masculine antimasculinity that answers to political hubris and pleonexia.

There is one more noteworthy episode in Socrates' political life— his refusal to escape from prison and from capital punishment. This refusal, too, may be seen as self-sacrificial morality: sacrificing oneself rather than doing injustice. The question is what principle covers Socrates' decision. In the *Apology,* the principle that covers his dissent and noncompliance is to avoid wronging the innocent (actual or putative), which he carries to a self-sacrificial length. He does not expect from any other person or any collectivity self-sacrifice for the sake of avoiding injustice. Nevertheless, Socrates' own integrity is partly defined by a willingness to risk death or loss of freedom in order to uphold a commonly accepted principle.

This principle is not only regularly breached in self-interested disregard of justice, but it also seems to allow people to suspend it if their own life or freedom is somehow endangered through no fault of their own—as when, for example, their choice is the one faced by Socrates: to be an instrument of injustice or to risk suffering a loss of life or freedom. He insists on preferring others to himself, preferring death to serving injustice. But what is involved in his staying in prison to face death, rather than escaping? It does not do to say that Socrates disobeys the state only when it acts with procedural irregularity and always obeys it when it acts with procedural regularity. It is not clear that he would ever obey, in any circumstances, a validly issued order to cease philosophizing with others. He is not a pure proceduralist. Procedural irregularity matters decisively to him when it is a device of substantive injustice. That it makes sense for us to speak of the inherent morality of procedural regularity is not relevant to the Socrates of the *Apology.*

He claims to know that he is innocent of the charges. He is innocent in his own eyes. He does not corrupt the youth by teaching new divinities, much less by teaching atheism. By not escaping he therefore becomes an instrument of political injustice, this time to himself. If before, especially in regard to the

Tyrants, he had risked death by his intransigent refusal to obey, he is now obedient unto death, his own unjust death. Why is he obedient? In the *Crito*, Socrates gives a number of reasons for his decision. Among them are two basic principles, as well as several considerations not neatly connected to either of the two principles. Socrates may stay to die, however, not because of any principle or consideration but because in his integrity he does not want to associate the practice of relentless questioning (in the name of dispelling errors) with anything less than heroism, physical heroism like that of Achilles in the face of certain death soon to come. Comparing himself with Achilles better suits the Socrates of the *Crito* than the Socrates of the two episodes in the *Apology*.

These reasons do not satisfy. They are thrown out in a rush as if to overpower the auditor and leave him little time to answer. Likening himself to the frenzied worshipers of Cybele, an earth goddess, Socrates says that his arguments sound in his ears like the music of flutes: "The sound of these arguments rings so loudly in my ears, that I cannot hear any other arguments."[21] This sound is not the sound of intellectual integrity. More important, the reasons do not satisfy because in moral complexion, the *Crito* is perhaps closer to the *Gorgias* than to the *Apology*. The *Crito*, like the *Gorgias*, gives too much to an almost masochistic severity to the self, to the practice of authoritative punishment, and to servile deference to properly constituted authority. Socrates opens up a vast gulf between what he allows political authority to do and what he allows individuals to do. This is not the same gulf as separates the morally allowable suspension of morality in cases of terrible risk for individuals and the insistence, for oneself, that one face terrible risk instead of being a party to treating others unjustly.

When we try to find the principle, two emerge. The first is the same one invoked in the *Apology:* a self-sacrificing avoidance of doing injustice or being its instrument. The second one is altogether novel: when treated unjustly by the state or others, an individual should never retaliate. The difficulty is to ascertain which of the two really covers Socrates' refusal to escape. I do not think that we can unambiguously determine the matter. The cause of the ambiguity lies in ascertaining the agent that is the recipient or beneficiary of Socrates' enactment of—submission to—moral principle. Is it the city and its laws? Or is it those men who, acting by means of a valid and intrinsically fair legal procedure, arrived at a substantively mistaken, perhaps maliciously motivated, and seriously unjust decision? (It was only by a comparatively small majority: if only thirty votes, out of five hundred or so, had changed sides, the outcome would have been different).[22] In his discussion with his old friend Crito, Socrates appears to shift the identity of the object of his self-sacrifice. He also seems to shift the identity of the source of the injustice done to him.

The upshot is as follows: If it is men, not the laws,[23] who visited injustice on him, then to seek to escape their judgment is to retaliate against them in the sense that he would treat them unjustly, as they had treated him. The whole avowedly novel and peculiar doctrine of nonretaliation is first enunciated in the *Crito*, with the implication that to escape would be to treat unjustly the jurors who had condemned him to death unjustly; to treat them as they had treated him. The retaliation is not in kind; rather, it repays an unjust effect with an unjust intention (vengeance). Retaliation is made to look worse than the initial act of injustice.

But it is not clear to me that the doctrine of nonretaliation as Socrates initially formulates it pertains to the mistaken and perhaps malicious jurors. Perhaps a more suitable referent awaits these unprecedented words:

> For there is no difference, is there, between doing evil to a man and acting unjustly? ... Then we ought not repay injustice with injustice or to do harm to any man, no matter what we may have suffered from him.... Are we to start in our inquiry from the premise that it is never right either to act unjustly, or to repay injustice with injustice, or to avenge ourselves on any man who harms us, by harming him in return.... I myself have believed in it for a long time, and I believe in it still.[24]

As an individual who is also an uncommon citizen but one who is not necessarily—or necessarily not—setting himself up as a model for collectivities and their leadership, Socrates says that it is right to abstain from punishing the *guilty*. To punish them is to harm or injure them in some sense, and to harm or injure them is to treat them wrongly or unjustly. (The distinctions between these notions tend to disappear.) To give those who have wronged oneself what the world thinks they deserve is to render them injustice. Socrates avoids injustice when he accepts it for himself. The idea is amazing, but it does not really refer unawkwardly to the jurors.

To what or whom can it refer less awkwardly, even if still not with a perfect fit? After the words just quoted, Socrates begins to speak of the city, not of the particular men who condemned him. If he escapes, he would harm the city; at least part of that harm consists of doing injustice to it. Is the city (condensed into its laws, which are then impersonated by Socrates to speak to him, but of course in words that he has composed and that may, in some respects, be unusual if not novel and unprecedented) — is the city, despite his express denial, guilty of injustice, or wrongdoing, to him? To try to escape would then be to retaliate, to return harm for harm, wrong for wrong. If the city, however, is not guilty, then the doctrine of nonretaliation, as I have said, would not be clearly illustrated by his refusal to escape. But Socrates never says flatly that the city is guilty; to the contrary, as we have seen.[25]

Perhaps the city is both guilty and innocent. That would mean that both the principle of nonretaliation and the principle of never wronging the innocent (cost what it may) would be needed to cover Socrates' refusal. If the city, is, from one perspective, innocent and only the jurors are guilty of injustice, a case could be made for saying that to escape is to harm the innocent. In accordance with Socrates' insistence that he will not harm the innocent, cost him what it may, he will accept the verdict and wait to die in prison. But if the city is, from another perspective, guilty, Socrates will accept the verdict and not retaliate, not return harm to the city for the harm it inflicted on him. He will not harm the innocent. Also, he will not harm — that is, punish or wrong — the guilty, no matter how much conventional opinion may think that the guilty should always be punished or harmed or wronged by the aggrieved party.

The city is innocent if men, not the laws, effected the miscarriage of justice. The city is guilty if its laws, despite their overall acceptability, could ever lead, through their failure to ensure against drastic human imperfection, to serious injustice. The city is perhaps guilty or perhaps innocent if it sincerely but mistakenly thought that it did the right thing.[26]

Whether the city is innocent or guilty or both or not quite

either, the harm done by escaping from its judgment is the encouragement given others to disobey a law whenever they thought they could safely do so and for any self-serving purpose whatsoever. Socrates has the laws say: "Do you think that a state can exist and not be overthrown, in which the decisions of law are of no force, and are disregarded and undermined by private individuals?"[27]

Socrates then supplements this generalized conception of harm with three considerations: if he were to escape, he would be guilty of three vices. First is the vice of ingratitude toward the laws that provided the framework within which Socrates was born and raised and educated. The laws deserve greater honor and obedience than one's parents do; the laws are more truly parents than biological parents are.[28] Second is the vice of faithlessness to an implied agreement to obey all laws and decisions. Socrates was free to emigrate without penalty, but he stayed, as if to say that he had freely chosen an allegiance into which he was born but did not have to retain.[29] Third is the vice of unfairness because Socrates was given a chance to persuade the city that it was wrong but he failed to take the chance.[30] (Apparently, Socrates did not regard his speech at the trial as an effort at persuasion, and he did not want others to see it as such, either.)

These vices are condemnable apart from any direct harm they may inflict. (But their example could prove contagious and thus eventually become a direct source of harm to the city and its laws.) Socrates' escape would display these vices. They would be imputed to him after the fact by a candid observer, himself or another, but they would not motivate the escape. Fear would motivate it, and perhaps also hatred and a spirit of revenge. Moral integrity precludes acting from such motives or passions, just as it precludes acting in such a way as to display major vices like ingratitude, faithlessness, and unfairness in the course of acting from fear or hatred or vengeance. Detestation of the vices should be enough to overcome the strength of powerful self-concerned emotions. But Socrates wants to avoid moral taint for his own sake and also for the sake of the city and for the sake of other individuals.

I have said that I do not think that Socrates' reasons (whether general principles or particular considerations) satisfy. They do not seem to cover suitably his decision not to escape from prison and death. Neither of the two principles is really appropriate to govern the relationship between an individual citizen and the city or its laws or even between an individual citizen and a group of citizens formally entrusted with an official responsibility (as the jurors were). In the *Apology,* after all, Socrates's concern is to avoid wronging innocent persons when they are the targets of official lawless action. He seeks to protect individuals against the state. But he sides with official injustice in the *Crito.* He treats the city as if it were a hounded and vulnerable individual and thus transforms political duty into a relationship of such personal intensity that it threatens to become malignant.

The principle of nonretaliation, however, shows a moral refinement that is even more extraordinary than the principle of never harming the innocent, cost what it may. But the view that nonretaliation is exemplified when a prisoner cooperates with an unjust punishment is a terrible stain on the very idea of moral integrity; it is a disfigured moral heroism. Such obedience, especially when it is defended by a refined principle, sets a worse precedent than does any kind of disobedience, however motivated, and it also outweighs the value of the example set when an independent thinker faces death alone in a triumph of physical courage. Martyrdom to principle is, of course, poignant. Without it, Socrates' hold on the imagination would be less. If Socrates had escaped into exile, what would Plato have written about him?

Does the Socrates of the *Apology* inevitably lead to the Socrates of the *Crito?* I have already indicated that the *Crito* seems closer to the *Gorgias* than to the *Apology.* I mean that Socrates' arguments in the *Apology* show a freedom of spirit that they do not show in the two other works. Only in the *Apology* does he defend dissent and noncompliance as justified. He seems to have invented these modes of individual citizenship and then compounded his moral originality by practicing these modes to the point of risking loss and destruction. Yet it may be possible, I do not deny, that there is some consonance of character between the Socrates of the *Apology* and the Socrates of the *Crito.* In both works, he is careless of death. In the *Apology,* he risks death to avoid being an instrument of injustice. In the *Crito,* let us say he goes to his death to avoid displaying the vices of ingratitude, faithlessness, and unfairness. Perhaps the avoidance of these vices matters more to the Socrates of the *Crito* than any abstract moral principle, even though adherence to one or the other principle is what provides the pretext for Socrates' moral gallantry. Perhaps he fears being thought a coward more than he fears anything else. Or perhaps the matter is simply that as Socrates says, a man who subverts the law by escaping from prison may well be supposed a corrupter of youth, and thus Socrates for the first time will have been proved guilty of the crime that originally he was falsely accused of.

The long and short of it is that Socrates shows moral integrity when he acts for others, not for an (as it were patriotic) abstraction like the laws or the city. I say *abstraction* because Socrates barely indicates that the institutions of the Athenian polity embody moral principles worth defending for their own sake, rather than because they happen to be the institutions of Socrates' own city. Devotion to one's city as such is devotion to an abstraction. In contrast, he acts for others, for other specific individuals, or for his fellow citizens as individuals when he dissents and refuses to carry out a murderous command and when he imagines himself choosing death or imprisonment rather than acceding to an offer to remain free and safe provided that he stops questioning others. He consummates his moral integrity when he self-sacrificingly practices the principle of not wronging the innocent, cost what it may. This principle is made vivid in the *Apology*, not the *Crito*.

I have said that his intellectual integrity is for Socrates a means to the end of his moral integrity and that he also tries to induce some intellectual integrity in others to reduce their proclivity to urge or support injustice at home or abroad. Yet to say that his own intellectual integrity is a means to this double moral end is not a formulation that I am certain of. Accordingly, I would like to point out some elements that are implicated in it but that do not all go in the same direction.

Socrates' moral integrity is most fully demonstrated when he risks himself rather than lending himself to injustice. Does his intellectual integrity show itself so riskily? Throughout his life "as a sort of a gadfly,"[31] he knows he incurred animosity. The old charges against him were that he studied and speculated about things in the heavens and beneath the earth, that he made the worse argument appear the stronger, and that he taught these practices to others.[32] These charges did not win him favor, only fear and ridicule. Socrates denies the old charges but thinks they provide a propitious background for the accusers and their new charges, namely, that he corrupts the young and does not believe in the same divinities that the state believes in, but in new ones.[33] He denies the new charges, too, but he also knows that animosity lies behind them, just as it lay behind the old charges.

Socrates, however, does not seem to say that he had ever thought, until the formal accusation against him, that he was risking death by his practice of persistent questioning and perpetual dissatisfaction with the answers. To be sure, he antagonized specific sectors of the Athenian population by showing the hollowness of their answers to the basic question of what human excellence is, or what it means to excel in what human creatures are naturally capable of,[34] or how it is possible to educate people to attain human excellence. Still, if he tended to brand as ignorant and presumptuous the answers offered by political leaders, poets, and craftsmen, if he could say that those with the highest reputation for wisdom were the most unwise "while others who were looked down as common people were much more intelligent,"[35] he did not think, it seems, that he was endangering his life or liberty or his continued ability to reside in Athens, despite some apprehensions.

Socrates' intellectual integrity becomes truly risky when he senses that the outcome of the trial could be his death, and yet he refuses to ingratiate himself with the jury or to plead for forgiveness or leniency. He also insists that if offered a dismissal of the charges on condition that he desist from his public philosophizing, he would refuse the offer. He would go on asking questions and finding the answers ignorant and presumptuous, even if told beforehand that his persistence would lead to his execution.[36] Indeed, "whether you acquit me or not, I shall not change my way of life; no, not if I have to die for it many times."[37]

It is at the end that intellectual integrity shows itself as self-sacrificing; Athenian tolerance lasted a long time, and it was not inevitable that Socrates would ever have had to face death for the sake of persisting in a life of questioning and not answering. Athens respected and even encouraged *parrhesia*, frankness. This is not to deny that Socrates would have persisted until the end, cost what it may, even if the end had come much earlier. So if intellectual integrity is the means to a moral end, it is nevertheless true that Socrates would have died for the sake of the means. The means are irreplaceable. But to be prepared to risk much or everything for the means is still not to make the means the end in itself.

Socrates risked death also for the sake of his end, which is negatively moral and consists in the will to avoid treating any individual unjustly. As we have seen, however, Socrates' moral integrity countenances his general political abstention: he would not die young in the wasted effort to change a tendency of policy and a masculinist system of culture that had to produce injustice on a large scale. His moral integrity is self-sacrificing only narrowly and episodically. He has never sought opportunities for moral self-sacrifice. But he has always sought opportunities to practice his intellectual integrity and to try to encourage it in others. He has tried to sow dissatisfaction with received opinion on what is good in life and what human excellence is. What is more, he has inhumanly neglected his own interests and remained poor so that he could engage others philosophically.[38] And then he dies, it appears, not because of original and independent moral integrity but because his intellectual integrity somehow catches up with him unawares, and fatally. He regrets nothing and would now deliberately face death rather than ceasing to philosophize with others. Isn't his moral integrity therefore only incidental and his intellectual integrity central? Isn't it more likely the case that neither is a means to the other? Isn't it certainly the case that intellectual integrity is not a means to moral integrity?

In spite of all, I believe that everything in Socrates' intellectual life is devoted to the moral end of reducing injustice in the world. He grants that he has stayed alive rather than participating actively in politics with its risk of death or exile or some unsustainable loss. We grant also that he does not try to be a systemic reformer. Rather, he stays alive to force people, one by one, or a few at a time, to face themselves. His every word, the whole method of ruthless examination (*exetasis*), is devoted to the questions of how to act, what to want, how to conduct a life, what to live for. He is trying to induce, by his perpetual dissatisfaction with answers, not skepticism but moderation. He is trying to erode the sources of pleonexia and hubris, which derive their force in part from unchallenged opinion about the goods and ends of life. If he has been generous, though parsimonious, in risking his life for the avoidance of injustice, still he has not wanted to die before he was old, so that he can continue to moderate Athens, at least to attempt to do so, with only a mild expectation of some small success. Perhaps the future Athens will vindicate him.[39]

In any event, nothing is finally important to Socrates but the struggle against injustice. His labor is animated by the conviction that a disabused mind favors a less raging heart. What is more, intellectual integrity is not required to know what injustice is. I do not see in Socrates a pure will to truth: error irritates him because it is usually an instigation to injustice or a rationalization of it. The most public and powerful errors of opinion concern the goods and ends of life: they all pertain to excellence or happiness. But they are productive mostly of injustice and eventual ruin. High idealism, always mistaken, is corrupting when publicly enacted. It is as if Socrates desires that the questions that social life incessantly raises, if only implicitly, should never be answered; as if he wants the whole subject of positive excellence and composed happiness to remain suspended so that people would concentrate their energies on living more moderately and therefore more modestly. The result would be some reduction of injustice at home and abroad. Socrates' method of intellect, like his whole self, is a sustained refusal to be an instrument of injustice.

Socrates examines others because they do not examine themselves. At best, under Socrates' pressure, they may ultimately learn to examine themselves a little, make their improvident conclusions into questions that are not readily answered. Although the phrase "the unexamined life is not worth living"[40] need not refer to self-examination, the context gives it such a connotation. People crave this or that worldly good. Socrates asks them and wants them to ask themselves, If they possess that good, is it really good? Does it really give happiness? Does it permanently allay the craving that led to its pursuit or, rather—in T. S. Eliot's words from "Gerontion"—does the giving famish the craving? If people do not have some worldly good or prize, Socrates wants to delay them in their pursuit so that they may ask themselves, Do I really want this? Couldn't I be happier or less unhappy without it or with less of it? Am I in a competition for no good end? Am I playing somebody's else's game?

Socrates' conception of self-knowledge is, therefore, inseparable from moderation or temperance. Critias, of all people, says in the *Charmides,* a dialogue about temperance, that the phrases "be temperate" and "know yourself" are equivalent.[41] The self-examining person can learn to say, "How many things I can do without!"[42] Self-examination therefore helps make life somewhat more worth living. But the practice of self-examination is uncommon. If it is odd, perhaps blasphemous, for Socrates to claim that he is guided by an inner and divine sign or voice,[43] it is at least as odd to practice self-examination, as he says he does,[44] and to encourage it in others. For a moral purpose, Socrates is inventing the practice of self-examination, and clearly, his practice of it is far in advance of that of his interlocutors.

From the perspective of this chapter, it is worth noticing that Socratic integrity, moral and intellectual, is dependent on division within the self, not on being at one with oneself, not on having a conventional psychological integrity or wholeness. Self-examination is self-division, and from self-division comes self-knowledge. Self-knowledge turns out to be mostly negative: Socrates discovers that he does not really want the worldly goods and prizes that he is supposed to want; his desires are for other things, which are not positively described. And he also learns to resist certain descriptions made of him; specifically, those of his accusers. He knows himself sufficiently so that they cannot overpower him into forgetting who he is,[45] even though he may not have a full understanding of who he is or think that he can define himself or be defined by others. The results of self-examination are what they are.

Self-examination is an uncompletable process. It should last until death. Socrates never claims perfect self-knowledge. It would be incompatible with having a self. The Socrates of the *Phaedrus* says that he does not know whether he is as proud as Typhon (a usurpatory monster with a hundred serpents' heads) or a more gentle creature: he is a question to himself.[46] He can imagine himself capable of the worst. This searching self-exploration, marked by some trepidation, that is formulated in the *Phaedrus* goes well with the Socrates of the *Apology*.

What is pertinent here is that by practicing self-examination, Socrates shatters his oneness. He breaks himself up into a watcher and a watched. The watcher is not always morally suspicious; it is not the Christian conscience. Although it is distinct from the inner voice, the watcher does reinforce the work of the inner voice, but this voice prohibits Socrates from doing anything that may be *personally* bad—injurious—for himself to do. Neither the inside watcher nor the inner voice is *directly* moral. What, then, is self-examination? The self examining itself may show something like "the ability to hold converse with myself" that Antisthenes, a friend of Socrates, says is the advantage of philosophy.[47] But a conversation needs more than one speaker. Is the self-examining self two selves?

In the *Apology*, Socrates does not say enough about self-examination for us to decide conclusively that it is a dialogue between me and myself (in Hannah Arendt's formulation).[48] If it is, however, does the watched self talk back to the watcher? Does Socrates internalize his public method of examination? If so, then the watcher or examiner is the superior, but not exactly as reason, in the *Republic*, is superior in dignity to the passions and appetites that when the soul is not trained, reason constantly battles and often loses to. Socrates does not refer to any special training or higher education, but only to self-examination and the kind of examination by others that may encourage self-examination.

Perhaps in its persistent retrospection, self-examination is similar to interpreting a dream one has: one's wakeful experience is like a flow of dreams, and only a kind of internal secession from the experiencing self permits one to understand what one was up to or what one has been pursuing without quite knowing why. Implicit is the hope, however, that the inside watcher or examiner is not altogether too much like the amorphous I in the dream that is dreamed along with the rest of the dream. The hope is that the inside examiner is not so entangled with the examined that there is no possibility of genuine distance and difference between these two aspects of the self, no possibility of genuine self-examination. The hope is that self-examination is not a trick of language, an incorrigibly contaminated process, from the start.

Socratic self-examination is not merely self-consciousness; it is not merely reflexive consciousness, the ability to speak sentences about oneself. It is not, at least to begin with, the ability to imagine oneself in the place of another or to imagine what it is like to be another. It is also not quite Thoreau's "doubleness," in which "I can stand as remote from myself as another" thanks to "a part of me, which, as it were, is not a part of me, but a spectator, sharing no experience, but taking note of it, and that is no more I than it is you."[49] Socratic self-examination may be one of the seeds, but Thoreau's doubleness is closer, I think, to late Stoicism (though still far from it in important respects).

Whatever Socratic self-examination is, whatever it is most like, and whether or not it is genuinely possible, it is a principal negative component of Socratic integrity and shows, once again, how such integrity is made from negatives. Self-examination can be difficult or painful or disorienting; it is almost unnatural. It surely is not nicely compatible with being splendidly virtuous, which contains nothing tentative or perplexed or self-doubting. It is not useful for self-realization or the display of aristocratic virtues. To become less disposed either to serve as an instrument of injustice or to lend one's strength to the initiation or maintenance of injustice is its ultimate end. The way to greater moderation or sanity is self-examination, joined to examining and being examined by others; the way is not Aristotelian habituation from an early age.

It is obvious that the moral origins of Socratic self-examination do not determine the later history of the practice. Socrates inaugurates thinking about the potentialities of inwardness, but its story in the West contains much diversity. Not all those who have strenuously practiced self-examination or who have theorized its practice are morally motivated, as Socrates is. Inwardness as the site of freedom or self-renewal or positive inspiration is an essential part of the Western fabric, but I do not think that the original conception of inwardness, which is Socratic, contains all these later developments. To say as much is neither to praise nor to reproach Socrates. His conception is what it tremendously is.

Why does Socrates care about injustice to the extent that he does? Why is he so passionate to see less injustice in the world and disposed to risk death rather than being an instrument of injustice? Why are his moral integrity, and derivatively his intellectual integrity, so intense? There is no conclusive way of answering these questions. I am not even sure that such questions should be asked; indeed, there is a sort of crass impertinence in raising them. Still, the temptation to speculate is hard to put down. The speculation I offer mixes references to Socrates' statements and to his psyche.

One can say simply that for Socrates, human beings, unlike other creatures, are capable of justice and injustice. That is their distinctiveness. Socrates does not know what full distributive justice is; he does not know humanity or any particular human being, even himself, well enough to know how to confer such justice. He does know what injustice is; he knows what undeserved and deliberately inflicted pain or suffering or dispossession is. He knows what people tend to shun or shy away from. He also knows that those who resent injustice when it is done to them are quite prepared to do it to others, whether initially or in retaliation.

From all this, a possible conclusion is that the truly significant aspect of human distinctiveness is the capacity to do injustice. Socrates' aim is to curb it: everyone agrees that certain kinds of pain or suffering or harm are bad. The badness is enough reason to curb it. Then add: to persuade people to be less unjust is not to take them closer to human excellence (one component of which would be the ability to confer full distributive justice), but it is to take in hand a distinctive human capacity—the ability to do injustice—and to transform it into a better expression of human distinctiveness, the ability to refrain from injustice. Such a line of reasoning is suggested by what Socrates says in the *Apology* in regard to the elusive nature of human excellence and the limits on human knowledge concerning it.[50]

One possible reason that Socrates cares (and that we should care) so much about injustice, then, is that the honor of being distinctively human in the most feasible way is at stake. But I do not believe that in thinking about Socrates, we should put too much weight on the idea of human distinctiveness. We may incorporate too much Plato or Aristotle into the Socrates of the *Apology,* even if we highlight the negativity of the manner in which he may conceive of human distinctiveness.

A related reason, present in the *Crito,* is taken up with an eye on eventually introducing the doctrine of nonretaliation. Socrates says that doing injustice is bad for the agent, not only for the victim. The agent harms himself in harming another. This would mean that Socrates has tried to abstain from injustice for his own sake, not that of others, and that he urges the same attitude on others: "For if we do not follow him [the wise man], we shall corrupt and maim that part of us which, we used to say, is improved by justice and disabled by injustice."[51]

The *Gorgias* intensifies the idea: it is better for oneself to be the victim of injustice than its perpetrator. But when Socrates in the two episodes must choose between being an instrument (never the initiator) of injustice and risking death, he does not say that he would rather be dead than impaired. Such an interpretation is possible. After all, when Socrates claims in the *Apology*—and it is a shocking statement—that an unexamined life is not worth living, he says something similar. But the choice of an examined over an unexamined (in a sense impaired) life is a choice that can usually be made without risk of death or of any other great loss. Only sluggish people refuse to choose an examined over an unexamined life; their lives are therefore diminished radically and needlessly. Their cowardice is moral, not physical. They choose their impairment amid ease and safety.

I think, however, that the point made by Socrates' conduct in the two episodes is that he will never assist injustice to save himself; he would rather die. Only when the issue is escaping unjust punishment and the city is likened to a parent greater than a biological parent does Socrates say by means of a rhetorical question that it is better to be dead than impaired: "Then is life worth living when that part of us which is maimed by injustice [i.e., by doing injustice] and benefited by justice [i.e., by doing justice] is corrupt?"[52] The *Crito,* however, as I have said, could be thought closer to the *Gorgias* than to the *Apology,* in which the perspective of the victim's suffering, not the advantage of the agent's soul, is paramount.

To be sure, Socrates does say in the *Apology* that if the Athenians (because of Meletus) put him to death unjustly, Meletus and they would do more harm to themselves than to him (or at least as much harm).[53] This probably means, however, that Socrates is more valuable to Meletus and Athens than life is to Socrates. On the one hand, Socrates is valuable because he is unique in his power to get people to think about why and how their pursuits and policies are making themselves unhappy and harming others; on the other hand, life matters less to him than it does to others. I do not think we can import into this sentence the comparative advantage or disadvantage to the soul of the agent, whether Socrates or the city, of doing and receiving injustice. By his assumption that he is not guilty, Socrates is saying that Athens does not have to choose between doing and receiving injustice, but between doing and not doing injustice.

If we stay with the *Apology* in pursuit of why Socrates is so passionate about injustice and why he prefers dying to being its instrument, we can say that Socrates has an opinion about death that leads him to make lighter of it than most people do. That he was over sixty at the time of the episodes of dissent and noncompliance and that he is seventy when he explains himself under accusation may have some bearing on his readiness to refuse to abet or do injustice to others, cost him what it may. But I doubt it. Xenophon does go so far as to have Socrates say that to die now at the hands of the state would spare him the hardest part of life (old age) and give him the easiest death (quick and painless poisoning).[54] Perhaps Socrates did put the matter in this way, if only to himself, but the prudence manifested in these words does not suit the Socrates of Plato's *Apology*. There is something tonally different from prudence when toward the end of Plato's *Apology*, he says, "I am persuaded that it was better for me to die now, and to be released from trouble."[55]

Socrates' old age does not really affect his heroism; most elderly people cling to life as ferociously as young ones do. Nevertheless, Socrates thinks about death in such a manner as to leave the impression that he has never cared too much about staying alive for its own sake. He does not love life with a blind attachment; he seems to need reasons to go on living. Perhaps the cause is temperament or some obscure distaste or revulsion. A more worthy reason would be the prevalence of injustice. We shall turn in a moment to a kind of explanation that Socrates himself provides. Whatever the reason, Socrates is continually unintimidated by death and not only when he is risking it in the name of avoiding injustice. Not dreading death absolutely, however, makes it easier for him to risk his life and then to face certain death with equanimity. This is not to say—Socrates does not say—that it was easy, routine, a smooth matter of course, for him to risk death. He sometimes speaks as if he felt danger, felt fear for himself, when he stood alone.

The *Apology* contains two main and interrelated points concerning death. The first is Socrates' contention that the good person cannot be harmed; the second is Socrates' assertion that either there is no afterlife or if there is one, it can be an opportunity for eternal conversation among the dead. Either hypothesis would help make it easier for Socrates to risk or face death. We leave aside the powerful but metaphysically laden utterances about the philosopher's affinity to death in the *Phaedo*, great as they are. The Socrates of the *Apology* has no positive soul-metaphysics of the sort found in the *Phaedo*.

Concerning harm to the good man, Socrates says: "Meletus and Anytus can do me no harm: that is impossible, for I am sure it is not allowed that a good man be injured by a worse."[56] He also says, even more unconditionally, that "no evil can happen to a good man, either in life or after death."[57] The first contention refers to the harms of (judicially imposed) death, exile, and loss of political status.[58] The second formulation refers to harm to the good person's affairs in general, but the central harm is (judicially imposed) death.

Although in his speech after conviction and before the penalty, Socrates calls imprisonment an evil and surely considers exile a terrible fate, especially for himself,[59] he concentrates in these two statements the claim that for himself, death and other judicial penalties—but especially death—are not harms, certainly when inflicted unjustly. Although not harms, they are still not things that Socrates actively seeks or unequivocally wants. He is, after all, a human being and only a human being. He takes pride in having risked his life by dissent and noncompliance, as if he felt the risk as a risk and the possible cost as a cost. Reconciliation to death, even though perhaps present throughout his adult life, is not fully consummated until the eve of his death.

We can distill his claim in this way: in devoting himself as an episodically active citizen, as a general nonparticipant in politics, and as "a sort of gadfly" to the cause of diminishing injustice and not lending himself as an instrument to its perpetration, he has labored to prevent people, at home and abroad, from being deprived of what is theirs. He has also risked much that is rightfully his in doing so, even though being deprived of what is rightfully his—especially life—does not matter too much to him. That kind of deprivation matters a great deal more to others. A really good person does not attach himself very tightly to even the rudiments of his existence or to his existence itself; a really good person also knows that often those he wants to protect are (or have been or will be) themselves initiators or instruments of evil.

In short, Socrates devotes himself to preserving people, who are not exactly worthy, in possession of those things that are not exactly important, except to their unimproved selves. (The preservation amounts to abstention from unjust taking.) For Socrates to be deprived of life or something else is not really to be harmed, but because people are as they are and because they will more or less likely remain so, despite Socrates' unstinting efforts, they will feel themselves harmed by such deprivations. Despite their incredible readiness for military self-sacrifice, people ordinarily want to go on living as long as they can and as prosperously as possible. They are within their right to do so. What people rightfully want, Socrates will try not to deny them, even if he himself must lose those things that people rightfully want.

Self-examination has made Socrates more moderate, less intensely attached not only to the prizes of the world but even to the level of day-to-day life that moderate people satisfy themselves with. Perhaps an initial disposition also has moved him in a self-denying direction. Then, too, the divine sign or voice never seems to deter him from risk or self-sacrifice, as if to give its negative blessing to Socrates' independent resolve to struggle in his own way against injustice. These elements all help detach Socrates from ordinary self-concern, including concern with his death from any cause but particularly his death from the injustice of others.

The question persists, however: why is Socrates, now and before, so calm about death? Why does he mind dying less than most people do, certainly than most people taken as natural individuals not disciplined into martial collective self-forgetful self-sacrifice? Socrates goes very far when he says, "For no one knows whether death may not be the greatest good that can happen to man" rather than the greatest evil, as most people think.[60] Why would anyone think, instead, that death may be the greatest good? The rate of suicide is low even among the desperate.

Socrates eventually answers this question when he addresses the jurors who voted to acquit him. The answer, however, seems to violate the heart of the claim that Socrates knows nothing that is worth knowing. His unashamed claim to ignorance has up to this moment rested on the view that the most important power— being able positively to live well—must depend on wisdom, and wisdom is knowledge of what being dead amounts to. He says:

> For to fear death, my friends, is only to think ourselves wise without really being wise, for it is to think that we know what we do not know. . . . And if I were to claim to be at all wiser than others, it would be because, not knowing very much about the other world, I do not think I know.[61]

His very last words at the trial express total ignorance: "But now the time has come, and we must go away—I to die, and you to live. Which is better is known to the god alone."[62] One is tempted to say that his search for wisdom all along has been to learn what others think death amounts to and how they adjust their way of life to their thoughts about being dead. Everywhere he turned he found not wisdom in the form of acknowledged ignorance, but ignorance presented as wisdom, with horrible consequences for self and others. Love of life is feverish because the thought of Hades is so appalling. We cannot be wise unless we know what being dead amounts to, and no one living knows that. Hence no one is wise, least of all Socrates, who at least is knowingly ignorant.

The trouble is that Socrates thinks he knows something about death. It is clear that he takes issue with a common view that in Hades souls survive in a condition of longing for life. At least, Socrates in Hades would not long for life. It is also clear that what he tells the jurors who voted for his acquittal comes from no divine source, no oracular priestess, no divine sign or voice and that what he says could not have come from self-examination or the method of examination used with others. At the end, Socrates, careful to deny that he has speculated about conditions beneath the earth, does just that. Perhaps this speculation has sustained him for a long time in his struggle against injustice. Perhaps his city thought that his aberrance—what we call his integrity—was underlain all along by an unorthodox idea of what being dead amounts to. To that extent, perhaps his old and new accusers were right.

When Socrates says that death is one or another of two states, he does not allow for the possibility of a third. Death is either nothingness or it is a "migration of the soul to another place" where the opportunity presents itself for endless conversation with and examination of the other dead.[63] Socrates would want to talk especially with the very types of human being that he, when alive, found especially wanting, poets and men of worldly affairs. The latter possibility is charming because it implies that a lifetime of experience—anyone's experience—could be the source of an endless duration of interpretation, though it would help if Socrates were on hand as midwife of interpretation. But this latter possibility, an unorthodox version of an orthodox view, does not suit Socrates as one whose intellectual integrity prohibits wishful thinking. However, the notion does suit him as one who, while alive, seems to aspire to be an undistracted, disembodied intellect.

Of course, we can never know for sure what Socrates thought. The first possibility, however, does perfectly suit Socrates' intellectual integrity. Death is nothingness; it is like not having been born yet; it is not a condition of any sort (personal or otherwise). Gregory Vlastos says: "So far from allowing Socrates a belief in the prenatal existence of the soul, Xenophon does not even credit him with the usual, old-fashioned, belief in the soul's survival in Hades."[64] Xenophon's omission is not proof of anything, but it is interesting that writings that Xenophon dedicates to the attempt to make Socrates as unthreatening as possible do not declare Socrates' acceptance of the soul's immortality.

A supposition that death is nothingness need not sponsor moral integrity; it can as easily go with libertinism or apathy. Socrates' case is different. He finds the prospect of nothingness appealing, not disgusting or disturbing. He does not repeat the saying of Silenus that it is best never to have been born, but he comes close. He says:

> if death is the absence of all consciousness, and like the sleep of one whose slumbers are unbroken by any dreams, it will be a wonderful gain. For if a man had to select that night in which he slept so soundly that he did not even dream, and had to compare with it all the other nights and days of his life, and then had to say how many days and nights in his life he had spent better and more pleasantly than this night, I think that a private person, nay, even the Great King of Persia himself, would find them easy to count, compared with the others. If that is the nature of death, I for one count it a gain. For then it appears that all time is nothing more than a single night.[65]

Only a few days and nights in one's life are sweeter than dreamless sleep or the nothingness of death, and they do not weigh as much as the other days and nights.[66] Being dead forever is nothing more for the dead person than a single night's dreamless sleep is for a living one. To risk or face death may be a little easier for a person who not only thinks that death is nothingness but also believes that life is a burden.

Surmising about death as Socrates does, why has he gone on living in the absolutely arduous way he has? Why didn't he lead a more ordinary life or a moderately pleasurable one? The answer can be, finally, that he could not help living as he did. I mean that he was driven irresistibly and from the beginning, from before the time the priestess gave her answer, which in any case Socrates did not have to construe in the activist way he did. Driven by what? By the one positivity that perhaps can be attributed to him: that he was driven by affection and compassion for others. Indeed, all Socrates' negativity stems from that one positivity and is dictated by it. It is his energy, his eros. He is more than just the friend of the Athenian jurors that he says he is.[67] The whole image of Socrates as a model of intellectual and moral integrity, as a supreme hero of self-denial and self-sacrifice, as a master of negativity, needs one, if only one, positivity, and that must be a positive commitment to others. He cared for them more than he cared for himself. He lived and died for them. He made them his superiors by deeming them worthy of his self-sacrifice. But he did not think that they were his equals, and this is precisely why he had to care for them and in the way that he did.

NOTES

1. Page 37a. All page number references are the standard margin pages of Plato's works and refer to the dialogue being discussed. I used the translation of the *Apology* and the *Crito* by F. J. Church, revised by Robert D. Cummings (Indianapolis: Bobbs-Merrill, 1956). I also regularly consulted the translation by G. M. A. Grube, *The Trial and Death of Socrates*, 2d ed. (Indianapolis: Hackett, 1981); and read the translations by Benjamin Jowett, *The Dialogues of Plato* (New York: Random House, 1937), vol. 1, 401–38; Hugh Tredennick, *The Last Days of Socrates* (Baltimore: Penguin, 1959); and R. E. Allen, *The Dialogues of Plato* (New Haven, Conn.: Yale University Press, 1984), vol. 1.

In thinking about the *Apology* and the *Crito*, I found instructive and helpful the following works: Hannah Arendt, "Thinking and Moral Considerations," *Social Research* 38 (1971): 417–46; Hannah Arendt, *Thinking*, vol. 1 of her *The Life of the Mind*, 2 vols. (New York: Harcourt Brace, 1978); Hannah Arendt, "Philosophy and Politics," *Social Research* 57 (1990): 73–103; Thomas C. Brickhouse and Nicholas D. Smith, *Socrates on Trial* (Princeton, N.J.: Princeton University Press, 1989); W. K. C. Guthrie, *Socrates* (Cambridge: Cambridge University Press, 1971); Richard Kraut, *Socrates and the State* (Princeton, N.J.: Princeton University Press, 1984); Alexander Nehamas, "What Did Socrates Teach and to Whom Did He Teach It?" *Review of Metaphysics* 46 (1992): 279–306; Josiah Ober, "Gadfly Ethics in Context: The 'Socrates and Athens' Problem in *Apology* and *Crito*," unpublished manuscript; Christopher Reeve, *Socrates in the Apology* (Indianapolis: Hackett, 1989); Gerasimos Xenophon Santas, *Socrates: Philosophy in Plato's Early Dialogues* (Boston: Routledge & Kegan Paul, 1979); Gregory Vlastos, *Socrates: Ironist and Moral Philosopher* (Ithaca, N.Y.: Cornell University Press, 1991); and A. D. Woozley, *Law and Obedience: The Arguments of Plato's Crito* (Chapel Hill: University of North Carolina Press, 1979). I have also learned greatly from my students at Amherst and Princeton, where I have been privileged to teach the *Apology* and the *Crito* over a period of forty years. My special thanks to Neera Badhwar, J. Peter Euben, Donald R. Morrison, and Alexander Nehamas for their criticisms and suggestions, and to John Cooper for many enlivening discussions of Socrates.

2. 37a.

3. 31c.
4. 17d.
5. 31d–32a.
6. 32e–33a.
7. 32a–c.
8. 32c–e.
9. 28e.
10. 28b–29a.
11. 40a–b.
12. 21a.
13. 29d.
14. Diogenes Laertius, "Socrates," in R. D. Hicks, trans., *Lives of Eminent Philosophers*, 2 vols. (Cambridge, Mass.: Harvard University Press, 1950), vol. 1, II: 31, 161.
15. 32e.
16. Thucydides, *The Peloponnesian War*, III: 41–48.
17. Ibid., III: 49–50.
18. 32b.
19. 49c.
20. 28516b–c.
21. 54d.
22. 36a.
23. 54b–c.
24. 49c–e.
25. 54b–c.
26. 51a.
27. 50b.
28. 51a–b.
29. 51d–e.
30. 51e–52a.
31. 30e.
32. 19b.
33. 24b.
34. 20a–b.
35. 22a.
36. 29c–d.
37. 30b–c.
38. 31a–b.
39. 39c–d.
40. 38a.
41. 164–65.
42. Diogenes Laertius, "Socrates," vol. 1, II: 25, 155.

43. 31c.

44. 29a.

45. 17a.

46. 230a.

47. Diogenes Laertius, "Antisthenes," in Hicks, trans., *Lives of Eminent Philosophers*, vol. 2, VI: 6, 9.

48. See note 1 for citations of Arendt. Arendt makes much of a passage in the *Gorgias*, in which Socrates says: "It would be better for me that my lyre or a chorus I directed should be out of tune and loud with discord, and that multitudes of men should disagree with me rather than that my single self should be out of harmony with myself and contradict me" (482b–c). See *Plato's Gorgias*, trans. W. C. Helmbold (New York: Liberal Arts Press, 1952), 50.

According to Arendt, Socrates' regular practice of self-examination is entwined with his dread of the self-reproach that wrongdoing would cause him: he stays blameless so that he can be internally harmonious. But I doubt the Socrates of the *Apology* believes that he can ever attain steady internal harmony, perfect freedom from self-reproach. Furthermore, Arendt assimilates self-examination too closely to conscience; she makes it too directly moral.

See also Bonnie Honig's thoughtful essay on integrity and self-division, "Difference, Dilemmas, and the Politics of Home," *Social Research* 61 (1994): 563–97.

49. Henry David Thoreau, "Solitude," in *Walden* (New York: Modern Library, 1937), 122.

50. 20a–b.

51. 47d.

52. 47e.

53. 30c, d.

54. Xenophon, *Recollections of Socrates and Socrates' Defense before the Jury*, trans. Anna S. Benjamin (Indianapolis: Bobbs-Merrill, 1965), 6–9, 146.

55. 41d.

56. 30c–d.

57. 41c–d.

58. 30d.

59. 37b–e.

60. 29a.

61. 29a–b.

62. 42a.

63. 40c–41c.

64. Vlastos, *Socrates*, 103.

65. 40c–e.

66. Why are most dreams bad dreams, and why are bad dreams continuous with most wakeful life? The Socrates of the *Republic* suggests that the reason is that dreams, like daily life, are the scene of temptation to wrongdoing. He says: "Our dreams make it clear that there is a dangerous, wild, and lawless form of desire in everyone, even in those of us who seem to be entirely moderate or measured" (572b). See Plato, *Republic*, trans. G. M. A. Grube, rev. C. D. C. Reeve (Indianapolis: Hackett, 1992), 242. Temptation makes life as well as dreams a burden to one whose sense of injustice is keen. There may be a connection to the Socrates of the *Apology*.

67. 29d.

PART II

INTEGRITY, CONSCIENCE, AND PROFESSIONALISM

6

INTEGRITY, CONSCIENCE, AND SCIENCE

JOHN KANE

Few people at the end of the twentieth century can have much doubt about the significance of science to modern life. We are a truly "scientific culture" if by that we mean we are, as a culture, heavily dependent on science. It can hardly be said, however, that a genuine understanding of science has penetrated broadly and deeply into the nonscientific community. This disparity between public dependency on and public understanding of the scientific community creates the possibility of dissonance.[1] People are often torn between respect and fear.

In this chapter I distinguish two, rather opposed, lay views of science that will allow me to address the issue of relations between scientific community and the public. I do not claim that these views are exhaustive, but they are convenient in that they also allow me to address the issues of integrity and conscience with respect to science. The first view sees science as a moral exemplar from which much may profitably be learned by society; the second sees it as a Pandora's box on which the lid cannot now be shut.

The first view rests on an admiring appraisal of scientific integrity and argues that the world would be a better place if it adopted more of science's values and methods to solve social and political problems. It concentrates more on the practices of science and the values they embody than on the products of science, and is

115

concerned with valuable lessons that the wider community may learn from the scientific community.

The second view is more pessimistic, or more ambivalent, about science. It admits our practical dependency but harbors worries about the material and social effects of scientific discoveries and the applications to which they are put. That is, it concentrates more on science's products than on its practices and is concerned mainly with the control of (or lack of control of) scientific discovery and invention. The relevant ethical category here, rather than integrity, is that of social conscience with respect to science. This ambivalent attitude has become increasingly predominant since the end of World War II.[2] Centrally at issue is a question of trust.

Traditionally, the degree of trust that laypeople have invested in the scientific community has been quite high. The sheer magnitude of science's success seems to argue that in their pursuit of truth, scientists are demonstrating rigorous standards of integrity. The integrity in question is, of course, professional integrity, internal to the practice itself, rather than the wider moral integrity that scientists may or may not possess simply as human beings. But there has always been a temptation to identify professional virtue with a wider ethical virtue, as though the internalization of scientific values by scientists in their training and practice makes them more trustworthy than the average person, certainly than the average politician. Because these values are centered on the search for the objective truth of things, as opposed to opinions, prejudices, or special interests, their assimilation can be imagined as producing in scientists a rare and habitual honesty. And if doing science makes them better people, it follows that public virtue might be improved by a wider inculcation of scientific values and that social problems might be better handled by the application of objective scientific expertise rather than through the messy interplay of political interests.

Over the last few decades, there has undoubtedly been significant erosion of this trust (or perhaps we should say faith). From the scientists' side, there is, of course, an instinctive mistrust of any lay interference in scientific practice, but the increasing demand for such interference (in the form of public regulation) is itself evidence of a deepening failure of public trust in science. To make matters worse, the professional integrity of scientists has recently been called into question inside the scientific community itself. Greg Sachs and Mark Siegler claim that scientific misconduct is now seen by scientists, the public, and elected officials as a potentially fatal cancer that threatens to destroy what they call the "exquisitely successful and productive marriage" between scientific community and public that has characterized the postwar period.[3]

These charges come at a time when the tide of opinion seems, for other reasons, to be running against the profession. Science is by no means an endangered activity, but there is no denying that compared with the recent past, it feels threatened. Evandro Agazzi no doubt overstates the case but perhaps reflects the feelings of many scientists when he writes that "an unlimited confidence, unshaken optimism and unconditioned [*sic*] approval for the growth and conquests of science and technology have been replaced in the last decades by widespread mistrust, fear, denigration and rejection. Our society seems to have passed from science to anti-science."[4]

No longer does the identification of science with human progress, forged in the Enlightenment and strengthened by the rise of industrial society, seem quite so self-evident to the public mind; no longer are the allegedly objective opinions of scientific "experts" received with automatic reverence; the special status of scientific truth itself has been questioned, even mocked, by some; and there has been a marked decline in faith in "scientific," technocratic solutions to social and political problems.

Some scientists have responded to all this by adopting a siege mentality, but this has not been constructive. It is important to see that not all these developments are necessarily a cause for lamentation. I argue that the decline of professional standards, if real, is serious enough, for it may have significant political consequences. But much of the decline in automatic trust can be interpreted as evidence of the public's growing maturity, which should be encouraged rather than bemoaned. Indeed, it must be encouraged if it is not to lead merely to disillusionment and cynicism.

I address these matters by exploring two questions extracted from the opposing attitudes to science noted earlier. The first asks whether any aspects of scientific practice may be regarded as generally and profitably applicable to public life, and the second asks about the degree of public trust that can or should be placed in scientists in their pursuit of scientific truth.

Since the latter question immediately raises the problem of the wisdom and possibility of publicly controlling or monitoring scientific activity, my two questions might be rephrased as "Can the public learn anything useful from scientific practice, and can science gain anything from greater public scrutiny of its activities?"

SCIENTIFIC VALUES AND SCIENTIFIC INTEGRITY

To address the question of whether the public can learn from science anything of ethical value, we first need to understand what the values of science are and how they inform the practices of scientists. We should note at the outset that these values, however admirable in themselves, are instrumental to the practice of science. They are upheld because they are deemed necessary for the successful prosecution of science's endeavor, which is the quest for reliable knowledge.

In 1973,[5] Robert Merton identified the four principal values of science as universalism, communalism, disinteredness, and organized skepticism. *Universalism* implies the indifference of science to the nationality, race, color, creed, or gender of its practitioners. *Communalism* means that scientific knowledge must be public and information freely exchanged with individual scientists responsible for the integrity of their work. *Disinteredness* denotes the requirement that results not be manipulated for the sake of profit, ideology, or expediency but be honest and objective. And *organized skepticism* ensures that nothing is accepted merely on the word of authority but that freedom always exists to question alleged truths and to test them against empirical evidence.

Each of these principles, I think, implies to a large extent the others, the real key being the requirement of publicity, which provides the material on which organized skepticism can get to work. If scientists in their practice need to be honest, color-blind, critical of others, and open to criticism themselves, it is because science is organized precisely to make scrutiny and replication of work as inevitable as it can possibly be made.[6] In its institutional wisdom, the scientific enterprise may have expected more than the usual honesty in its practitioners but has never entirely depended on it. Science has never presumed that individual conscience alone could be relied on to ensure scientific integrity. Science, indeed, might be thought to have institutionally adopted H. L. Mencken's definition of conscience as "the still, small voice which tells you someone may be watching." In science, someone generally is watching, if only after the fact.

None of Merton's values of science has ever been fully realized or ever will be. Universalism and communalism are compromised by national divisions, even in this post–cold war world (who now, in the United States, will dare share nuclear knowledge with Iraq?), not to mention the competitive race of industries for the profitable patent. Neither can the disinteredness of scientists any longer be taken for granted, however prone some of them may still be, in argument, to pulling superior rank in this. Scientists are just as likely as anyone else to have their views warped by petty jealousy, envy, ideology, self-interest, or hopefulness. They can also, as a group, be just as silly as anyone else, as the extraordinary frenzy generated a few years ago by the so-called discovery of cold-fusion[7] (by Martin Fleischmann and Stanley Pons of the University of Utah) showed. Stephen Fletcher, a senior Australian research scientist who, with a substantial grant from industry, attempted unsuccessfully to replicate the Fleischmann and Pons results, later commented that "the cold-fusion debate has taught us more about the sociology of science and the way in which the press and groups of scientists respond to announcements of 'breakthroughs' than about the possibilities of alternative energy."[8]

But silliness is not the worst fault of which scientists can be accused. Conscious subversion of the values of science of the kind recently reported is far more serious. The problem is not one of major fraud (whose occasional, highly publicized detection can be argued to show that science is on its mettle, safeguarding its ethic) but of what might be termed "ordinary" cheating. That most serious transgression of the scientific ethic, the fabrication of data, is, according to scientific publishers, increasingly commonplace, if only in the minor form that goes under the slang terms *cooking* or *trimming and fudging*. Plagiarism is apparently on the increase (including covert self-plagiarism, in which authors republish a single piece of work in various formats and forums).[9]

Recent studies conducted independently by Judith P. Swazey for the National Science Foundation and by the Massachusetts Institute of Technology reveal disturbing attitudes among graduate students and science faculty members.[10] Again, the practices uncovered—fudging data, plagiarizing, misusing research funds, taking credit for the another's work, and the like—constitute misdemeanors rather than crimes, but the troubling part is how widespread they appear to have become. If not exactly condoned, they are at least implicitly accepted by many people as an everyday occurrence, as part of the game.

In England, physiologist Harold Hillman coined the term *parafraud* to describe an undiscussed phenomenon that he claims has become ordinary practice in the profession.[11] He cites as examples those scientists who refuse to answer challenges crucial to their beliefs, researchers who do not report experiments or observations that are incompatible with their beliefs, the expectation of supervisors that they will share the authorship of research work to which they have made no contribution (but who then quickly repudiate responsibility if fraud is detected), and scientists who fail to carry out control experiments crucial to the validity of their results.

If this trend is something more than a perceptual myth, the explanation for it is unclear. Some commentators have pointed to greater competition for scarcer research funds and positions and to the movement of scientists out of their formerly cloistered and amateurish world toward the success-oriented realm of big business.[12] The scientific establishment, at any rate, seems to be taking the problem seriously. In the United States, many funding agencies, like the National Institutes of Health, now tie research funding to mandatory ethics training for students and issue guidelines for handling cases of detected fraud.[13] In addition, research institutions in many parts of the world have begun to issue codes of conduct for research, which is hardly surprising in view of the important practical consequences, political and intellectual, that might result.[14]

The political consequences concern the danger to continued funding. Science needs to maintain its public image of more-than-ordinary integrity because the continued funding of its research programs may partly depend on it. In an era of so-called fiscal crisis, Western governments are on the lookout for soft targets for proposed expenditure cuts. Nowhere are the cuts likely to be more savage than in the United States, where a Republican Congress, determined to outscrooge Scrooge, plans to slash basic science funding by $24 billion by the end of the century. The Republicans argue that the scientific establishment is bloated, and they support their case by pointing (with no more deference to honest credibility than one might expect) to examples of "silly science," in which public funds are spent on arcane topics of no clear benefit to society.[15] In these circumstances, adverse public attitudes toward science, whatever their source, are a boon to the slashers.

The intellectual consequence of a failure of integrity is, of course, the impact on the credibility of scientific findings generally. Revelations of widespread misconduct inevitably place a question mark over the soundness of scientific results. The opportunity to misbehave without much risk of detection may, for some species of unethical conduct, be greater in some disciplines than in others, greater, for example, in social science than in physics (as I will discuss shortly). However, Hillman notes that the failure to carry out control experiments is occurring even in important physiological work relating to the understanding of, among other things, cancer, multiple sclerosis, and muscular dystrophy. He writes that "the failure to carry out crucial controls means that the experiments are incomplete, and it puts at risk all findings, theories and treatments based on these experiments."[16]

How serious is the threat to knowledge that such failings represent? The answer is that no one really knows, for it is impossible to tell with any accuracy how widespread these corrupt practices may be and to what extent they have contaminated published findings. Colleagues of Hillman's admit that what he calls *parafraud* is widespread, but they tend to downplay its significance by arguing that one should not expect academics to behave more morally than the general public and that, anyway, truth will triumph in the end.

The first of these claims is questionable, if on no grounds other than the purely prudential one of the risk to continued public funding, as noted earlier. The loss of a reputation for more than average integrity may have, for science, very tangible costs. As for the second claim, that truth will triumph, there is a reason for accepting that in science, at least in the long run, this may well be the case. Whatever the corruption, science as an institutionalized activity cannot be imagined as surviving long if it ceases to generate genuine knowledge, and in the end the profit will go to those scientists who, applying their scientific craft with suitable rigor, actually manage to do this.

We must accept, though, that for some areas of knowledge the long run may be very long indeed. The effectuality of publicity and replication in countering silliness, distortion, and parafraud depends on the object of study and the ease with which it can be manipulated. In the case of cold fusion, for example, the procedure for checking was relatively simple: it involved setting up the experimental apparatus as specified by Fleischmann and Pons and replicating their procedures. The failure to reproduce their results, despite the money and effort invested by numerous agencies, soon cooled the initial ardor of scientists (though a few optimists continue to experiment). In areas where possible causes may be confoundingly complex and conditions do not lend themselves to neatly confined laboratory testing, the opportunity for systematic bias is much starker. Such areas include environmental themes like the global-warming debate, much of astrophysics, and most of sociology.[17]

We should not doubt that scientists are as prone to bias, whether conscious or not, as anyone else is. Mark Diesendorf[18] contends that we should be especially alert to bias when scientists apply themselves to "real-world problems," such as in matters of energy, health, pollution, social change, and economics. Here the inherent complexity of the subject matter requires making value-laden assumptions about unknown variables, and this fact, combined with the inevitable institutional and political pressures, tends to produce "findings" that are seldom as objective as they are usually presented. In this kind of applied science, Mark Twain's dictum about "lies, damned lies, and statistics" still has a point, and we are right to be extremely skeptical of all claims to "objectivity."[19]

Some people might want to go further. They could argue that

what has been said so far supports the charges of those who hold that science's claim to "objective knowledge" is wholly spurious and that it is just another culture-bound "knowledge system" on a par with, say, so-called creation science or the cosmology of the ancient Egyptians. But then it would be difficult to account for science's unique ability to deliver knowledge that is not only surprising but often counterintuitive and that, moreover, is so productive in application.[20]

In other words, science more often tends to disconfirm our prejudices than to confirm them, unlike most other so-called knowledge systems. The fact that in daily practice, scientists sometimes, perhaps often, fail to live up to their own standards of objectivity and are swayed by self-interest, ideology, and politics hardly undermines the credibility of all scientific knowledge. Science is a human activity, and scientists are merely human, but science has a rein on human cupidity through its institutionalization of skepticism and critique, which work constantly to prevent the closure of science as a system of knowledge.

Theodor Adorno once said, apropos of Marx, that great thoughts should be criticized, not idolized, and in this he expressed the essential scientific spirit. In science there is a place for the respect of significant work, but never for idolatry. When scientific beliefs become closed to critique and testing, they become idolatrous and cease to be scientific. In idolatry, people bow to authority and interpret the world according their idol's vision; in science at its best, people try to allow the world to determine belief, painful though this sometimes is to fondly held prejudice.[21] It is therefore an enduring characteristic of scientific knowledge that it cannot be fixed, once and for all, but must remain open and progressive.

It is true that there may be a great deal of unpredictability, even illogicality, about scientists' openness or otherwise to new knowledge claims. Sometimes they may accept, en masse, a new theory before it is adequately tested while they may reject other theories for a long time even when they seem evidentially supported. When I was an undergraduate student of biology, the theory of continental drift on tectonic plates was only just beginning to emerge from the category of "crackpot" to that of "interesting"; now it is universally accepted by scientists as true and is the foundation for much recent work in biology and geology. The evidence, finally, seemed irrefutable, and all resistance ended. Science never proceeds smoothly and continuously, and factions may nurse favored and competing theories for very long periods. But in the end, however far away the end may be, the only thing that matters is a theory's success in providing a convincing explanation of phenomena, one that accounts for the available evidence and can withstand the challenge of new evidence and argument and that thus may justify our belief in its descriptive truth.

LESSONS FROM SCIENTIFIC PRACTICE

If even scientists cannot be fully relied on to observe their own standards of integrity, what lessons can scientific practice have for a general public wholly unconstrained by the discipline and aims of science? There is at least one important lesson, I think, which I will expound by means of a true moral tale.

In Australia in the 1980s, there occurred an extraordinary national psychodrama centering on the events surrounding the notorious "dingo case."[22] This was the case in which a couple, Lindy and Michael Chamberlain, were convicted and jailed for the supposed murder of their baby, Azaria, who, they claimed, had been taken by a native wild dog (dingo) during a camping trip in central Australia in 1980. The nation became passionately and noisily divided over the couple's guilt or innocence. Evidence at the scene fully supported the couple's version, but a train of events and rumors led to an eventual trial in which the "expert" evidence of forensic scientists played a crucial part. Pathologists argued that a spray pattern under the dashboard of the couple's car was "classic arterial blood spray" consistent with spurting from a baby's throat; testing of the spray pattern and of the carpets with the chemical orthotolidene, used for blood screening, found traces of "fetal hemoglobin"; and zoologists confidently asserted that the jaws of even the biggest dingo were incapable of a gape large enough to pick up a baby's head. Ken Crispin, who represented the Chamberlains at one point, wrote scathingly about "the scientists whose theories about what 'must' have happened were obviously perceived to be scientific fact, but ultimately proved specious."[23] The spray pattern turned out to be present on other cars of the same make and was, in fact, a Dulux sound-deadening compound; orthotolidene proved to be reactive with copper dust in the same way as with blood (the Chamberlains came from a copper-mining town); and dingoes were filmed picking up frozen chickens much larger than a baby's head.

The lesson to be drawn from this case (and no doubt from many similar ones) is perhaps obvious. It is that a measure of skepticism regarding "expert" scientific opinion is advisable until all the evidence is in. That is, the deference that is properly due to specialist knowledge must be tempered with caution and an awareness of the likelihood of error or, at least, of the expectation of the nonunanimity of opinion among scientists. In the scientific community, as we have seen, a pronouncement by any one scientist is supposed to be an occasion for scrutiny, double-checking, criticism, and (frequently) disagreement as peers bring their own expertise to bear on the claims being made. Although this attitude is, as I have argued, fundamental to scientific progress, it ensures that there is almost always a penumbra of doubt surrounding the truth value of any scientific claim, whatever the rhetorical force with which it may be presented.

And this, I think, is the lesson worth learning from scientific practice. The constructive skepticism of science is as valuable in public life as it is in the laboratory. The objectivity for which science strives and that is central to its endeavor cannot be thought to be unproblematically validating of the truth of statements by individual scientists, whether these be made intra- or extracurially. Or to put it another way, we should be wary of accepting any important pronouncement simply on the authority, scientific or otherwise, of the pronouncer.

Even scientists, of course, must accept many things on trust— one cannot do everything, and progress would be impossible otherwise (which is why the phenomenon of parafraud is so worrying). But in science, nothing, nothing at all, can rest finally on any authority other than consistency with the evidence. The eminence and authority of the asserter may be factors for consideration in assessing the likelihood of the truth of a statement, but they can never be decisive. Of course, laypeople are at a disadvantage when confronted by experts of any kind, and they cannot be expected to test opinions in an expert way. But they do not have to. They have only to realize that science is neither monolithic nor final and that there usually are dissenting expert opinions to weigh in the balance. This may make for difficult and uncomfortable choices, but that is preferable to the error of automatic genuflection to authority.

It is probably fair to say that the public has, anyway, become less naive about scientific "experts" and more street-smart in general. The reasons are no doubt complex and entangled in the whole postwar social history of the West, but the result is that we live in an antiheroic age.[24] The public no longer grants respect simply on the basis of position or professional qualification.[25] Consequently, it has become harder to get a predictable response by pushing old, well-tried buttons. Dressing a TV actor in a white lab coat and calling him a scientist might have been sound advertising strategy in the 1950s, but in the 1990s it is more likely to raise a cynical eyebrow than to sell a bottle of aspirin. The automatic deference that advertising agencies once took for granted is simply no longer there.

The real insight at the heart of postmodernist views may be the recognition of this general loss of faith. Postmodernists sometimes misrepresent it as the discovery of the relativity of all beliefs, which somehow licenses a freedom to think, do, be, and feel as one chooses. But it is instead both the realization that unquestioning faith in authority is always misplaced and a consequent shifting of responsibility onto individuals to assess independently the truth values of all claims and the practical value of all suggested norms, whatever their source. This is, one might say, a more democratic attitude. It discourages those hierarchical authoritarian structures that once dominated social, professional (including scientific),[26] and political life.

It is true that a loss of public faith in these structures often leads to bewilderment and cynicism rather than to mental independence. But if science teaches anything, it is that skepticism can be principled and reasonable rather than cheaply cynical, that withholding assent can be more than a mere reflex of mistrust. It is an attitude that must be learned, that demands education, and that is dependent, of course, on the publicity requirement to ensure the full availability of argument and evidence. But this attitude would seem worthwhile inculcating in laypeople as much as in scientists if it would encourage the formation of that eternal dream of democracy, a critically informed public able to make up its own mind and to withhold assent to propositions inadequately supported by evidence.[27]

Given that this is much the same line argued by John Locke under the impress of the new science, some three hundred years ago, we should perhaps not be overly optimistic about its practical promise.[28] But if scientific skepticism can teach that justified conviction is a thing hard won and even when won not immune to further argument, it is no doubt a lesson that would be well learned by society at large.

SCIENCE AND SOCIAL CONSCIENCE

It should be clear from the foregoing that we need not seriously entertain the naive notion that scientists as a group are ethically superior to the rest of us, despite the rigor of their training. They are no doubt as variable as any other group of humanity in this respect. This is not to say we may not justifiably have a measure of trust in the institutions of scientific training and practice that encourage in this variable humanity some degree of conformity to ethical standards. But we must realize that trust, though necessary, may not always be vindicated.

It is unlikely, however, that the general public has been much exercised about whether standards of scientific integrity are being maintained and the extent to which, if they are falling, the intellectual products of science have been rendered unreliable. The accumulation of knowledge is too widely trumpeted and too visible in their daily lives, in the shape of novel techniques and applications, to admit doubt. But the benefits of this cumulative knowledge are not always clearly outweighed by the potential hazards. The question of trust that arises most frequently, therefore, is how far scientists may be trusted in their freedom to endlessly pursue new and possibly dangerous knowledge. And this incipient distrust would in no way be allayed by an assurance that standards of scientific integrity were being (even perfectly) maintained, for it is the products of this practice that worry the doubters.

The debate currently taking place over bioethical research is illustrative.[29] The questions raised concern the potential uses— for either good or ill—of this enlarged knowledge of human genetics and the advancing technological capacity for genetic manipulation. Is it socially and politically possible to ensure that the good may be achieved and the ill simultaneously avoided? If it is not, may it not be that this form of research must be limited, which would be to argue that in some areas of life it is better to maintain our ignorance? And even if this were answered affirmatively, is such control possible? All these are questions about science that cannot be answered wholly from within science. Scientists cannot defend a liberty to pursue unhindered such research by appealing to scientific integrity.

I noted earlier that the internal ethic of science is largely instrumental to the achievement of its end, the accumulation of reliable knowledge. If technical procedures are meant, broadly, to safeguard against the contamination of results by error, faulty design, or bias, the ethical ones are intended to safeguard against fraud and the closure of inquiry. When scientists argue for their unfettered liberty to pursue scientific truth, they must, perforce, step beyond this professional ethic to the wider universe of ethical discourse. Typically they point to the value of the end of science, knowledge, or truth, and more often in terms of its intrinsic value than its instrumental value. The reason may be that the instrumental argument, even though it might give scientists the credit for beneficial applications of knowledge, would also make them responsible for the horrors. As Julius Stone explained it,

> The scientist in our tradition is dedicated to the advancement of knowledge and he has refused to compromise with the demands made in every generation that this or that line of inquiry shall not be pursued because of some supposed evil that may come from new knowledge gained. The scientist's answer has been that the scholar's pursuit of knowledge is for its own sake, that such pursuit is his duty and his liberty, and that whether the resulting knowledge is put to good or evil is not for him, but for society generally to decide.[30]

Thus scientists defend their freedom of inquiry in the exalted terms of the pure value of knowledge, perhaps founded on an ineradicable human curiosity (one scientist contended that the "acquisition of knowledge by the human brain is part of protean nature").[31] There is undoubtedly some disingenuousness in such arguments, relying as they do on an absolute distinction between pure and applied science, as though applied scientists were not equally scientists and theoretical scientists had nothing to do with the development, for instance, of the atom bomb.

Even so, the point must be admitted in principle. We generally do regard knowledge as a value in itself. Arguments from an alleged transcultural human curiosity, or protean nature, may be deeply suspect, but few will argue that scientists in their work are not pursuing the truth of things and that truth is not a fundamental ethical value. Lying may sometimes be expedient, and ignorance may be bliss, but by and large the onus of proof lies on those who would defend the telling of lies or the maintenance of ignorance, not on those committed to truth and knowledge. Pointing out that a person's attitudes and actions are based on demonstrable falsehoods is invariably a criticism to which the person inevitably feels obliged to respond in some way.[32] As the great champion of liberty of thought, John Stuart Mill, put it, "To discover to the world something which deeply concerns it, and of which it was previously ignorant . . . is as important a service as a human being can render to his fellow creatures."[33] There seems to be, as Shapiro observed, "a basic human interest in knowing and acting on the truth, in acting authentically."[34]

To say, then, that science is dedicated to the pursuit of truth makes it seem like a fundamentally ethical pursuit, and in part, of course, it is. Shapiro writes further that

> it is to the human interest in knowing and acting on the truth that the project of science appeals. We might even go so far as to say that this interest supplies all science with its impetus and rationale. Science holds out the hope that we can get beyond the welter of conflicting opinions and ideological claims to the truth of the matter.[35]

But this is perhaps to exaggerate the ethical component of scientific pursuits and underplay the purely instrumental role of scientific truth. The vast sums spent on research and development by nations and corporations can scarcely be imagined as wholly driven by an ethical interest in human knowing. True knowledge is sought for its tangible payoffs, laudable or otherwise—better treatments for disease, more effective weaponry, prestigious achievement (e.g., landing on the moon) or more marketable products.

No doubt science's status as a convenient cash cow presents certain ethical problems. We cannot expect that science, any more than sport, can serve both God and mammon without suffering some ethical stress. But we need to be realistic here, for there is limited utility in regret. Science is a human artifact, an important institution in a complex human social and political world, and its motive force is power and money as much as, and more than, the desire for knowledge for its own sake. But who could imagine that the funds available for scientific research would have been so great over the years if scientific knowledge could not be turned to a multitude of purposes. And scientific knowledge, for its part, has undoubtedly been substantially advanced (even if skewed in certain directions) by such pragmatic connections and by the competitive needs of states and firms.

A corollary of this, however, is that many research projects are in fact determined extrascientifically, by the demands of governments and business. Research generally follows the dollar, as the old saying goes. Therefore, when scientists take the high moral ground in their defense of an unfettered liberty of research and assert that "scientists acting independently are the best judges of what should be the goals of pure research" or that "the alternative to scientific autonomy is politically and bureaucratically regulated science,"[36] their pronouncements should be taken with the tiniest grain of salt. Their further argument that it is anyway impossible to prevent the flow of research in an area once commenced might also be read as a tribute to the power of money rather than to some protean human drive to knowledge.

The fact is that there is no such thing as an unfettered liberty of anything. Even if we concede that scientists should have the liberty to pursue those research projects that seem to them the most promising or interesting, it does not follow that they should necessarily be granted the means to do so. The allocation of funds for research is a political and economic matter and so is susceptible to the usual analyses of propriety, fairness, political demands, likely returns, and so on. It is true that important scientific discoveries cannot be programmed but often come from unexpected research and that therefore there is wisdom in providing sizable funds for "pure science," even for "silly" science (what if cold fusion had been real?). But even this argument, insofar as it sways a fund provider, is as likely to do so on the basis of a calculation of material returns as on arguments about the advancement of pure knowledge.

All of this is to argue that scientists should come down from their high horse and admit that the extrascientific world has a genuine interest in, and a degree of determination of, their practice. It is not to argue, however, that funding restraints should be placed on scientific research in which new knowledge is perceived to present new dangers. A good deal has been written recently about what "scientific responsibility" requires and about the ethical demands and restraints that might justifiably be placed on scientific activity and how these restraints may be enforced— whether through self-regulation, legal regulation, the adoption of risk-assessment procedures, and so forth.[37] Some of the recommendations seem sensible and unobjectionable, but it is not my wish to comment on them here. I merely want to note that the fear of dangerous consequences is not, in general, a good argument for limiting or halting the growth of knowledge in a particular area. (It may be limited in practice by a failure to allocate funds, owing to the determination that money would be better spent elsewhere, but that is a different matter.)

However much the patterns of scientific discovery may be skewed by the realities of funding and vested interest, it remains true that the advancement of knowledge remains a good in itself. As in the rest of life, the argument that ignorance is better than knowledge might occasionally be successful, but the presumption is generally against it. The onus must be heavily on those who argue for the maintenance of ignorance to prove their case. With regard to science, this will be difficult to do, since the benefits and dangers of a particular discovery may be largely unforeseeable or, even when foreseeable, may be so balanced as to make a clear decision impossible.

The real challenge is to manage the dangers of all scientific discovery and application while securing what benefits we can.

This is more likely to be successful if the wider public is included in such management. Much is talked in private and public management these days about the need for the consultation and participation of "stakeholders" and "clients" when major policy measures are being planned. This is not just for social justice reasons, but for the sake of ensuring policy success. There is no reason that the same arguments should not apply to the development of potentially risky scientific applications, in which the public is generally a major stakeholder.

John Durant points out that public participation usually improves decision making, for it provides a wider perspective than does the narrow technical one to which scientific experts usually confine themselves.

> One important reason why professional and lay estimates of risk so often differ is that lay perceptions frequently embody intuitive assessments of the trustworthiness of particular institutions responsible for the safe management of risk. In this sense the concept of risk dissolves the boundaries between science and the wider society; for technical and social judgments are both equally relevant to lay risk assessment.[38]

Another way of putting this is to note the ancient distinction between knowledge and wisdom. Scientific knowledge may be the peculiar preserve of the scientist, to which the public may have only limited access (even though access should be encouraged to the greatest extent possible), but there is no reason to presume that scientists thereby possess the requisite practical wisdom to turn that knowledge to safe use in society.

Durant does not think it utopian to seek greater public participation in science, asserting that the ideals of democracy and justice rest on a fundamental faith in the' public to cope with even the most complicated issues. He points to a form of such participation, called a *consensus conference,* pioneered by the Danish parliament. This is a dialogue between laypeople and experts, in which a panel of lay volunteers investigates a scientific or technological issue by cross-examining experts and later presents its published conclusions at a press conference. Findings on matters such as food irradiation, human genetics, and childlessness have influenced public debate and policymaking. Durant speculates whether this might help explain why, in studies conducted throughout Europe, the Danes show a relatively high level of confidence in their public authorities as sources of information about biotechnology.[39]

Scientists and public have a common interest in both the advancement of knowledge and the management of the risks of applying that knowledge. The promotion of wider channels of communication between them and of greater public participation in decision making on scientific issues is therefore to be encouraged. Scientists have an interest in maintaining public trust in the good faith and good works of science and therefore in subjecting their work to more frequent and more intense public scrutiny, even if not to public censorship.

CONCLUSION

I have offered answers to my two initial questions. On one hand, the public may learn from scientific practice a measure of caution about a too-ready reception of "expert" opinion. Walking the delicate border between appropriate respect and constructive skepticism may be a difficult art, but it is one worth learning. Science, on the other hand, has advantages to gain from allowing greater public access to its work and from allowing public participation in decision making even in "expert" areas.

These things are connected, indeed, through the medium of trust. Laypeople must often place their trust (though not their blind faith) in expert scientific opinion, but then so must other scientists. In science, practitioners must have reasonable confidence that the institutional safeguards against bias or fraud are operating correctly if their trust is to be maintained, and it is crucial to science that it be so maintained. It is hardly less important that the trust of the lay community be fostered and maintained. A public that has become more skeptical about everything can no longer be taken for granted or treated with high-handedness but must to some extent be won over. This argues the wisdom of providing regular mechanisms of public participation and channels of open communication on which reasonable trust may be founded.

Most people continue to have great respect for the achievements of science, even if they cannot fully understand them. Greater admittance to and familiarity with scientific work should deepen their appreciation of science's problems and constraints without necessarily diminishing that respect. Science, whatever the motives of those who fund it, whatever bad faith may exist among its practitioners, and whatever baffling problems its discoveries sometimes present, remains by virtue of its capacity for generating knowledge a powerful ethical force in the world. Being realistic about its inevitable impurities should not blind us to this truth.

Noted physicist Freeman Dyson, while accepting that science has been driven largely by the forces of mammon, nevertheless argues that for many ordinary as well as for supremely gifted scientists, the chief reward is not power or money but "the chance of catching a glimpse of the transcendent beauty of nature."

> There is no necessary contradiction between the transcendence of science and the realities of social history. One may believe that in science nature will ultimately have the last word, and still recognize an enormous role for human vainglory and viciousness in the practice of science before the last word is spoken. . . . To my mind, the history of science is most illuminating when the frailties of human actors are put into juxtaposition with the transcendence of nature's laws.[40]

And it is, indeed, the nature of all human endeavor to be a confusing mixture of the transcendent and the mundane, the pure and the sordid, the divine and the worldly. It is the beginning of wisdom to understand and accept this, for scientific practice as for every other.

NOTES

1. Traditional representations of scientists in popular fiction have perhaps not significantly improved understanding. A recent book on some recurring images in Western literature discerned three: the hero, the hubristic overreaching madman, and the nerd. See Roslyn D. Haynes, *From Faust to Strangelove: Representations of the Scientist in Western Literature* (Baltimore: Johns Hopkins University Press, 1995).

2. John Durant cites the Media Monitor Project in Britain that took a random sample of daily newspaper reporting of science from 1946 to 1990: it showed that coverage had moved "from the celebratory to the critical and then backwards to the ambivalent." See his "Why Science Needs the Public's Ear," *Times Higher Education Supplement,* reprinted in *The Australian, Higher Education,* February 21, 1996, 25.

3. Editorial Committee of the Council of Biological Editors, "Teaching Scientific Integrity and the Responsible Conduct of Research," *Academic Medicine,* December 1993. This work argues that there are now armies of researchers, all dependent on acquiring substantial but limited funds and all desperate for the status that only publication brings. The pressure is on to cut corners.

4. Evandro Agazzi, "Responsibility: The Genuine Ground for the Regulation of a Free Science," in W. R. Shea and B. Sitter, eds., *Scientists and Their Responsibility* (Canton, Maine: Watson Publishing International, 1989), 203. Certainly there now exists a vocal antiscience contingent that would like to see science's pretensions punctured. The champions of what Paul Davies calls the "new ignorance" have gone on the offensive in recent years, attacking science and scientific values with evangelical fervor, even in academia itself. See *The Australian,* July 8, 1992, 17. Paul Gross and Norman Levitt listed, in a recent book, literary and cultural theorists, poststructuralists, postmodernists, radical feminists, black separatists, Afrocentrists, deep ecologists, and animal liberationists among the modern enemies of traditional science. See their *Higher Superstition: The Academic Left and Its Quarrels with Science* (Baltimore: Johns Hopkins University Press, 1994).

5. Robert Merton, *The Sociology of Science* (Chicago: University of Chicago Press, 1973).

6. One must wonder in this case at the status of knowledge claims in political science, in which a debate over the need to replicate work has been going on for a few years and in which a recent study showed that 90.1 percent of published political science research is never cited, much less replicated. See David P. Hamilton, "Research Papers: Who's Uncited Now?" *Science,* January 4, 1991, 25.

7. This was the alleged generation of excess heat energy from a small amount of electricity passed through heavy water using palladium electrodes. Governments, corporations, and research centers, spurred by the prospect of endless, cheap, and safe power, poured money into attempts to replicate the findings, but without success.

8. Cited in Peter Davis, "Fusion Debate Generates More Heat Than Light," *Campus Review,* September 29–October 5, 1994, 11.

9. See Editorial Policy Committee of the Council of Biological Edi-

tors, *Ethics and Policy in Scientific Publication* (Bethesda, Md.: Council of Biological Editors, 1990), xi.

10. Cited in Dorothy Zinberg, "Misconduct Raises a Stink in the Labs," *The Australian, Higher Education*, November 16, 1994, 35.

11. Harold Hillman, "Peccadilloes and Other Sins," *The Times Higher Education Supplement*, reprinted in *The Australian, Higher Education*, November 8, 1995, 14.

12. Zinberg, "Misconduct Raises a Stink."

13. See Editorial Policy Committee, *Ethics and Policy*, 9–10.

14. In my own part of the world, the University of Melbourne recently issued one of these prefaced by a "Statement of Guiding Principles." This states that research is "the pursuit of truth" and that "research workers should, in all aspects of their research, demonstrate integrity and professionalism, observe fairness and equity, avoid conflicts of interest, and ensure the safety of those associated with the research. Research methods and results should be open to scrutiny and debate." Cited in *Campus Review*, July 28–August 3, 1994, 17.

15. Dorothy Zinberg, "Science Run through the Woodchipper," *The Australian, Higher Education*, June 14, 1995, 29.

16. Hillman, "Peccadilloes and Other Sins."

17. At a lecture in London in the early 1980s, Peter Medawar remarked that in general, the greater the difficulty of obtaining reliable empirical evidence, the more fanciful and suspect the theories that are generated.

18. Mark Diesendorf, "Science under Social and Political Pressures," in D. Oldroyd, ed., *Science and Ethics* (Kensington: New South Wales University Press, 1982), 49.

19. In politically charged areas (e.g., studies of differential intelligence among racial groups), the formal and statistical apparatus of science may be hardly more than a cloak of "objectivity" flung over a blatant prejudice. But even in less obviously politically charged fields, it is important to be alert to the way in which the underlying agenda may inform the work.

John Cornwell warns that we should be particularly wary of works of popular exposition of scientific ideas that come "replete with the tricks and compromises, hidden agendas and sleights of hand familiar in other literary genres." See his "The Difficulty Keeping Body and Soul Together," *The Australian, Higher Education*, May 25, 1994, 26–27.

This comment occurs in Cornwell's review of a book on the nature of the mind, entitled *The Astonishing Hypothesis: The Scientific Search for the Soul*, by Francis Crick, Nobel Prize winner for his codiscovery of the double-helical structure of chromosomes. Cornwell notes particularly "the tendency to pose as a single, infallible oracle by flaunting past distinction for experimental discoveries" and the bolstering of scientific argument by "campaigning atheism." Cornwell writes that "Crick's protest that his strategy is confined to empirical data merely as a secure starting point, is hardly corroborated by a subtext that rumbles through his book like bottled thunder. For Crick's astonishing hypothesis is as much a sustained attack on religious belief as it is about neuroscience."

20. For a vigorous defense of science's "scientificity," see the book by the fundamental-particle physicist Alan Cromer, *Uncommon Sense: The Heretical Nature of Science* (Oxford: Oxford University Press, 1994).

21. This is not, of course, a simple matter of holding up a theory and comparing it with the world to see how it conforms. The ingenuity of science is precisely in devising painstaking methods and strategies for extracting from the world the evidence that will help evaluate hypotheses about the way things are.

22. For parallels, particularly with regard to the psychological involvement of ordinary citizens, think of the Dreyfus case in France at the turn of the century or, more recently, to the O. J. Simpson trial in Los Angeles.

23. Ken Crispin, "An Australian Witch-Hunt," *The Weekend Australian*, December 16–17, 1995, 23.

24. Even our celluloid heroes have become so obviously fantastic in their exploits that we are clearly not intended to believe in them, just to enjoy the mayhem.

25. Remember the reverence with which our parents or grandparents treated even a humble general practitioner, who as a member of the "noble profession" was akin to a god.

26. Scientific research institutes, like medical and other institutes, were typically organized on the Victorian authoritarian model, in which the chief scientist was a god whose word was law and subordinates were cowed into obedience and submission. A recent scandal in an Australian university laboratory, involving the physical assault by a chief scientist on a research fellow, revealed the nature of the changes under way. Preliminary accounts described the conflict as a result of a clash of wills between an old-style autocratic leader and a young turk (fresh from Canada) used to a more democratic organization of research (News Program, ABC radio, March 2, 1995).

27. In truth, this is a lesson that could be learned from any critical discipline, for most of what is said here about "science" applies to other academic pursuits not normally thought of as falling under this appellation. Intellectual integrity in a scientific culture demands certain standards of argument, evidence, and good faith that do not differ across disciplines. It is worth remembering that many of the critical standards

we normally think of as "scientific" were first formulated not in natural science but in the hermeneutical study of texts in the discipline of philology.

28. John Locke, *An Essay Concerning Human Understanding,* especially the introductory Epistle to the Reader.

29. For essays on some of the ethical issues raised, see D. J. Kevles and L. Hood, eds., *The Code of Codes: Scientific and Social Issues in the Human Genome Project* (Cambridge, Mass.: Harvard University Press, 1992), part III.

30. See Julius Stone, "When Politics Is Harder Than Physics: Sketch of a Code for Science," in David Oldroyd, ed., *Science and Ethics* (Kensington: New South Wales University Press, 1982), 95.

31. Geneticist Maxine Singer, cited in Stone, "When Politics Is Harder," 103.

32. Not necessarily rationally, of course.

33. John Stuart Mill, *On Liberty* (London: Everyman, 1962), 89.

34. Ian Shapiro, *Political Criticism* (Berkeley and Los Angeles: University of California Press, 1990), 265.

35. Ibid., 274. Scientists themselves, especially when defending their freedom to pursue research as they see fit, frequently appeal to the "natural curiosity" of human beings as justification. But the assertion of such a cross-cultural and transhistorical impulse can only doubtfully stand up to serious scrutiny (at least without elaborate defense and qualification). This is not to say that knowledge as a value in itself is indefensible but to argue that this as defining the central rationale of science is suspect, even if many, or most, scientists would regard it as their primary motivation.

36. Professor J. Ben David, cited in Stone, "When Politics Is Harder," 96.

37. See Stone, "When Politics Is Harder"; Agazzi, "Responsibility"; Hanbury Brown, *The Wisdom of Science: Its Relevance to Culture and Religion* (Cambridge: Cambridge University Press, 1986); Greg Sachs and Mark Siegler, "Teaching Scientific Integrity and the Responsible Conduct of Research," *Academic Medicine,* December 1993; and the following papers in Shea and Sitter, eds., *Scientists and Their Responsibility,* 203: Marcello Pero, "Should Science Be Supervised, and If So by Whom?"; Peter Saladin, "Should Society Make Laws Governing Scientific Research?"; and Andrea Degginger, "Freedom of Research and Basic Rights."

38. Durant, "Why Science Needs the Public's Ear."

39. Ibid.

40. Freeman Dyson, "The Scientist as Rebel," *New York Review of Books,* May 25, 1995, 33.

7

TRUST IN SCIENCE AND IN
SCIENTISTS: A RESPONSE
TO KANE

KAREN JONES

John Kane's "Integrity, Conscience, and Science" advances two
main claims: First, the public would do well to borrow from science a stance of constructive skepticism and so refuse automatic
trust to those who claim expertise, especially including those who
claim scientific expertise. Second, science would benefit from
opening itself up to greater public scrutiny and control. Both
these conclusions have the air of common sense—so much so
that it is hard to find fault with them, at least when we think of
them just as practical prescriptions, that is, as ways of combating a
tendency toward gullibility on the part of the public and a tendency toward unaccountability on the part of science. In this
chapter, I focus on the first claim: Although the prescription
against gullibility is salutary, in arguing for it Kane assumes a
problematic cognitive individualism.

The cognitive individualist is suspicious of all claims of cognitive authority, assigning to each person the responsibility to examine the evidence in favor of a claim and to make up his or her
own mind about it. This position, skeptical of cognitive authority
and demanding cognitive independence, sees itself as advocating
"cognitive autonomy." [1] It seems that Kane is drawn to cognitive
individualism out of concern that we display autonomy and not

abdicate our epistemic responsibilities, especially when faced with questions that have important practical implications. However, because of the need for a division of cognitive labor, cognitive individualism is untenable. Once we dispense with it, we are forced to face the issue of how to be wise in our deference to experts. The central question to be addressed here is "What default stance should we adopt with respect to accepting a statement on the basis of expert say-so?" Should we have toward experts a presumption of trust, of distrust, or of neutrality?

I argue for a variable default stance with respect to accepting testimony from scientific experts. My purpose is not so much to disagree with the practical conclusions of Kane's chapter, for across a wide range of cases, we arrive at the same practical conclusions. Instead, my purpose is to place Kane's prescription against gullibility on a firmer theoretical foundation by showing it to be compatible with the sort of deference to experts required by the cognitive division of labor. The cognitive authority granted to experts can be shown to be compatible with an ideal of cognitive autonomy, properly understood.

Kane shows some ambivalence in his advocacy of constructive skepticism, appearing now to endorse cognitive individualism, now not quite willing to commit to it. On one hand, Kane says that he means to follow Locke in Locke's rejection of authority and thus, presumably, in his refusal to borrow knowledge from others.[2] Furthermore, Kane appears to endorse "the realization that unquestioning faith in authority is always misplaced and a consequent shifting of responsibility onto individuals to assess independently the truth values of all claims and the practical value of all suggested norms, whatever their source." On the other hand, Kane reminds us that "laypeople must often place their trust (though not their blind faith) in expert scientific opinion, but then so must other scientists." No Lockean can accept that beliefs formed on the basis of trust in the word of others can count as knowledge. Even when it does not amount to "blind faith," such trust is at odds with the injunction to assess independently the truth value of claims that one would accept.[3]

There is a way to reconcile the apparent tension between these two strands of Kane's position. Perhaps Kane means to advocate cognitive individualism as a regulative ideal. Conceived as regulative ideal, cognitive individualism would be something that we have a duty to approximate as closely as we can. Someone who advocates cognitive individualism as a regulative ideal can acknowledge that given our cognitive limitations, we sometimes need to rely on others. However, insofar as we can, it is incumbent on us to limit our dependence on other people's opinions and to attempt to reach our own conclusions. Sometimes we must fall short of the individualist ideal, but our cognitive practice should be governed by the attempt to attain such an ideal. Furthermore, any deviation from that ideal is regrettable—it would be better if we could instantiate the ideal rather than merely approximate it.

Even when considered as something to approximate, cognitive individualism is misguided. In a series of papers, John Hardwig argues that those who insist on epistemic independence risk cutting themselves off from the best available reasons for holding beliefs.[4] Often a layperson (or someone working outside her own, possibly very narrow, area of expertise) is not able to assess the reasons an expert has for believing what she believes. Moreover, if the layperson were to try to form beliefs on her own concerning a domain outside her competence, there would typically be less reason for her to be confident in her own opinion than there would be for her to be confident in expert opinion. Nor is it usually an effective use of time for someone in a position to gain individual access to the relevant evidence to set about doing so. For example, a mathematician who could bone up on an area outside her area of research and so check the results that she takes on trust in her own research would not be advised to do so.[5] Taking cognitive individualism as a regulative ideal would slow the pace of knowledge acquisition to a standstill or a near standstill.

More radically, requiring that our epistemic practice be guided by an ideal of cognitive individualism would make it impossible to acquire some kinds of knowledge at all. Hardwig reports the case of an experiment measuring the life span of charm particles that took 280 person-years to perform and was reported in a paper with ninety-nine authors.[6] No one person has, or could acquire, the expertise necessary to vouch for all the parts of the experiment even if it were physically possible for the experiment to have been conducted single-handedly.

Given that the acquisition of knowledge can progress as fast as it does only because such acquisition is a social rather than an individual enterprise and given that some things are knowable only because of cognitive specialization and teamwork, it would be perverse to claim that departures from cognitive individualism are regrettable departures from an ideal. Indeed, cognitive individualism is not a genuine ideal. Granting cognitive authority to others and deferring to their expertise enables secondhand access to whole realms of reasons that are not available to us individually.

Once we have abandoned cognitive individualism, we face the question of how to be responsible in our deference to expert opinion. When should we trust expert opinion, and when should we not? It may seem that there is little philosophically interesting to say here. Sometimes we should be willing to defer to the authority of experts, and sometimes we should not. Although it takes judgment to know which cases are which, philosophy can tell us nothing about what is involved in having good judgment in these matters—that is a task for whatever disciplines are needed to assess the trustworthiness of the experts testifying on a particular occasion. However, I think this position overlooks an important question that should be settled before approaching the details of a particular case. That question concerns the appropriate default stance, or the question of how much and what kind of evidence we must seek before we accept expert testimony.

There are four possible default stances with which to approach the testimony of experts: trust, distrust, neutrality, and a variable stance. A default stance of *trust* is a rebuttable presumption in favor of accepting expert say-so. This presumption can be defeated by evidence that the expert is incompetent or insincere or is likely to be unreliable for other reasons that do not imply culpability. Responsible use of a default stance of trust requires that one be alert to indications of insincerity or incompetence, but one may trust as long as there are no such indicators; that is, the mere absence of reasons to distrust justifies trust.

A default stance of *distrust* is a rebuttable presumption against accepting expert say-so. To rebut that presumption, we must seek out substantial positive evidence in favor of the expert's trustworthiness. The kind of evidence needed here depends on the context, but it typically includes evidence relating to both the content of the expert's testimony and her credentials as an expert. We may wish to check on both what the expert says and the expert herself. Thus, for example, we may want to seek out corroboration of her testimony and to investigate her past record on the matter in question.[7]

A default stance of *neutrality* is the absence of presumptions either in favor of or against accepting testimony. We should be unwilling to accept or reject expert testimony without an even-handed investigation into the testifier's trustworthiness. The difference between neutrality and distrust as default stances is not a difference between, on the one hand, withholding belief in what an expert says and, on the other hand, disbelieving it, for the appropriate response to an unrebutted default of distrust may well be to withhold belief. Rather, what distinguishes them is the weight of evidence needed before we are warranted in accepting the expert say-so. With a default of distrust, we need to amass evidence sufficient to rebut a presumption against acceptance, whereas with neutrality there is no such presumption that needs rebutting.

Trust, distrust, and neutrality are not the only options to adopt with respect to expert say-so. We may find it inappropriate to approach all cases of expert testimony in the same way and instead prefer to distinguish among the classes of expert testimony and approach some with a default stance to trust, some with distrust, and some with neutrality. Call this the *variable* default stance. Such a stance, in effect, denies that expert say-so constitutes an epistemic kind.

In a recent paper, Foley defends a default stance of trust with respect to all testimony, including expert testimony. Foley prefers to put the point in terms of the distinction between fundamental and derivative authority. Derivative authority "is authority generated from my reasons for thinking that your information, abilities, or circumstances put you in an especially good position to evaluate the claim." Fundamental authority, in contrast, is authority granted to others "even when we have no special information indicating that they are reliable."[8]

Foley's argument in favor of granting fundamental authority to the word of others is a consistency argument: Given that we have fundamental trust in our own epistemic capacities, we are obliged to trust the epistemic capacities of others, and hence—absent worries about sincerity—we are obliged to trust their word. Our most basic intellectual faculties are such that we cannot defend their reliability without using the very faculties in question; hence our trust in them must be fundamental. Thus, given that other people's capacities are much like our own and the environment in which they operate is much like our environment, we must trust them if we trust ourselves. Foley acknowledges that this presumption of trust in the word of others can be defeated, and will be so defeated, when I have a belief that conflicts with the belief of another—the trust I have in my own abilities here undermines my trust in the other person. I may decide to trust him or her after all, but now I need special reason to do so, whereas before I did not.[9]

It is a consequence of taking conflict with our own beliefs to be the chief defeater of a presumption of trust in the word of others that the more ignorant we are about a subject matter, the less evidence of trustworthiness we need to justify deference. Thus deference to experts is built into Foley's account:

> Still, in general it will be the case that the fewer opinions I have about a set of issues, the more likely it is that I have reasons to defer to the opinions of others. For example, if I am new to a field, I'm unlikely to have very many opinions about the field and hence there won't be many opportunities for conflicts between my opinions and those of others. Thus, there is plenty of room for deference.

Of course, there can be other defeaters: "I can have special reasons to distrust their opinions—perhaps their track record on such issues isn't very good or perhaps they lack the relevant training." For the nonexpert, however, there is a presumption in favor of acceptance.[10]

I believe that Foley's argument mistakenly assumes that the inability to give a reductive, or noncircular, defense of our reliance on our fundamental epistemic capacities implies a presumption in favor of relying on them in any particular case. This presumption is then extended to our reliance on the capacities of others. In other words, Foley confuses the issue of reductionism with the issue of default stance. But the issue of reductionism concerns whether our dependence on testimony can be reduced, without remainder, to reliance on other modes of epistemic access to the world—such as memory, perception, and inference—whereas the issue of default stance concerns the responsible epistemic starting point in a particular case. These are not the same.

For example, it is not incoherent to suppose that we might discover that perception is not to be relied on in certain circumstances unless we have a special reason for thinking that it is reliable. It is true that to find this out, we must rely on perceptual evidence, evidence that is, for the purposes of this inquiry, taken to be reliable, even though we may later revisit that evidence and question why we should rely on it. Similarly, it is not incoherent to suppose that we could find out that it was sometimes, or even always, wise to begin from a default stance of distrust with respect to testimony and conclude that we should always have positive evidence of the reliability of a particular speaker before accepting what he or she says.[11]

The task of investigating which default stance we should adopt with respect to expert testimony does not have to begin from scratch, for it turns out that we already have a body of commonsense theory about the reliability of testimony and about the kinds of circumstances in which we are warranted in beginning from a default stance of trust and those in which we are not. The body of commonsense theory about when to trust testimony falls under our commonsense theory about when it is appropriate to trust. This is not surprising, since trust in the word of another is one instance of trust in another. Indeed, what distinguishes testimony from argument is that it is the testifier herself who vouches for the truth of what she asserts. In contrast, when an argument is fully transparent and complete, there is no need to rely on the arguer; we can assess for ourselves whether the conclusion follows from the premises.[12]

Furthermore, trust in the word of others has the two features universally accepted as hallmarks of trust, namely, that the one who trust opens herself up to harm should the one she trusts turn out to be unreliable and that the one who trusts is typically unable to monitor the one trusted.[13] But if the question of which default stance to adopt with respect to testimony is a special case of the question of which default stance to adopt with respect to trusting others more generally, then we can employ insights gained from reflecting on trust in general for the question of trust in expert testimony.

Elsewhere, I have argued that we cannot defend a universal default stance with respect to trust in others.[14] The reason is that the appropriate default stance is sensitive to the following four variables: climate, domain, expected disutility of misplaced trust or distrust, and our own reasonable assessment of the tendencies in our own trusting and distrusting.

Some climates foster untrustworthiness, perhaps by penalizing motives for trustworthiness through, for example, promoting conflicts of interest. Other climates foster trustworthiness, most notably by harmonizing potentially conflicting interests. In climates or subclimates in which institutions and social norms and expectations work to create a confluence of motives for trustworthiness, we can be justified in assuming that those we encounter are, by and large, trustworthy. In climates or subclimates in which motives against trustworthiness are rewarded, an assumption of untrustworthiness may be warranted. What sort of climate or subclimate we inhabit thus affects whether a default stance of trust or of distrust is warranted and how much evidence we need to justify moving away from such an initial default stance.

The trust we have in others is seldom global but typically extends to some more or less restricted domain of interaction.[15] For example, the domain across which our trust in strangers extends is generally small and may consist merely of trusting them not to harm us as we go about our business. With friends, in contrast, the domain is extensive, though here, too, usually not without limits. Some domains are such that trustworthy performance within them requires nothing more than minimal decency and competence. For example, it takes only minimal decency to refrain from harming strangers. Thus we may assume—supposing the climate is not horrible—that most people can be trusted to that extent. In contrast, trustworthiness with respect to some domains can require considerable moral sensitivity and strength of character. For these reasons, whether a default stance of trust, distrust, or neutrality is warranted should depend, not surprisingly, on the domain over which our trust extends.

The default stance is also dependent on the expected disutility of misplaced trust or distrust. When the consequences of trusting and being let down are severe, we need more evidence of trustworthiness than we do when the consequences are slight. So when the stakes are high, it may be appropriate, even in favorable climates, to begin from a default stance of distrust.

The fourth variable that affects which default stance is warranted concerns the degree to which it is reasonable for us to trust our trust or our distrust. The appropriate metastance of trust or distrust in our trustings and distrustings should affect our default stance for the following reason: If I know, or should know, that the reason that I distrust a certain sort of person across a certain domain is not related to indications of untrustworthiness but has some other source, I should not be willing to trust my initial inclinations to distrust. This in turn should make me willing to reevaluate my default stance. In this context, consider the racist distrust of African American men.[16] Many whites approach African American men with a default stance of distrust, a default stance determined by prejudice and stereotype rather than by reliable indications of untrustworthiness. Default stances with such origins should be resisted.

Because the appropriate default stance with respect to trust is affected by climate, domain, expected disutility, and the metastance toward our own trusting, any generalizations about the default stance are necessarily limited. For this reason, we cannot expect to defend a default stance with respect to trust in testimony in general, given differences in context, subject matter, and testifiers. For some subject matters, in some contexts, a default stance of trust is warranted; for others, a default stance of distrust is recommended. But if this point holds for testimony in general, then it holds equally for expert testimony. Whether we should approach expert testimony with a presumption in favor of acceptance or with a presumption against acceptance likewise depends on the climate.

Is the institution of science working to create a confluence of motives toward trustworthiness, or is it, as Kane suggests, working to militate against such motives? Domain matters, too. Expert testimony with the most relevance to public policy frequently involves subject matter for which there is a real possibility of ideological distortion, a possibility, that is, that practitioners— even those of competence and good character—will defend views that ratify existing social relations.

Furthermore, as Stephen Jay Gould documents so ably in his account of scientific investigation into human intelligence, the consequences of misplaced trust, in terms of human misery, can be great.[17] Finally, reflection on our past patterns of trust in expert testimony, or at least trust in testimony regarding many of the more controversial domains of expertise, should make us suspicious of our own tendencies toward trust in expert testimony. A default stance of trust with respect to expert testimony may sometimes be warranted. It may, for example, be appropriate for a layperson to form beliefs about planetary motion or chemical structure on the basis of such simple trust. In most cases, however, a default stance of distrust is merited.

The observation that the appropriate default stance with respect to the deliveries of science is dependent on how well the institution of science operates to create a confluence of motives toward trustworthiness suggests an interesting possibility. Could we replace our trust in scientists with trust in science considered as an institution?[18] There is evidence that we cannot now replace our trust in individual scientists with trust in the institution of science. For example, whistle-blowers are often punished more severely than perpetrators of fraud, and there is little funding available to repeat the fraudulent work.[19] But the fact that we cannot now replace trust in scientists with trust in the institution of science does not mean that we cannot move in the direction of doing so through institutional reform.

Kane seems to suggest that if only we could make the institution of science force its practitioners to live up to the standards of their profession, then science would be trustworthy. If only, that is, individual scientists would act with what Kane calls "professional integrity," then in the long run at least, science could be counted on as a reliable source of knowledge.[20] But there is reason to think that this is not so. Across a range of topics, the history of science shows that science is not self-correcting. For example, what knowledge we have about gender (and we probably do not have much) is knowledge made possible by the feminist movement and the critiques of scientific discourse on gender that it generated. If this is correct, the lesson is important: science is not made trustworthy merely by the professional morality of its practitioners.

I have argued that for a wide range of topics, we should begin with a default stance of distrust in expert testimony. My conclusion is thus similar to Kane's: We should be more skeptical of expert authority, at least concerning many questions that have practical implications. However, the defense of a prescription against gullibility no longer rests on cognitive individualism. In most cases, we must approach expert testimony from a default stance of distrust, and we must satisfy ourselves of the speaker's competence and sincerity. In satisfying ourselves about the speaker's credentials, we are not required to "go it alone." We can call on the resources of other knowers, including other experts.[21] And this is just as well, for we are generally not in a position to assess independently either the content of expert say-so or the credentials of experts.

There remains one more question: Is the account of what we need to be responsible in our deference to experts an account that is compatible with *an* ideal of cognitive autonomy? Not surprisingly, our answer to this question depends on our account of cognitive autonomy. I propose that we borrow insights from discussions about the nature of autonomy in moral and political contexts to address the question of how best to conceive of cognitive autonomy. Gerald Dworkin suggests, as a constraint on an adequate account of autonomy, that such an account explain why autonomy might be thought to be something desirable and that it not be an account that makes autonomy fundamentally incompatible with other important values.[22] Such a constraint seems as appropriate in an epistemological context as in a moral and political context.

According to Mackie's account of cognitive autonomy, the knower "should know whatever it is off his own bat; he must be an authority; he must have discovered it, or worked it out." Testimonial knowledge is thus in apparent conflict with the ideal of the autonomous knower. The two can be reconciled, however—but only if such knowledge can be brought back under the umbrella of things known firsthand:

Knowledge that one acquires through testimony, that is, by being told by other people, by reading, and so on, can indeed be brought under the heading of this authoritative knowledge, but only if the knower somehow checks, for himself, the credibility of the witnesses. And since, if it is a fact that a certain witness is credible, it is an external fact, checking this in turn will need to be based on observations that the knower makes himself—or else on further testimony, but, if an infinite regress is to be avoided, we must come back at some stage to what the knower observes for himself.[23]

The autonomous knower here is conceived of as someone who has, at the end of the day, discharged her cognitive dependency on others. The resulting picture is what I call *cognitive individualism.*

Just as autonomy-as-independence accounts of autonomy in the moral and political context violate the constraint that an adequate account must show why autonomy might be considered as something valuable, so do accounts of cognitive autonomy as cognitive independence.[24] Such accounts are, as I have shown, incompatible with the cognitive division of labor, which requires cognitive dependence. But we surely do not want to say that any sort of dependence is acceptable. Some dependencies are slavish and thus incompatible with any reasonable ideal of autonomy, but other dependencies are not. How then, can our account stake out some middle ground between refusing all dependency and advocating any sort of dependency whatsoever?

It might be thought that the answer is already contained in our discussion of default stances: As long as we begin from a default stance of distrust, our eventual trust will be compatible with an ideal of cognitive autonomy, because our eventual dependence will be the result of a rigorous critical examination of the likely trustworthiness of the other. It will be critical dependence. Knowers who begin from a default stance of distrust are autonomous knowers, whereas knowers who begin from a default stance of trust or of neutrality are not.

However, this answer seems to have the unfortunate consequence that too little of our borrowed knowledge would count as compatible with the ideal of cognitive autonomy. Although it is not part of my project to argue that just any borrowing will do or even that most of our actual borrowings are acceptable, this answer rules out borrowings that result from a default stance of trust even when we have good reason to think that a default stance of trust is appropriate in the circumstances. The fact that sometimes we have good reason to think that a default stance of trust is appropriate shows us where to look for a solution. Dependencies resulting from default stances that can be endorsed after a process of critical reflection are dependencies that we should think of as being compatible with cognitive autonomy, properly understood. Slavish dependencies cannot pass this test, but dependencies resulting from a default stance of trust may. This suggestion is also of a piece with contemporary discussions of autonomy in the moral and political context that stress the importance of agents' having the capacity both to reflect critically on their preferences and desires and to modify them in the light of such reflection.[25]

NOTES

1. What I call *cognitive individualism,* Frederick Schmitt calls *cognitive autonomy.* See his "Socializing Epistemology: An Introduction through Two Sample Issues," in Frederick Schmitt, ed., *Socializing Epistemology: The Social Dimensions of Knowledge* (Lanham, Md.: Rowman and Littlefield, 1994), 6. Since I am arguing that epistemic dependence is compatible with cognitive autonomy properly understood, I prefer the label *cognitive individualism.*

2. John Kane, "Integrity, Conscience, and Science," 127. See John Locke, *An Essay concerning Human Understanding,* ed. Peter H. Nidditch (Oxford: Oxford University Press, 1975), I. iv. 23, for a trenchant rejection of borrowing knowledge from others.

3. Kane, "Integrity, Conscience, and Science," 126, 133. Kane identifies this as the "real insight at the heart of postmodernist views," which is curious, given that it is so modernist in tenor.

4. See John Hardwig, "Epistemic Dependence," *Journal of Philosophy* 82 (1985): 335–49; John Hardwig, "The Role of Trust in Knowledge," *Journal of Philosophy* 88 (1991): 693–708; and John Hardwig, "Towards an Ethics of Expertise," in Daniel Wueste, ed., *Professional Ethics and Social Responsibility* (Lanham, Md.: Rowman and Littlefield, 1994), 83–101.

5. For this argument, see Hardwig, "The Role of Trust in Knowledge," 696.

6. See Hardwig, "Epistemic Dependence" and "The Role of Trust in Knowledge."

7. These two kinds of checking up are distinguished by Gerald Dworkin in *The Theory and Practice of Autonomy* (Cambridge: Cambridge University Press, 1988), 27.

8. C. A. J., "Egoism in Epistemology," in Schmitt, ed., *Socializing Epistemology*, 53–73, 55.

9. Ibid., 58–63, 65.

10. Ibid., 68, 67–68.

11. On a related point, Elizabeth Fricker argues that it is coherent to suppose that testimony-dependent empirical investigation could show testimony to be unreliable. See her "Telling and Trusting: Reductionism and Anti-Reductionism in the Epistemology of Testimony," a critical notice of C. A. J. Coady's *Testimony: A Philosophical Study*, in *Mind* 104 (1995): 408.

12. Thus Coady says, "When we believe testimony we believe what is said because we trust the witness." See his *Testimony: A Philosophical Study* (Oxford: Oxford University Press, 1992), 46.

13. For this minimal account of trust, see Diego Gambetta, "Can We Trust Trust?" in Diego Gambetta, ed., *Trust: Making and Breaking Cooperative Relations* (New York: Basil Blackwell, 1988), 213–37.

> Trust (or, symmetrically, distrust) is a certain level of subjective probability with which an agent assesses that another agent or group of agents will perform a particular action, both *before* he can monitor such action (or independently of his capacity ever to be able to monitor it) *and* in a context in which it affects *his own* action. (217; italics in original)

Stronger accounts of trust that require relying on the good will of another must also concede that accepting testimony typically requires trust in the testifiers. The reason is that we seldom have the kind of information about or control over the testifier that would enable us to rely on other aspects of her psychology.

14. See Karen Jones, "Trust as an Affective Attitude," *Ethics* 107 (1996): 4–25.

15. The point captured in terms of the variability of domain can also be captured by, as Annette Baier does, analyzing trust as a three-place relation: "A trusts B with valued item C." See her "Trust and Anti-Trust," *Ethics* 96 (1986): 231–60.

16. For a moving discussion of the effect of this sort of distrust, see Laurence Thomas, "Next Life, I'll Be White," *New York Times*, August 13, 1990, p. A15. The problem is discussed further in Laurence Thomas, "Moral Deference," *Philosophical Forum* 26 (1992–93): 233–50.

17. Stephen Jay Gould, *The Mismeasure of Man* (New York: Norton, 1981).

18. Russell Hardin makes the case for the role of institutions in underwriting trust in individuals in his "Trusting Persons, Trusting Institutions," in Richard Zeckhauser, ed., *Strategy and Choice* (Cambridge, Mass.: MIT Press, 1991), 185–209.

19. Hardwig points this out in his "The Role of Trust in Knowledge," 702–6.

20. Kane, "Integrity, Conscience, and Science," 121–24.

21. Of course, Kane himself does not deny this; see his "Integrity, Conscience, and Science," 125. My point is only that his official grounds for endorsing it are tainted by cognitive individualism.

22. Dworkin, *The Theory and Practice of Autonomy*, 8.

23. J. L. Mackie, "The Possibility of Innate Knowledge," *Proceedings of the Aristotelian Society* 70 (1969–70): 254.

24. See Dworkin, *The Theory and Practice of Autonomy*, 22–25, for a discussion of the compatibility of autonomy with some forms of dependence.

25. See, for example, ibid., 20. Such accounts seem to capture better the nature of autonomy than do accounts that see it as merely a matter of the relation between higher-order and lower-order desires (for what if the higher-order desire is itself corrupt?). The best-known hierarchical desire account is that of Harry Frankfurt, "Freedom of the Will and the Concept of a Person," *Journal of Philosophy* 68 (1971): 5–20. I do not mean to endorse the details of Dworkin's account, for there is much to be said against his picture of what such critical reflection needs to amount to.

8

MORAL OPPORTUNISM:
A CASE STUDY

KENNETH I. WINSTON

Moral integrity is a quality of persons only in a nonideal world. We commend someone for acting with integrity, typically when the person has been exposed to an enticement or temptation to act contrary to principle—and has resisted. Both the temptation to violate principle and the resistance to doing so are crucial. A person of integrity stands firm in the face of pressures and opportunities to do otherwise.

However, the world is nonideal in a deeper way: The fit between moral integrity and the achievement of moral good is not neat. On some occasions, the only way to act for the best, morally, is to do something that violates a settled moral principle. This should not be surprising. Integrity, after all, is a virtue of form, like sincerity or authenticity. Although the connection to moral goodness is presumably positive in the long run, it is still contingent. This contingency is evident in the way that circumstances make a difference in our assessment of what a person ought to do. For example, we do not judge someone harshly if desperate conditions, such as extreme deprivation, preclude even ordinary moral decency.

In this chapter, I am concerned about a different way in which circumstances matter. The idea is that circumstances sometimes provide opportunities for moral goodness that otherwise might not be realized and a person may be deemed to have failed morally for not exploiting such opportunities, even if they entail significant moral costs. If this is correct, a realistic account of the moral life must make room for a kind of moral responsiveness— *moral opportunism,* I call it—in relation to which the concern to preserve one's integrity is only an obstacle. In its ordinary sense, opportunism yields to immediate desires or short-term goals, thereby placing long-term values at risk. With moral opportunism, important value is achieved, but only at significant moral cost. Because of this cost, the moral opportunist does not receive the unequivocal praise or admiration garnered by the person of integrity. Moral opportunism does not entail inner peace or leave much room for moral self-satisfaction. Yet it is morally worthy, so I shall suggest.

To explore this idea, I discuss a single case of moral opportunism. Elsewhere I have suggested that moral theorizing should be rooted in the study of real cases if it is to avoid being sterile (having no practical application) or artificial (too easily producing alleged solutions to real problems).[1] I am aware that real stories involve risks. For one thing, they carry the potential of overwhelming any theoretical account if new facts or new implications are discovered. Also, they make generalization across cases more problematic, as our convictions in each instance may depend on peculiar combinations of factors. Nonetheless, I believe that responses to real cases are more firmly rooted in moral experience and are therefore more reliable.

At the same time, there is no reason to privilege my convictions over anyone else's, so enough of the story needs to be presented to allow readers to test their own responses and draw their own conclusions. In this respect, my method reflects a limited convergence with what Robert Ames reports to be a characteristic feature of texts in Chinese philosophy: Rather than seeking to persuade readers by consecutive argument, the author attempts to evoke in them their own reflective philosophizing.[2] I would be pleased to be able to make that claim here, but it would not be quite accurate. What is similar is that I present sufficient detail about the institutional setting and the main events to enable readers to engage in their own ethical analysis. At the same time, my imprint is on everything. Although I begin an explicit examination of defenses only in the final section, it will be clear to readers that my moral argument starts on the first page and continues uninterrupted throughout.

The story concerns a lawyer in the solicitor general's office who was able to exploit his access to a U.S. Supreme Court justice and have a decisive influence on one of the most important legal decisions of the twentieth century, *Brown v. Board of Education*.[3] In relating this story, I first introduce readers to the solicitor general's office, about which few U.S. citizens know very much. The importance of this institutional detail is that the operative norms of the solicitor general's office help us identify the main features of professional integrity for anyone working there. I then offer an account of the crucial events that transpired, focusing on the violation of a norm that is a core component of fair judicial procedure, the rule prohibiting ex parte communications. Finally, I offer reflections on some of the considerations in any moral assessment of this violation.

THE MODEL OF A MODERN SOLICITOR GENERAL

The solicitor general (SG) is a political appointee who serves at the pleasure of the president.[4] The person holding the office works for the attorney general as the latter's legal expert. Although the SG is the only government official required by statute to be "learned in the law" and thus might be regarded as most qualified to make decisions about the government's participation in lawsuits, everything the SG does is subject to the general supervision and direction of the attorney general, who can decide which cases to argue and which position to adopt in those cases. In fact, the attorney general retains the legal authority to displace the SG and assume the role at any time. So, in formal terms, the SG is a subordinate officer in the Department of Justice.

If we look only at the lines of formal authority, however, we will fail to understand the special role of the SG as it has developed over time. In general, there are two standard ways of describing an institutional function or office, which we might call *positivist* and *naturalist*. A positivist account is rule centered and focuses on explicit (usually written) directives; it emphasizes the chain of command. A naturalist account is practice based; it focuses on operative norms, tacit assumptions, and settled expectations, especially those that diverge from the formal rules. If the divergence is sufficiently wide, we could end up with two quite different accounts of the same office.

A practice-based account of the SG's office centers on the degree to which the distinction between law and politics has become a matter of settled expectation in the Department of Justice. The attorney general has explicit political responsibilities, is often a close adviser to the president, and is not expected to exercise unvarnished legal judgment. Even so, the attorney general is responsible for safeguarding the department's legal mission by protecting it on appropriate occasions from political intrusion. Different occupants of the office have, of course, been more or less successful at this task, but the expectation has remained fairly constant. The SG is still further removed than the attorney general from politics, and the control of professional norms is correspondingly stronger.

Although a political appointee, the SG has no political duties. Rather, the task of the office is to conduct appellate litigation for the government. Being learned in the law, the SG is expected to exercise that responsibility with dispassionate legal judgment. So, in practice, as the office evolved (and as the best SGs provided models of dispassionate judgment), the expectation developed that the attorney general would generally defer to the SG's opinion in specific cases. This expectation was reinforced at the next level of the hierarchy by the SG's deference, in turn, to the small cadre of high-quality career lawyers who work in the office, where the norms of professionalism are at their strongest. (Serving in the SG's office is generally regarded by members of the legal profession as one of the most prestigious jobs a lawyer can have in the United States.)

Thus, a practice-based account of the office serves as an important corrective to a positivist account. At the same time, it runs the danger of exaggerating the SG's independence from politics. This is too often done, even by former SGs. The reality is more complicated. In many cases that reach the SG's office, the best judgment of the career lawyers is that as a matter of law, the decision could go either way. This should not be surprising, since a case is unlikely to make its way to the Supreme Court unless it is a close call. For many of these cases, then, the question legitimately turns on a matter of political morality, and it is entirely appropriate for the attorney general and the president to be involved. In these cases, indeed, one could say that the SG's obligation is to make certain of their participation.

The independence of the SG, therefore, consists of maintaining an often delicate balance between a fiduciary duty to the law and accountability to a particular administration. The SG's office is respected for its independence, not when it has no master, but when it places its commitment to the one master on a par with its commitment to the other.[5] Maintaining a balance is reasonable because the SG is not an elected official and has no standing, separate from the appointing officer and the statute that created the office, as an official decision maker. Total independence would mean a lack of democratic accountability and would quickly subject the office to political pressures. Paradoxically, it is the attorney general's formal authority to overrule the SG that protects the SG in exercising the fiduciary duty. So, even in ideal terms, the SG should be answerable to the attorney general (and thus the president) at the same time that as a matter of practice, the attorney general should generally defer to the SG's legal judgment.

The fiduciary duty is exhibited in the patterns of expectation that govern the SG's office in its dealings with the Supreme Court. The Court expects the SG to be a guardian of the law, a counselor to the Court, the legal conscience of the government and not (simply) an agent of the current administration. This means the SG looks beyond the interests of the administration as well as beyond the interests of the immediate parties in a case, to guide the Court in taking the long view toward an orderly development of decisional law. Thus, the SG's job is as much to protect the Court as to persuade it. Likewise, in meetings with administration officials, the SG should give voice to the views of the Court and the law.

With the Court relying so heavily on the SG, the SG has correspondingly weighty responsibilities to the Court. The SG can be effective only if the justices have confidence in the SG's integrity and legal judgment. Whether they have such confidence is in great part a function of the SG's evident commitment to professional norms and the skill with which the SG assists the justices in meeting what they understand as their own responsibilities. Thus, effectiveness does not refer to success in winning cases but to success in serving the Court and the law. John W. Davis, one of the most distinguished SGs in U.S. history, explained the SG's fiduciary duty: "Whenever the case is decided right the government wins."[6] The SG, of course, should be trying mightily to get things right.

Craft is essential to maintaining credibility and shows itself in a number of concrete ways. One is to take seriously the legal issues in a case and to keep them distinct from partisan political issues. Ideology predominates when the SG's brief to the Court downplays lawyers' issues and becomes a "position paper" on public policy. There is, needless to say, much skepticism in our culture about the capacity of individuals to exercise dispassionate judgment. This skepticism is reinforced by the studies of political scientists that "confirm that government litigation in the Supreme Court tends to conform to the ideological direction of the current administration."[7]

These studies should be treated skeptically themselves, however. First, it takes only a small number of cases to display a "tendency" in an "ideological direction." I have already pointed out that a large number of cases reaching the Supreme Court are close calls and turn on questions of political morality to which the administration is legitimately a party. These cases would display the tendency in question. Second, "ideological direction" is too crude as a measure of the SG's independence, which is exercised in ways to which this measure is not sensitive. For example, legal judgment, as opposed to political judgment, is demonstrated by determining the scope of an argument or principle brought to the Court. The attorney general may want a sweeping declaration of policy; the SG may instead formulate a narrowly tailored rule, even one based on a technical point rather than the substance of the case. (Thus a case on racial equality may turn on the interpretation of a standard of evidence.) But the outcome will be in the same "ideological direction."

If independence in relation to the SG's superiors is maintained by adhering to the distinction between legal and political judgment, it also is maintained in relation to government clients by refusing to support petitions for review, by submitting a brief while declining to endorse its argument (e.g., by a well-placed footnote), or by completely rewriting an agency's brief and employing only those arguments deemed worthy by the SG. In rare cases, SGs have even refused to sign the government's brief or have refused to argue a case themselves, an act that sends a message to the Court. Even more dramatic is the long-standing practice of "confessing error," that is, arguing to the Court that a lower-court decision was a mistake, even though it favored the government.[8]

More generally, the Court's confidence in the SG's office is based in large part on its willingness to exercise self-restraint, for example, by refraining from using cases to raise issues that go beyond the dispute between the parties, by refraining from asking the Court to address a major issue without careful intellectual preparation, and by refraining from asking the Court to reverse itself on a settled matter in the absence of compelling legal reasons. An argument for reversal becomes compelling only when it is preceded by thoughtful lower-court decisions and changes in the intellectual climate of the legal profession, reflected perhaps in law-review articles showing serious reconsideration of Court precedents—not simply when the president's agenda calls for it.

Having described the dimensions of professional integrity in the SG's office, I confess that there is much more I am eager to say about it (and will on another occasion). In particular, I have omitted any discussion of the SG's office during the Reagan presidency, when the Department of Justice made a strenuous effort to transform the office into an agent of the president's agenda before the Court. These attempts were largely unsuccessful, I believe, because the two people appointed as SG during those years, Rex Lee and Charles Fried, understood the nature of the threat and combated it effectively. Although there is much to learn from reviewing their efforts, it would not affect the account I have provided.

THE STORY

In 1944, Philip Elman joined the staff of the SG's office and, until 1961, handled all civil rights cases before the Supreme Court in which the United States was a party or was involved as amicus curiae. Given the tradition of deference to the career lawyers in the office, Elman exercised great influence over the development of civil rights law during this period. The specific moment of interest here is the early 1950s, when the Court was handing down major rulings on racial segregation in educational institutions and was working its way toward a decision in the cluster of cases known as *Brown v. Board of Education*. It is generally agreed that during this time, Elman "was perhaps the most knowledgeable and strategically placed Court-watcher in Washington."[9]

One reason for this strategic placement was Elman's intimacy with U.S. Supreme Court Justice Felix Frankfurter. In the early 1940s, Elman served for two years as Frankfurter's law clerk, at a time when justices had only one clerk each. From that point until Frankfurter's death in 1965, they maintained a close, even familial relationship. Elman reports, for example, that Frankfurter would call him almost every Sunday night to talk about the week's events: "We'd have a long, relaxed, gossipy conversation for an hour and a half sometimes."[10] The gossip was often about other justices and the Court's business. Thus, in connection with *Brown*, Elman reports that Frankfurter told him about discussions in the Court, including what was said during the justices' weekly conferences to which even their clerks were not admitted.

The details of this relationship became public when Elman was interviewed for the Columbia University Oral History Project and the transcript was published in the *Harvard Law Review*.[11] In the oral history, Elman suggests that in some ways, he never ceased to be Frankfurter's law clerk, and several times he refers to himself as "law clerk emeritus." A few years later, in a letter to me when I was arranging to include an excerpt from the oral history in a judicial ethics casebook, he portrayed himself as a close friend of Justice Frankfurter:

> When the Justice and I talked about the cases, he was talking to an old friend, an intimate confidante, whose lips were sealed—*not* to a lawyer for a party (or even amicus) in the cases. . . . For all practical purposes, he might have been confiding in Dean Acheson, Paul Freund, or some other old, trusted friend—that was *my* position when FF talked to me.

But Elman was also a lawyer in the SG's office with responsibility for writing the government's briefs in pending cases. Whether Elman had any conscious sense at the time that his conversations with the justice might raise legitimate questions of propriety is uncertain, but once the oral history was published, it was apparent to others. Thus, the *New York Times* was moved to write a damning editorial. Carrying the stinging title "With All Deliberate Impropriety," the editorial took Elman to task for his high-mindedness in exploiting a "back channel" to the Court for partisan ends, thereby undermining the fairness of the judicial process. Even if the segregationist states were engaged in hateful conduct in defending the "separate but equal" doctrine, the *Times* said, they deserved a fair tribunal. But that was denied them because in their private conversations, Frankfurter informed Elman about the "leanings and prejudices" of the other members of the Court. This information enabled Elman, when writing the government's brief, to craft the kind of argument that he could be confident would win at least a majority if not the unanimous support of the Court. The *Times* conceded that although the *Brown* decision was "the most important constitutional decision of modern times," neither "loftiness of purpose" nor "concern for the national interest" provides an acceptable defense of the impropriety.[12]

The *Times'* case against Elman is clear and powerful. Even so, I am inclined to disagree with its conclusion, as I will indicate in due course. Here I want to focus on the *Times'* picture of what happened. Its reading of events is consistent with the assumption that Frankfurter had a settled position on *Brown* and was strategizing with Elman about how to persuade the rest of the Court to agree with their view. Elman himself stresses that in Frankfurter's judgment, the Court in 1952 (when the first of the *Brown* cases reached it) was nowhere near ready to overrule *Plessy*. Frankfurter could not count five sure or even probable votes, so he engaged in delaying tactics because he wanted a unanimous decision "so that the Court as an institution would best be able to withstand the attacks that inevitably were going to be made on it." According to this reading, Frankfurter was firm in his commitment to overrule *Plessy* but realized that a fractured decision "would [have] set back the cause of desegregation; . . . would have hurt the public school systems everywhere; and . . . would have damaged the

Court." That is why he needed Elman to control the timing of the government's push for desegregation and to make the right sort of argument in the government's brief.[13]

The situation on the Court, as portrayed in this account, had a parallel in the SG's office. The current SG, Philip Perlman, was not himself prepared to recommend overruling *Plessy*. Although he had supported black plaintiffs (and the NAACP) in several prior "separate but equal" cases involving law schools and dining cars on trains, he drew the line at the racial integration of public schools. Because of Perlman's position and with the approval of Attorney General J. Howard McGrath, the government initially declined to participate in *Brown* as amicus. Thus the most Elman could do was to plan for a time after Perlman had left and been replaced by a more sympathetic SG. That happened in late 1952.

However, the impropriety portrayed in the *Times* editorial, although evident, does not appear to be particularly egregious. It is true, given the prestige of the SG's office, that it would have been helpful if the government's brief had contained an argument that could be assumed to be effective. But commentators agree that Elman did not need Frankfurter to tell him the opinions of the other justices or what sort of arguments would work with them. So in my judgment, the *Times* seems to have been overreacting to what it construed the situation to have been.

The *Times* missed the heart of the story, however, which is that Frankfurter had not made up his mind about *Brown*. The principal reason he attempted to delay a decision, I believe, was that he himself was not convinced that *Plessy* should be overruled. Elman understood this and took it as his task to persuade Frankfurter otherwise. In the oral history, Elman makes it clear that Frankfurter had doubts about whether the time was ripe for integration. He was leaning to the view that the recent "separate but equal" decisions (which effectively placed blacks in white institutions, since the black institutions were not equal) should be given a chance to have an effect. He also thought that if integration were mandated, the southern states would have to send white students to inferior schools, which would invite massive resistance. He wanted to allow liberal leaders in the South the opportunity to move everyone along at a gradual pace.

Reinforcing Frankfurter's gradualism was Justice Hugo Black's dire prediction that if the Court mandated integration, southern liberalism would be finished, and the segregationists would take over. "The Bilbos and the Talmadges would come even more to the fore, overshadowing the John Sparkmans and the Lister Hills."[14] Although Black himself favored overruling *Plessy,* his talk about the effects of doing so alarmed many of the justices, including Frankfurter. As Elman recounts Black's message: "There would be riots, the Army might have to be called out—he was scaring the shit out of the Justices, especially Frankfurter and Jackson, who did not know how the Court could enforce a ruling against *Plessy.*"

Furthermore, as a leading proponent of judicial modesty, Frankfurter was intellectually and temperamentally attracted to the position of Justice Robert Jackson. Jackson's view was that the integration of public schools was a task for the Congress, not the courts. Section 5 of the Fourteenth Amendment specifically gives to Congress the responsibility for enforcing its provisions. It is true that the Congress had so far abdicated its role, but that did not mean that the Court should fill the vacuum. Rather, the Court should tell the Congress to take it on. As Jackson saw it, the task was a political one, involving the massive restructuring of state educational systems in nearly half the states. (One should remember, of course, that a powerful group of southerners dominated much of the Congress's agenda.)

The most revealing line in the oral history comes when Elman says: "*I remember arguing with Frankfurter.* He was very sympathetic to Jackson."[15] Elman then relates how he made the case against Jackson's view. He emphasized that the Fourteenth Amendment had been written to protect freed blacks, to guarantee that they had the same rights as whites. Yet since 1868 the Court had found violations of equal protection only in cases involving Chinese or aliens or corporations, everyone but blacks. When the one group for whom the amendment was written came to Court, Jackson wanted to say: " 'Yes, your constitutional rights have been violated. But don't come to us . . . [G]o across the street and ask Congress to give you relief.' " After he heard this argument, Elman reports, "Frankfurter was torn."

In his letter to the *Times,* Elman describes Frankfurter as having had "enormous difficulty" supporting the abolition of school segregation by judicial decree, and in this respect he lumps Frank-furter together with Justices Jackson, Frederick M. Vinson, Stanley F. Reed, and Thomas C. Clark. (One of the fascinating aspects of the story of the *Brown* decision as it has been written by historians over the last forty years is the constantly changing account of which justices stood where and when.) The private conversations Elman was able to have with Frankfurter—which he carefully "never mentioned . . . to anyone"—gave him the opportunity to persuade Frankfurter otherwise. We still might ask whether these ex parte conversations were really necessary. Could Elman have made the arguments he needed to make to Frankfurter simply by placing them in the government's brief? I think not. The issues in *Brown* touched some of Frankfurter's deepest beliefs. To turn him in the right direction required extended argumentation, with a lot of give-and-take, from someone whom he trusted and with whom he felt free to entertain disturbing ideas.

Even given his opportunity for uninterrupted conversation, Elman knew that he probably could not move Frankfurter all the way over to the position he favored: overruling *Plessy* and ordering immediate remedial action to eliminate segregated schools. Frankfurter's worries about the Court's reputation and about the effects in the South were too formidable. Elman describes his task accordingly: "So I began looking around for something [i.e., a legal strategy] that would get Jackson, *that would hold Frankfurter,* that would even get a strong majority to hold racial segregation unconstitutional but would provide some kind of cushion [to mitigate the effects in the southern states]." [16]

Elman's solution was "with all deliberate speed," that is, the idea of separating the affirmation of constitutional principle from the provision of a remedy. He formulated the idea initially in the brief submitted to the Court in December 1952, with the approval of the acting SG, Robert Stern, and repeated it in the govern-ment's 1953 amicus brief, which Elman also wrote. The phrase itself, "with all deliberate speed," was first used by Assistant Attor-ney General J. Lee Rankin in oral argument before the Court in December 1953, and it was Frankfurter who later recommended its insertion in the Court's opinion in the remedial phase (*Brown* II).

The dubious legality of "with all deliberate speed" is an im-

portant part of the story, but I will say only a word about it
here. Elman characterizes the idea—in retrospect, but probably
reflecting his view at the time—as "entirely unprincipled," "simply indefensible," and "just plain wrong as a matter of constitutional law." [17] It was just plain wrong because the Court had held
repeatedly that constitutional rights were personal. This means
that if a right is violated, the individual is entitled to immediate
relief. Elman's idea was instead to delay relief so as to give segregated school systems time to adjust to a new constitutional regime.
In any case, as we know, the *Brown* plaintiffs had long since
graduated from their segregated schools before the restructuring
began.

Why did Elman propose this unprincipled, indefensible idea?
His account is about means and ends: It was crucial to attaining a
unanimous vote on the Court. "None of this was based on what I
thought was right [for the plaintiffs]—I had no idea whether
it would have been better educationally or politically to do it
immediately—I was simply counting votes on the Supreme
Court." So the immediate goal was to secure a ringing declaration
of principle, getting the Court to overrule *Plessy* and to reject the
doctrine of "separate but equal." At the same time, Elman must
have known that even though his strategy might achieve unanimity on the principle, it would not necessarily move the Court
toward agreement on a remedy. It would still allow Jackson to say
that now that the Court had declared the meaning of the law (in
Brown I), Congress should enforce it. So in that regard, the formula only postponed the difficulty. Perhaps Elman thought that
unanimity on the remedy was not critical, or perhaps he was
hoping that the circumstances would change. And indeed they
did; Jackson died a few months after the 1954 decision.

If a declaration of constitutional principle was Elman's immediate goal, his larger purpose was ending segregated schools. In this
regard, his self-conception calls to mind Justice Louis D. Brandeis's vision of the lawyer who rises above advocacy and becomes
"counsel to the situation." [18] In his letter to the *Times,* Elman
noted that when the United States finally entered the case in
1952, "it was not as an adversary party but as an amicus curiae, a
friend of the court and proponent of the national interest." This
perspective also emerges in the oral history. When the interviewer

finally grasps the impropriety of Elman's conversations with Frankfurter and presses him about it, Elman responds in a way that crystallizes his basic argument: "I considered it a case that transcended ordinary notions about propriety in a litigation. This was not a litigation in the usual sense. The constitutional issue went to the heart of what kind of country we are. . . . [*Brown*] was an extraordinary case, and the ordinary rules didn't apply." [19]

Aside from "transcending" the ordinary rules of propriety and proposing an "indefensible" resolution of the case, Elman, by his own judgment, acted deviously in getting the Republican administration to support his position. He knew that the chances for a favorable outcome would be greatly enhanced if the Eisenhower administration added its support to the already declared support of the Truman administration. Elman might have acknowledged that a case that speaks to "what kind of country we are" turns on the deepest questions of political morality; therefore, the White House had a legitimate claim to be involved in the deliberations regarding the government's brief.

But Elman did not trust the Republicans to make the right decision by themselves. He mentions two subterfuges he engaged in regarding the second brief (submitted in 1953). First, in the section on the legislative history of the Fourteenth Amendment, he slanted the account of congressional intent to make the history regarding school segregation seem more favorable to his view than he knew it to be. Second, he entitled the new brief "Supplemental Brief," which meant to the Court that it did not replace the first (1952) brief but was to be added to it. Regarding this last maneuver, Elman says that it "slipped by my [Republican] superiors, [Assistant Attorney General J. Lee] Rankin and [Attorney General Herbert] Brownell." And he adds: "You can be sure the folks in the White House didn't realize its significance." [20]

If the president and attorney general were legitimately involved in fashioning the government's position in *Brown*, Elman was wrong to exclude them or to attempt to manipulate them into signing on to his view. As it happens, there is reason to believe that the Republicans were not deceived in the slightest by Elman's machinations. Indeed, Elman's comments reveal more about him than actual events do. But the full irony of this part of the story emerges only with Richard Kluger's observation that in the summer of 1953, when Brownell was delaying the decision whether to answer the Court's request for a second brief, Elman became increasingly anxious about what the Republicans would do, and tensions developed between him and Rankin. Kluger reports:

> To Elman, the Republicans seemed unsophisticated and sanctimonious. "They've been out in the wilderness [so long] . . . they've come to believe their own propaganda," he confided to Felix Frankfurter. "Rankin, for example, thinks that there is a distinguishing characteristic of the 'New Deal–Fair Deal' type of person. Such a person, he told me, believes in the philosophy that the end justifies the means. The Republicans—and this was said with a straight face—do not share that philosophy." [21]

The implication is that Elman thought the Republicans did share that "philosophy" and could say otherwise only because they had been out of power for so long. Only naïveté or sanctimoniousness could get in the way of affirming the maxim that the end justifies the means. Is this right? Is this a case in which application of that maxim is warranted?

ELMAN'S DEFENSE

A lawyer's integrity is bound up with process values. The craft that lawyers exercise and take pride in is not just constrained by but is also informed by their commitment to fair procedures, public deliberation, respect for affected parties, and so on. The constitutional scholar Alexander Bickel—who, coincidentally, was Frankfurter's clerk in 1952–53—captured this idea when he suggested that the highest morality is almost always the morality of process. [22] The *New York Times* understood this point and rightly took Elman to task for his ex parte conversations with Frankfurter, even though the *Times* did not fully realize the extent of Elman's deviance.

Yet as I have indicated, I believe that Elman acted for the best, morally. Although the morality of process is generally most compelling, it is not always so. The good to be achieved in this case was too important for Elman not to take advantage of his unique opportunity to influence the Court's decision in *Brown*. At the same time, I think the wrong he committed was not simply canceled or annulled by the greater good he helped realize. He incurred significant moral costs that warrant deep regret. In other words, in my view, Elman has "dirty hands."

Elsewhere I have identified different types of dirty hands and have described in a preliminary way the circumstances that give rise to them. This is not the place to review that ground.[23] Nor will I attempt here to reach any definitive judgment about Elman. There is a large repertoire of excuses he could have invoked in his defense, and each would need to be examined with care. Instead, I will focus on only two of these excuses, both of which Elman employed explicitly, and offer some observations about what place they might have in an assessment of Elman's deed.

I. He Believed He Was Doing the Right Thing

Perhaps sensing the difficulty of offering a plausible justification of his deed, Elman asserted: "I don't defend my discussions with Frankfurter; I just did what I thought was right."[24] But this is, of course, a defense, or an attempt at one.

Claims of conscience. When he says, "I don't defend what I did," Elman could mean "I *can't* defend what I did; that is, what I did was indefensible, it was simply wrong." But if he believed that, could he also say that he did what he thought was right? Could he have thought (to himself, perhaps) that the act was right even while thinking that there was no way to defend it (to others)?

Let us refer to such a view as *ethical privacy.* It involves giving credence to an inner voice (e.g., Socrates' daemon), to which no one else has access. The authority of the voice is based solely on the status conferred by the person who hears it, not necessarily on the reasonableness of what it says. So it carries moral weight for that person, regardless of facts and arguments and regardless of the views of others. A private moral belief, we might say, is one whose warrant rests solely on the believer's conviction as to its inherent validity. An extreme—but clear—example would be Kierkegaard's Abraham, who could not speak to others, even Sarah, about the purpose of his journey to Mount Moriah, because he knew they would not find intelligible the distinction between sacrificing Isaac, in obedience to God's command, and murdering him. As Kierkegaard himself says elsewhere: "In a merely subjective determination of the truth, madness and truth become in the last analysis indistinguishable."[25]

Conscience, as conventionally understood, is not ethically private in this sense. A tacit presupposition of our respect for personal conscience is that it meet a public standard of reasonableness. At a minimum, we require consistency of thought and absence of the merely self-serving. Some requirements are more substantive, involving concern and respect for other people. Whatever the standards are, the point is that claims of conscience are not immune to challenge. As Philip Selznick observes, the space we create for liberty of conscience has more to do with our regard for moral identity than the validity of individual moral judgment. Within limits, we respect the right of individuals to fashion self-defining moral commitments, but not to construct autonomous codes of conduct.[26] Thus, if Elman were making a claim of conscience, it would mark the beginning of our inquiry, not the conclusion. In the context of public action, the first step in such an inquiry, I suggest, is to distinguish two conceptions of conscience: narrow and wide. This distinction provides a basis for determining whether someone has the moral competence to be a public official.

In the narrow sense, conscience consists in the personal moral convictions by which one guides one's own life.[27] It matters little— except to the person whose conscience it is—what the sources of these convictions are or whether they are shared by anyone else. As long as the conditions of reasonableness are met, it is not a concern to the rest of us that a person's moral beliefs and values may reflect the contingencies of his or her individual circumstances. If the beliefs and values happen to be idiosyncratic or peculiar or even based on (what are to the rest of us) unfathomable sources, that is a matter of indifference to us. Once in the public realm, however, a person no longer has the luxury of idiosyncratic moral conviction. Principles that are important, even foundational, to oneself do not necessarily have a claim on anyone else. Accordingly, sincerity of conviction is not an acceptable basis of public action. Since public officials fashion and implement policies that affect others, including those who have different or even opposite convictions, there is an obligation to reach out beyond what is personal to what can be shared and agreed to by others.

Conscience in the wide sense captures this idea. It may take self-defining principles as starting points, but it inevitably moves beyond them. A conscientious public official in a democratic polity is one whose grounds of decision making are beliefs and principles that citizens are generally committed to or could be committed to after deliberation and reflection. Take the example of Abraham Lincoln. If the goal of emancipating blacks from slavery had been based on Lincoln's idiosyncratic convictions, there would have been no moral ground for calling on the nation to endure the great sacrifices necessary in prosecuting the war against the rebellious South. But Lincoln's appeal was based on the ideal of equality expressed in the Declaration of Independence, the nation's self-defining statement of moral principle. Even though he saw implications in that statement that not everyone saw, the logic of his argument was public, not personal.[28]

Lincoln's case is apt here, since Elman could also claim to be standing on the shared ideal of equality and moving it forward in accordance with its own inexorable logic. Certain elements of the story indicate his awareness of this point. For example, he saw the importance of bipartisan support for the *Brown* brief, even if he was, in his own view, manipulative in attaining it. The decision he sought was also not based on an abstract philosophy common at best to only a small group of ideologues alienated from fifty years of legal development (as could be said, for example, about Reagan's Justice Department). Indeed, there was no contempt for recent Court decisions and no plea to reverse them. Elman understood, as other legal observers did, that the NAACP's legal strategy in such cases as *Henderson, Sweatt,* and *McLaurin* was an attack, even if indirect, on the "separate but equal" doctrine even while it employed that very formula. Thus the central argument in *Brown* built on the underlying rationale of these cases, reflecting an emergent perception of the meaning of equality that was gradually pervading the legal profession and elite opinion generally.

In sum, if the moral basis of Elman's deed had been personal, it would have carried no moral weight. Personal beliefs and convictions do not give government officials a mandate for action. They do, of course, generate felt imperatives, and they may legitimately function as starting points, as the focus from which an official reaches out to others, in search of the shared values that would support collective action. But the discovery of such common ground is indispensable. It follows that one of the moral capacities necessary for responsible public decision making is the ability to adopt a nonpersonal or, better, impersonal point of view, to regard one's own opinion as only one among others and not decisive simply because one holds it. People who lack this ability are not effective, let alone legitimate, public servants.[29]

It does not follow, of course, that public officials do not exercise individual judgment; they do not divest themselves of moral agency. As Richard Neustadt pointed out: "Who else but they can choose what they will do?"[30] It is a mistake, however, to think that the only alternative to basing judgment on personal conviction is exercising no judgment at all. The source of confusion here may be the word *impersonal* which, when applied to public officials, is sometimes taken to mean that they are fungible (mere "functionaries"), as though experience and expertise and reflection make no difference. But that is not what is meant. Both personal and impersonal judgments are made by persons, and they are distinguished by their grounds, the kind of considerations taken into account, the point of view from which they are made—and all that leaves room for differences in judgment.

In Elman's case, it is evident that he exercised his professional judgment as to the state of elite opinion and the law, in light of recent Court decisions. Accordingly, I interpret "I just did what I thought was right" as expressing an impersonal, not a personal, point of view. I propose, therefore, that his conduct meets the first test of conscientiousness. At the same time, it was devious and had to be done in secret, a clear indication of the absence of public affirmability. So a grounding in wide conscience is only the first hurdle for a public official. A second factor is institutional mandate.

The moral entrepreneur. A person occupying an official position acquires new reasons for action, including new duties. Acting conscientiously means attending to those duties and giving them priority over other considerations. Moreover, since each official is typically only one among others in a complex arrangement of powers and responsibilities, each is assigned more or less well defined—and therefore limited—ethical tasks distinct from those of officials in other, complementary roles. The dispersion of assignments is thus accompanied by a division of ethical labor. Instead of asking "What should be done after all ethically relevant factors are considered?" the more relevant questions are "What should I do within the compass of what I am authorized to do? Which part of this situation falls within my assignment, and which actions must I bar from consideration because they are the concern of another official or agency?"

The idea of the division of ethical labor deserves a more extended analysis than I can offer here.[31] Instead, I shall use an illustration of it as the context for thinking about Elman as a moral opportunist. One feature of moral opportunism is violation of the division of ethical labor; the opportunist attempts to act on the basis of an all-things-considered judgment.

Consider the incident related by Herbert Wechsler that occurred when he was an assistant attorney general in the SG's office.[32] He helped prepare the government's brief supporting the constitutionality of President Franklin D. Roosevelt's orders to forcibly move persons of Japanese ancestry from the West Coast to relocation camps. Wechsler reports that he was deeply distressed by this policy and supported Attorney General Francis Biddle's vigorous opposition when Roosevelt was debating whether to proceed with it, as well as Biddle's refusal to allow responsibility for executing the policy to fall to the Justice Department rather than the War Department. But once the president had made the decision and it had to be defended before the Supreme Court, his professional judgment told him that it was good law and would be sustained—as indeed it was.

Despite his misgivings, Wechsler participated in the legal defense. (I am assuming that his distress about the internment policy did not rest on beliefs peculiar to him but, as in Elman's case, was founded on beliefs about racial equality that he took to be defining ideals of the nation.) In response to the question of why he did not resign his office, Wechsler said, "It seemed to me that the separation of function[s] in society justified and, indeed, required the course that I pursued." The responsibility to order or not order the Japanese evacuation rested with the president, not with the attorney general or his assistant. Nor was it up to him to make the actual determination of constitutionality; that was the job of the Court. Rather, Wechsler's responsibility was to exercise his professional judgment about the state of the law.

If our concern is impersonal belief as the basis for public decision making, Wechsler's response may appear to beg the question. An official may avoid judgment on a substantive policy and instead defer to a superior, but not without a judgment about the acceptability of deference. So invoking the division of ethical labor as a reason for not resigning only shifts the point at which the judgment is made. Wechsler still chose to work within a system that sometimes leads officials to support policies they think violate public values. Wechsler's response, however, could be that a person's structure of beliefs and commitments is more complicated than this objection reveals.

The division of ethical labor has an impersonal justification, just as racial equality does. Part of it is that given human fallibility, especially about moral matters, a complex society needs settled institutional roles in which individuals willingly cooperate in a hierarchical arrangement of decision making, entailing limits on judgment and checks on action. (Wechsler himself adds that the division of ethical labor helps society avoid "what might otherwise prove to be insoluble dilemmas of choice [for individuals].") [33] If that is correct, then from an impersonal point of view, moral entrepreneurship is properly discouraged even when it expresses public values. We could conclude, therefore, that Elman's deed, in contrast to Wechsler's, resulted from his failure to grasp the force of the overriding justification for the division of ethical labor.

But perhaps this inference is too hasty; perhaps I have misconstrued the nature of an official's mandate. Although it is true that the impersonal must supersede the personal point of view, there is another dimension of an official mandate that leaves more room than I have indicated for the excuse "I just did what I thought was right." The idea is this: The mandate of a public official is not something settled beforehand but is always in play, always something to be negotiated as the official moves from task to task. "The moral authority to act is nothing more or less than what in fact the political process allows [the official] to get away with."[34] According to this view, the official's job is largely defined by the official whose job it is. A mandate, in other words, is a self-created agenda, at least to a degree, and therefore is highly dependent on who occupies the office. If there are constraints on action, they do not derive from the division of ethical labor but from the agenda itself, which ought to be pursued with as much prudence as is necessary for success. In this view, public officials are moral entrepreneurs.

Elman is a good candidate for this account. He had an agenda that he pursued vigorously. Prudence required that he act in secret if he wished to be successful. He did succeed, and the outcome was widely applauded. However, a moment's reflection reveals difficulties in applying this account to Elman. His assignment in the SG's office was neither ambiguous nor changing continuously with the occupant of the office. In fact, it is only because his official mandate was clear—and because he clearly violated it—that his case is ethically interesting. His case also cannot be placed in the category of civil disobedience, which we could construe as another type of moral entrepreneurship. Although his activity was motivated by a desire for justice, Elman did not believe, and had no reason to believe, that the rules regulating his official conduct were unjust or illegitimate and hence should be violated for that reason. Furthermore, civil disobedience is a public act aimed at overturning a hated law or policy. But Elman's deed was secret and aimed, one might say, at leaving the SG's mandate in place. Elman was not in fact attempting to defy those in authority; he was attempting to persuade them to follow a certain course of action.

To summarize my argument to this point: The warrant, if there is one, for Elman's opportunistic role departure must turn on the impersonal appeal of his cause; it cannot be simply that he personally believed the cause to be overwhelmingly important. The point of the division of ethical labor is, in part, to override such personal judgments. The cause must embody a public value publicly affirmed—or affirmable. Furthermore, the division of ethical labor is so deeply entrenched that even an appeal to impersonal principle is disfavored and must carry a special burden of argument if it is to succeed. Thus, Elman's statement "I don't defend what I did" would have to be construed in this way: "I violated the duties of my office (hence, the act cannot be defended in those terms), but I was acting for the best in violating those duties because the cause of racial equality is so important that from an impersonal point of view, it outweighs even the division of ethical labor." Would that be persuasive?

II. It Was for a Good Cause

I accept the view that Elman was a moral entrepreneur or, better, a moral opportunist who exploited his close relationship with Justice Frankfurter and violated the duties of his office in a successful effort to ensure a desirable outcome in *Brown*. Although he says he cannot defend what he did, I believe there is a plausible defense available to him, and I shall devote the remainder of this chapter to exploring certain aspects of it. Elman himself comes close to suggesting this defense in the passage quoted earlier, in which he expresses his amusement at the "unsophisticated and sanctimonious" Republicans who, by 1952, had been out of office so long that they had forgotten that the end justifies the means. Elman, however, had not forgotten. The claim about ends and means emerges again in a more specific, if somewhat more ambiguous, formulation in the oral history, when Elman says that *Brown* was an extraordinary case "and the ordinary rules [of propriety in litigation] didn't apply." Can he appeal to this maxim in his defense?

Almost anyone who is asked point-blank—but abstractly—whether the maxim "the end justifies the means" is an acceptable ethical principle will deny it. Yet it is one of the most common, if most abused, justifications in political life. In a limited sense, as John Dewey pointed out, the maxim is perfectly sound.[35] Good consequences do provide a warrant for the means employed to achieve them. The problem is that the means may produce other, undesirable consequences, independent of what is aimed at. In the usual case, the maxim is thought to work only because a narrow focus on the desired outcome results in the neglect of other detrimental outcomes produced by the same means. A sound moral judgment, Dewey says, must take into account all the consequences. But Dewey's point leaves us with this question: How do we assess situations in which we have a mix of moral consequences? A moral opportunist like Elman deliberately sacrifices one thing of moral value in order to attain something else of moral value. If good outcomes do sometimes warrant the means employed to achieve them, do they cease to do so when the means involve significant moral costs?

The question is too large to deal with here, and besides it is a theorist's question. Since my concern is to stay rooted in moral experience and hence to keep the discussion as case centered as possible, I regard it as sufficient work for an ethics day laborer like myself just to identify some "provisional fixed points" that any theory construction would have to build on.

Let me begin by observing that reflection on Elman's story leads me to want to reformulate the maxim. It is not the case, so it seems to me, that however the moral opportunist acts necessarily involves wrongdoing; in that sense, the opportunist is not faced with a tragic choice.[36] Elman had the option of not engaging in the conversations with Frankfurter, or at least not discussing any Court business related to *Brown,* and he would not have committed any wrong had he taken that course. But the circumstances were such that the unethical deed was a means to a great good, and Elman was in an especially favorable, probably unique, position to realize that good. Thus his situation had, we might say, a certain moral urgency. The unethical deed was not unavoidable, but it was nonetheless compelling.

We cannot understand what Elman did unless we keep the sense of moral urgency at the forefront. The problem is that although his deed was morally compelling because of the good to be realized, the duties of his office did not cease to be compelling, too. If we were to employ the language of justification in this situation, we would be saying that the good to be realized not only outweighs or overrides but also cancels the violated ethical duty. Therefore, no moral residue would remain for us to worry about. "Justifiable wrongdoing" is, after all, an oxymoron. But if, rather, the ethical duty remains compelling, as I believe it does, we need to employ a moral vocabulary that expresses that fact. We can do this if we reformulate the guiding maxim: It is not that the end justifies the means; it is that at best, the end *excuses* the means.[37]

Admittedly, this correction makes the task of applying the maxim even more difficult than it appeared at first. In general, the application of "the end excuses the means" has six elements: (1) the postulation of a morally compelling end; (2) a causal claim about some act as a means to achieving the end; (3) the acknowledgment that using the means entails significant, perhaps irreparable, moral costs for violating a compelling ethical duty; (4) a practical claim about available alternatives, that no other means are (reasonably) available, that is, the choice of means is a practical necessity; (5) a normative claim that performing the act is "for the best" despite the moral costs; and (6) the normative conclusion that the person employing the means is excused for acting out of such practical necessity. The moral significance of saying that the agent is excused, rather than justified, is that we hold on to the fact that as a practical matter, acting for the best required wrongdoing. This is a source of deep regret, not just because circumstances sometimes require terrible choices (situation regret), but also because the agent should feel guilty for engaging in the wrongdoing, even though it was the morally best thing to do (agent regret).

In determining whether these elements are present in Elman's case, there are numerous ways of going wrong. In keeping with the themes of this chapter, I will briefly discuss certain epistemic and moral difficulties of the sort I have already identified.

Assessing the end. In his letter to the *New York Times,* Elman indicates that he saw himself acting as a "proponent of the national interest." In his case, this is a minimal condition for warranted application of the excuse. But in whose judgment is it true?

I have already discussed two obstacles to relying on personal judgment. First, there is the matter of protecting ourselves against moral mistakes. Individuals are not privileged sources of insight into the public good. Even people who are well educated and professionally trained are fallible, and this condition does not change when they enter public service. (Specifically, in this case, many wise observers share the view expressed by Randall Kennedy, that the troubled history of southern school desegregation provides no basis for self-satisfaction about the strategy chosen or for chastising others who favored other strategies.) [38] Accordingly, citizens have an interest in officials not acting on the basis of their idiosyncratic determination of the public good, for there is too much at stake.

Second, there is the moral consideration that even if sufficient knowledge and cognitive ability can be assumed, in a democracy one person's idea of the public good has no more standing than anyone else's. Thus, exploiting an official position to realize one's own particular idea of the good amounts to promoting a personal agenda. No official has a mandate for that.

The needed corrective to the personal point of view is public deliberation. Only judgments made under favorable institutional conditions, having withstood rigorous examination, can be considered reliable. There are no guarantees even then, of course, but public deliberation provides accountability, and the person who engages in good-faith deliberation is epistemically, as well as morally, responsible. Elman's deed, however, was designed to short-circuit established mechanisms of deliberation, which he deemed—plausibly, in my view—insufficient for the job of persuasion that was needed. He conversed with Frankfurter in secret. Is there any way for him to defend his determination of "the national interest" as a responsible act?

At a minimum, Elman could respond that public deliberation is not confined to government institutions. The failure of the Congress to act to end racial segregation, for example, was not decisive. Public deliberation occurs at many levels and in many settings throughout society; what occurs in the Congress is often only a pale, inadequate, and much delayed reflection of society's considered judgments. But what tests are available for building securely on public deliberation in the absence of governmental validation? Suppose there had existed widespread, even if not universal, public support for a change in constitutional principle, a kind of grassroots democratic mandate reflecting informal deliberation, which had not yet been expressed through official channels. Would that be sufficient support? Alternatively, suppose that public support was uncertain (but not clearly negative) and could reasonably have been anticipated to be favorable because of emergent opinion in influential elite groups such as the legal profession (in which, again, deliberation would have taken place)?

Obviously, the case for civil rights cannot depend on actual consent by a majority of citizens. Yet at some level there must be a connection to what any reasonable citizen would accept. Although there has always been some dissension concerning the wisdom of *Brown*, its status as the most important decision of the Supreme Court in the twentieth century—a "Himalayan fact," as Charles Fried calls it[39]—suggests that Elman may have met the burden of epistemic responsibility.

Assessing the means. Just as it is too easy for someone to overestimate the good to be realized, so it is too easy to underestimate the damage that will be done by the use of unethical means. Here, too, individual persons are not well positioned to judge, for the reasons I have identified.

This is especially true for a well-entrenched moral convention like the rule against ex parte communications. It is a central element of one of our most distinctive institutions. It is the outcome of reflection and mutual deliberation over many generations and even across cultures. It regulates one of the more constant and fundamental interests of citizens: to receive a fair hearing before an impartial tribunal in disputes with other citizens. Indeed, because the rule is so well entrenched and its moral status so fundamental, it seems reasonable to assume that its violation is likely to involve deep and unanticipated—and perhaps indiscernible—moral loss. In light of the epistemic incapacities of human beings, it is also reasonable to accord the rule such presumptive validity that anyone who proposes to violate it not only has a very heavy burden of argument, but also the burden is never entirely lifted even when the violation appears warranted. That, at least, would explain the intuition that any violation of the ex parte rule generates an ineradicable moral residue.

In general terms, we might conceive of entrenched moral conventions like the ex parte rule as remedies for problems of information faced by citizens who are not in a position to determine all the relevant consequences of their acts. (The illusion—engendered by philosophers and propagated by economists—is that a knowledgeable person could apply an algorithm to make the appropriate calculation. I do not understand Elman to have engaged in any such exercise, even tacitly.) Moreover, even if the existing moral conventions are not ideal, they are widely recognized and followed. We all know what they are and reasonably expect others to conform to them. If a single person violates a convention, other citizens have relied on it to their detriment. Epistemic cautions are therefore reinforced by fair play. For both reasons, we may say that entrenched moral conventions retain their force even when there are compelling reasons for violating them.

The result of these observations is that the presumption is so strongly against Elman's departure from the ex parte rule that it is difficult to see any moral space for defending his deed, even if we hold on to our recognition of the moral costs only by excusing it. My hypothesis is that the construction of a defense begins with the recognition that rules or rule formulations, no matter how wise and how enduring, are also fallible. Even if they are reliable in the general run of cases, they do not necessarily offer decisive guidance in extraordinary circumstances. At such moments, other capacities of individuals, besides the ability to follow a rule, must be brought to bear. These are second-order competences (or virtues) that enable people to recognize occasions when following rules has become problematic: they include reflectiveness, sympathy, and prudence. In a world of uncertainty and fortuitous happenstance, these competences are crucial to being an effective moral actor, and I believe that Philip Elman exhibited them in this case.[40]

NOTES

1. Kenneth I. Winston, "Teaching Ethics by the Case Method," a document written for (and available from) the Case Program at the John F. Kennedy School of Government, Harvard University (1995).

2. Robert Ames, *The Art of Rulership: A Study of Ancient Chinese Political Thought* (Albany: State University of New York Press, 1994), xxi.

3. 347 U.S. 483 (1954) [*Brown* I] and 349 U.S. 294 (1955) [*Brown* II].

4. Although it is flawed in places by partisan sniping, Lincoln Caplan offers an extended, lively, and informative account of the SG's office in his *The Tenth Justice: The Solicitor General and the Rule of Law* (New York:

Knopf, 1987). For an academic study, see Rebecca Mae Salokar, *The Solicitor General: The Politics of Law* (Philadelphia: Temple University Press, 1992).

5. For this apt formulation, see Philip Heymann, *The Politics of Public Management* (New Haven, Conn.: Yale University Press, 1987), 72.

6. William H. Harbaugh, *Lawyer's Lawyer: The Life of John W. Davis* (New York: Oxford University Press, 1973), 90.

7. Cornell W. Clayton, *The Politics of Justice: The Attorney General and the Making of Legal Policy* (Armonk, N.Y.: M. E. Sharpe, 1992), 60.

8. One of the most important segregation cases before *Brown* involved such a reversal. *Henderson v. U.S.,* 339 U.S. 816 (1950), challenged a ruling of the Interstate Commerce Commission (ICC) upholding segregation on trains traveling across state lines. Initially, the Justice Department argued the case on behalf of the ICC, but on appeal it "confessed error" and argued for the first time that the precedent case, *Plessy v. Ferguson,* 163 U.S. 537 (1896), should be overturned.

9. Richard Kluger, *Simple Justice: The History of Brown v. Board of Education and Black America's Struggle for Equality* (New York: Random House, 1975), 291.

10. This quotation is from Norman Silber, "The Solicitor General's Office, Justice Frankfurter, and Civil Rights Litigation, 1946–60: An Oral History," *Harvard Law Review* 100 (1987): 844. Much of the oral history is reprinted in John T. Noonan, Jr., and Kenneth I. Winston, eds., *The Responsible Judge: Readings in Judicial Ethics* (Westport, Conn.: Praeger, 1993), 67–84.

11. See n. 10.

12. Editorial, "With All Deliberate Impropriety," *New York Times,* March 24, 1987, A30.

13. Silber, "Oral History," 823, 828–29.

14. Kluger, *Simple Justice,* 593, 594.

15. Silber, "Oral History," 841 (italics added).

16. Ibid., 829 (italics added).

17. Ibid., 827, 829.

18. See Melvin I. Urofsky, *Louis D. Brandeis and the Progressive Tradition* (Boston: Little, Brown, 1981), 12, 65, 111–12.

19. Silber, "Oral History," 843.

20. Ibid., 835.

21. Kluger, *Simple Justice,* 650.

22. Alexander Bickel, *The Morality of Consent* (New Haven, Conn.: Yale University Press, 1975).

23. See Kenneth I. Winston, "Necessity and Choice in Political Ethics: Varieties of Dirty Hands," in Daniel E. Wueste, ed., *Professional Ethics and*

Social Responsibility (Lanham, Md: Rowman and Littlefield, 1994), 37–66.

24. Silber, "Oral History," 843.

25. Soren Kierkegaard, *Concluding Unscientific Postscript*, trans. David F. Swenson (Princeton, N.J.: Princeton University Press, 1941), 173–74. Kierkegaard discusses the story of Abraham and Isaac in *Fear and Trembling*, trans. Walter Lowrie (Princeton, N.J.: Princeton University Press, 1954).

26. Philip Selznick, *The Moral Commonwealth: Social Theory and the Promise of Community* (Berkeley and Los Angeles: University of California Press, 1992), 529–31.

27. The discussion in these paragraphs draws on my review essay "The Religious Convictions of Public Officials," *Canadian Journal of Law and Jurisprudence* 3 (1990): 129–43.

28. See Garry Wills, *Lincoln at Gettysburg: The Words That Remade America* (New York: Simon & Schuster, 1992), esp. chap. 3. Although Wills appreciates the distinction between public and private values in Lincoln's case, he fails to appreciate it in Mario Cuomo's case. See Garry Wills, "Mario Cuomo's Trouble with Abortion," *New York Review of Books* 37 (1990): 9–13.

29. For a general defense of this view, see Thomas Nagel, *Equality and Partiality* (New York: Oxford University Press, 1991), esp. chaps. 1 and 4–6.

30. Richard Neustadt, *Presidential Power and the Modern Presidents* (New York: Free Press, 1990), 38.

31. Thomas Nagel introduces the idea in "Ruthlessness in Public Life," in his *Mortal Questions* (Cambridge: Cambridge University Press, 1979), 85, and elaborates it in his *Equality and Partiality*.

32. Herbert Wechsler, "Some Issues for the Lawyer," in R. M. MacIver, ed., *Integrity and Compromise: Problems of Public and Private Conscience* (New York: Institute for Religious and Social Studies, 1957), 117–28, 124.

33. Ibid., 124.

34. See Arthur Applbaum, "Democratic Legitimacy and Official Discretion," *Philosophy and Public Affairs* 21 (1992): 248–49. Applbaum dubs this idea the "political realist" ethic. He argues that although there is some truth to it, we have defensible criteria for evaluating the moral acceptability of exercises of official discretion.

35. John Dewey, *Theory of Valuation* (Chicago: University of Chicago Press, 1939), 40ff. See also Dewey, "Means and Ends," in his *Their Morals and Ours* (New York: Pathfinder Press, 1973), 67–73.

36. On tragic choices, see Winston, "Necessity and Choice," 40–47. Since Elman's act does not involve inevitable wrongdoing, it falls outside the analysis offered by Christopher W. Gowans in *Innocence Lost: An*

Examination of Inescapable Moral Wrongdoing (New York: Oxford University Press, 1994).

37. The moral clarity of Machiavelli on this point exceeds that of most of his commentators. For example, in discussing the killing of Remus by Romulus, Machiavelli consistently employs the language of excuse, not justification. He says: "If [Romulus's] deed accuses him, its consequences excuse [*scusi*] him. . . . Romulus deserved to be pardoned [*scusa*] for the death of his brother. . . . Romulus should be forgiven [*iscusa*], not blamed." All these assertions take for granted that Romulus did something wrong. See chapter 9 of *The Discourses on Livy,* excerpted in David Wootton, trans. and ed., *Selected Political Writings* (Indianapolis: Hackett, 1994), 107–10. Even Michael Walzer—who in the opening sections of his famous essay on dirty hands recognizes the significance of Machiavelli's language of excuse—slides into the language of justification when he formulates the "Catholic" account of dirty hands, which he is inclined to favor. See Walzer, "Political Action: The Problem of Dirty Hands," reprinted in Marshall Cohen et al., eds., *War and Responsibility* (Princeton, N.J.: Princeton University Press, 1974), 62–82.

38. Randall Kennedy, "A Reply to Philip Elman," *Harvard Law Review* 100 (1987): 1947.

39. Charles Fried, *Order and Law: Arguing the Reagan Revolution* (New York: Simon & Schuster, 1991), 18.

40. I am indebted to Dean Judith Areen of the Georgetown University Law Center for access to the center's library while I was working on this chapter. For helpful comments on a previous draft, I am grateful to Cary Coglianese, Philip Selznick, Ian Shapiro, Dennis Thompson, and Michael Wald.

PART III

INTEGRITY AND CONSCIENCE IN THE LAW

9

CONSCIENCE AND THE LAW: LIBERAL AND DEMOCRATIC APPROACHES

DAVID DYZENHAUS

INTRODUCTION

The question "Is the law legitimate?" has become increasingly central to political philosophy in our secular and pluralistic age. Law may seem to offer a legitimate way of binding ourselves to a common order of values when appeals to transcendent moral standards or to tradition are generally regarded with suspicion. The question is, of course, also central to legal philosophy, in which it is often debated in rather technical terms.

In this chapter I show that a focus on the role of the individual conscience in legal order illuminates the question of the legitimacy of law in both legal and political philosophy. Our understanding of that role, of the appropriate moral reaction of the individual to the law, raises the question of the moral weight we should accord to the law even when we disagree with it. And this question draws attention to a prior question of whether law as such has moral weight, whatever its content.

As we will see, there are two perspectives of conscience in political philosophy, the liberal one that emphasizes the conscience of the judge and the democratic one that emphasizes the conscience of the citizen. To complicate things further, both the idea of "legitimacy" and the idea of "law" are inherently ambiguous, a problem fueling debates in legal philosophy between positivists and antipositivists.

In this chapter I also argue for the merits of an approach like Jürgen Habermas's to the legitimacy of law, one that is both antipositivist and democratic.[1] I start with a sketch of the positivist/antipositivist debate. I then set out some reasons for moving beyond what seems to be emerging as the dominant liberal account of the legitimacy of law. Finally, I describe an alternative Habermasian account to suggest why a democratic understanding of the role of conscience advances the debate about the legitimacy of law.

Positivists and Antipositivists on the Legitimacy of Law

Legitimacy can be taken to be legitimacy by virtue of what a group of people happen to believe is legitimate. Alternatively, it can mean legitimacy by virtue of the right standards, in which the quality of rightness, whatever its source, does not depend merely on the fact that a group of people happen to believe that the standards are right.

"Law" can mean positive law—the law of a jurisdiction that has been validly enacted, that is, enacted in accordance with this legal order's criteria for valid law.[2] We can also understand law from an antipositivist stance: Law is not limited to positive law, since it includes suprapositive standards that are necessarily part of the material of law. Their status as law is not dependent on either prior enactment or determinacy of content.

Contemporary legal positivists distance themselves from what they regard as crude positivistic command theories of law—theories that say that law is just the legally framed commands of an uncommanded commander.[3] They say that to understand law as command pure and simple is to miss out on its normative character. No legal order can be reduced to a set of commands that come with sanctions attached in case of disobedience. There are forms of law that are fundamentally important to any legal order, since they make legal order possible, but that are not commands. These forms prescribe what procedures must be followed for an act of lawmaking power to succeed in creating valid law. They can and often do exist in the absence of both prior enactment and sanctions for noncompliance. All that is needed for their existence is a settled practice of following them, a practice dependent in part on the continued acceptance of the forms by at least a core of key participants in legal practice.

Contemporary positivism holds, then, that law is normative at least in that a legal order requires some fundamental forms of law whose existence and efficacy must be partly explained by the fact of their acceptance as prescribing what one ought to do if one wishes to make law. Such a normative theory does concede that some legal standards do not depend for their existence on prior enactment and, furthermore, that they are standards of fundamental importance, since they prescribe the criteria for the validity of law. But this theory does not concede what legal positivists take to be crucial to an antipositivist position—that criteria of legal validity are necessarily also substantive moral constraints on political power.

Those who think that law is legitimate are generally antipositivists. They think that the suprapositive legal standards are also morally sound standards. The legitimacy of law stems thus from the influence of these standards on the positive law. But one can be a positivist and hold that law is legitimate. For example, one can hold that positive law is the only way of effectively establishing public and enforceable standards of collective life in the face of the fact that there are no standards of morality apart from what particular groups believe to be moral. Such a position was articulated by Thomas Hobbes, the founder of legal positivism, and similar positions on legitimacy and legality were put forward by Max Weber and Hans Kelsen.[4]

In general, though, contemporary positivists hold that positive law is never in itself legitimate because they also adhere to a separation thesis—that legitimacy is a matter of meeting moral standards that transcend both the positive law and what particular groups happen to believe is right. These standards are the standards of liberalism. Since many actual legal orders are profoundly illiberal, they are not legitimate.

It is this last fact that more than anything else bedevils the best-known challenge to legal positivism, Ronald Dworkin's interpretative theory of law.[5] Dworkin focuses on judges' ubiquitous reliance in interpretation on legal standards whose status as such does not depend on prior enactment. He also relies on the judicial sense that despite frequent controversy about the interpretation of these standards, there is in principle one right answer to questions of interpretation. Dworkin combines this focus with the striking claim that right answers at law generally coincide with the prescriptions of liberalism.[6] The rule of law is rule in accordance with liberal values, and he gives pride of place to the conscience of the individual judge in deciding whether a particular law does in fact so accord.

Positivists are generally regarded as having had the better of this debate. They share with Dworkin the view that the standards of legitimacy are not just what people happen to believe but, rather, the standards of liberalism. They also share the view that the judicial conscience should be informed by liberal values. But sheer facts of the matter about illiberal legal orders seem to show that any connection between law and legitimacy is contingent on a legal order's being part of a liberal political culture.

In sum, it is the separation thesis that legal positivists take to be crucial to their position and not the claim that there are legal standards, even fundamental ones, that have that status despite never having been enacted. Indeed, the debate between the positivists and Dworkin has hardly focused on the standards providing the criteria for the validity of law but has instead concentrated on the substantive moral standards—which Dworkin calls *principles*— that inform judicial interpretation. Here, too, the positivists have been willing to concede the existence of such standards. But again, they claim that the substance of the standards is contingent on the political culture in which the particular legal order is situated. If the political culture is a wicked one, that will be reflected in the law of that jurisdiction, and hence conscientious judges might have to lie about the law if they are to be true to liberalism.[7]

One result of this positivist reaction to Dworkin's challenge is that the possibility that it is legal form rather than moral substance that makes law legitimate has hardly received attention. But before I offer reasons to focus on form, I want to show why legal positivism seems to play an ever more important role in the debate about the legitimacy of law.

LIBERALISM, LEGITIMACY, AND DEMOCRACY

As we have seen, liberal philosophers can hold either positivist or antipositivist positions on the nature of law while agreeing that the legitimacy of law depends on the law's coincidence with the standards of liberal morality. Recently, many liberal philosophers have chosen a kind of legal positivism.[8] Their position is the result of their "discovery" that it is the *political* morality of liberalism on which the legitimacy of law depends and to which the judicial conscience owes its allegiance.

The most prominent elaboration of this idea is John Rawls's *Political Liberalism.*[9] He defends liberalism on the basis that it stakes out the terrain of politics in a manner that can command an "overlapping consensus" in the liberal democratic societies of the West.[10]

Political liberals recognize that their societies are in fact deeply divided on many important issues. They are troubled by the divisions because these might contain the seeds of violent conflicts like the great religious wars of the past. Hence liberal philosophers have posed for themselves the question of how stability is possible for a liberal society. Their answer is to have liberalism retreat to a plateau of consensus on fundamental political principles. Because of the controversial nature of any liberal idea of the good life for the individual—Kant's idea of autonomy or Mill's idea of individualism—political liberals think that the plateau must exclude such liberal ideas as well as more obvious candidates for exclusion, for example, religious doctrines that aspire to state enforcement. All such ideas are part of, in Rawls's terminology, comprehensive positions whose comprehensiveness is marked by the assertion that the particular vision of the good life articulated is the true or right way to live. Since there cannot be consensus about such matters, they, and all other comprehensive positions, are to be barred from the terrain of politics.[11]

Once the politics of a society have been purified of the truth claims of comprehensive positions, that society can be said to be neutral between different comprehensive positions. Neutrality does not mean here that the society takes no moral stand. Its moral stand is to ensure neutrality. Nor does it mean that all comprehensive positions will be on a level playing field. Those who wish their comprehensive positions to win political influence must be "contained." And even if those who hold antipluralist positions do not strive for political power, they will nevertheless find their positions undermined by the public culture of coexistence with a plurality of different comprehensive positions. All that neutrality means is that political power cannot be enlisted in support of a comprehensive position.[12]

A society that is neutral in this way is a legitimate one. However, Rawls does not stop at the equation of neutrality with legitimacy. In his quest for stability, he also claims that one can reasonably expect endorsement by the citizenry of a society ordered on these lines. The "liberal principle of legitimacy" is that "our exercise of political power is fully proper only when it is exercised in accordance with a constitution the essentials of which all citizens as free and equal may be reasonably expected to endorse in the light of principles and ideals acceptable to their common human reason."[13]

The idea of reasonableness here is ambiguous. Is it that citizens are expected to endorse a constitution because its values are justified values? Or is reasonable to expect endorsement because most citizens already accept the values?

Rawls clearly does not want to rest his theory on the contingent fact that the values are already accepted. Even though such a fact makes credible the claim that there will be stability, it seems to reduce the idea of justice to whatever values are widely accepted in a society and thus promise a basis for stability. Such a basis would be a mere modus vivendi, a contingently overlapping area of agreement.

Rawls rejects the modus vivendi basis partly because he wants ongoing stability and he is rightly doubtful about the staying power of values that we happen to hold in common here and now. The stability of such values depends on our not changing our minds. The values of the overlapping consensus must therefore exhibit the justificatory structure required by the liberal principle of legitimacy. They must appeal to the common reason of free and equal citizens.[14] So Rawls wants to say that political liberalism is justified on moral grounds and that is why it is reasonable to expect endorsement.

But the justification is not offered to the free and equal citizens of a democracy for their deliberation and decision. Rather, the justification tells us the limits to which free and equal citizens, who are also reasonable by the lights of political liberalism, will agree to in advance of deliberation.

Notice that these limits are political limits on deliberation in the public realm only in that they limit the decision-making power of democratic assemblies. The limits do not apply to the private realm or, as Rawls calls it now, the *social realm.*[15] Political liberals recognize, of course, that standard liberal freedoms, especially the freedoms of speech and association, must permit public, political advocacy of comprehensive positions. Day-to-day politics should not, indeed, cannot be purified by curtailing these freedoms. Rather, the purity of politics is ensured by having in place a constitution that requires neutrality and a supreme court that can test legislation for its conformity to neutrality, as understood by political liberals. Individuals can debate with one another whatever they like, but the state may not enforce any view that rests on a comprehensive position.

The limits of public reason are not, then, limits on what citizens can debate but on what conclusions can be legitimately enforced. They are limits on deliberation only in the sense that the test of legitimacy for the results of public debate is whether those results can be justified by public reason—by a process of deliberation that remains within the bounds of the overlapping consensus. Put differently, political liberalism sets the limits of democracy, and judges police those limits.[16]

As Charles Larmore, who coined the term *political liberalism,* put it:

> The liberal freedoms set limits to democratic government, and in
> particular to the form it usually takes, majority rule. Nor is this
> ranking a mere makeshift. On the contrary, democracy is made
> subordinate to liberal principles precisely because the value of
> democratic institutions is held to lie chiefly, if not exclusively, in
> their being the best *means for guaranteeing* liberal freedoms.[17]

To those who do not accept these limits, Rawls's answer is, it seems, that the values of political liberalism are simply so great, so important, that they have been taken "once and for all" off the political agenda. The values are the ones to which we are already committed, as is evidenced in our practices, including our law. So all we can do in the face of fundamental challenge is to assert their truth.[18]

In sum, the position of political liberalism on both law and democracy is that these are instrumental to the values of political liberalism.[19] To those who disagree, the answer is that they will find themselves outside the limits of the law, and therefore of political society, as it is.

This position has two curious features. First, its strength is meant to consist of the retreat to the plateau of values that no reasonable individual could contest. But since reasonableness is defined by agreement with those values, the population of the unreasonable sorts includes not only fundamentalists who wish to establish their doctrines politically but also liberals who think that comprehensive liberal doctrines should influence public policy. It also includes gays and lesbians who want public affirmation of the worth of their sexual orientation. All these people are unreasonable just because they want their particular comprehensive position to be given weight in public decisions.

Finally, political liberalism seems to refuse quite arbitrarily to take the next step that libertarian liberals think is required if liberalism is to retreat to a plateau of political consensus. Libertarians say that the great controversies about state involvement in the distribution of wealth show that a retreat from state involvement in such distribution is required for the sake of neutrality. They often offer as the reason for the state's not being involved in wealth distribution that distributive schemes are always premised on comprehensive positions. But political liberals are content to leave the issue of wealth distribution to politics.[20]

In short, political liberalism is puzzling because the values about which it claims consensus and that form the basis for its neutrality are both controversial and partisan.[21]

It is perhaps because of this first feature that a second curious feature arises. At least in the political culture of liberal democracies, political liberalism seems to be committed to a kind of positivism regarding both morality and the law. It is committed to a kind of positivism regarding morality because its answer to those who disagree with the way in which it limits democracy is simply to assert that the values of political liberalism are in fact the values of our political order. And it is committed to a positivism regarding the law because it is also asserted that the prime site of these values is in the Constitution that our founding fathers, as a matter of fact, gave us.[22]

Political liberalism, then, retreats to a kind of positivist position regarding morality and law in the face of fundamental challenge. But the positivist position to which it retreats is one that claims legitimacy for the law—the law of that particular society. The legitimacy that it claims is the legitimacy of a match between the values of the overlapping consensus and the values contained in the (constitutional) law of the society. The judicial conscience is then given pride of place in liberal legal theory because it is judges who are the guardians of the liberal political morality already contained in their law.

This second feature is curious only in that a position that was first articulated by Ronald Dworkin as an antipositivist position turns out to be a positivist one, after all. This will hardly seem to be a surprising turn to many positivists, who thought all along that Dworkin's position concealed a positivism in regard to American constitutional law. They always thought that his position depended on a claim that the values of fundamental law more or less coincided with what he understood to be sound political morality, a claim that was plausible as a matter of fact about the American legal order.

HABERMAS ON THE DEMOCRATIC FORM OF LAW

Habermas thinks that political liberalism is too ambitious because it draws the limits of legitimate democratic debate much too tightly. He also says that it is not ambitious enough in that it makes its justificatory claims too contingent on context and culture.[23] My interpretation of political liberalism supports his suggestion. Indeed, I suggested earlier that the excess of contingency (or positivism) is political liberalism's way of dealing with the fact that the consensus it claims is so contested.

Habermas's own account of the legitimacy of law looks to the form of law to establish a connection between law and morality. To disinter that account is no easy task, but its important message is that law's form imposes a logic on the exercise of political power that secures both the public and the private autonomy of the citizen. For Habermas, there is no rivalry between public and private autonomy because they are "co-original." To disinter that account also is no easy task, and I suspect that Habermas lacks an argument at one of the most crucial points in his book, a point to which I will return later.

The thesis of co-originality seems to mean at least the following.[24] First, there is a claim that is both conceptual and historical. It is that the ideas arise at the same time that we as individuals are authors of our moral values and that we have to decide collectively what these values are. They arise when each individual is thought to be the best final arbiter of moral values, but it is also recognized that people have to decide together on the terms of a common life.

With these ideas, there arises the view that positive law is the mechanism for making the results of collective reason public in a way that can ensure general compliance. Positive law is necessary to compensate for what Habermas calls the "deficits" of reason regarding morality under conditions in which no individual, or group of individuals, can be said to have unique access to the truth about morality.[25] In addition, sound moral rules do not on their own attract general compliance. Positive law is a necessary complement to morality because it provides a mechanism for both settling the content of morality and ensuring compliance with that content. But Habermas is anxious to emphasize that the practical necessity of positive law does not supply us with its justification. Positive law is justified when, and only when, it respects the equal moral status of public and private autonomy. Law must, as Habermas frequently says, respect the individual in his or her dual role as both the addressee and the author of positive law.

A second respect in which public and private autonomy appear to be co-original has to do with Habermas's list of basic categories of rights that must exist under the rule of law. He stipulates that all those rights that protect the sphere of private autonomy— rights against the state—are rights that we must collectively agree on. They are therefore, he says, the product of an exercise of public autonomy. Similarly, it seems that the rights of public autonomy—rights of participation in the political process—are also rights that must be produced through an exercise of public autonomy that is legitimate, that is, that does not infringe on private autonomy.[26] In making this claim, Habermas is also asserting that there is no "competition" between public autonomy and private autonomy,[27] and I suggest later that this part of his position must be rejected.

Habermas signals clearly, however, that even a legitimate exercise of public autonomy does not conclude the question of the citizen's obligation to obey the law. He wants to preserve some distinction between law and morality. Positive law is legitimate when it is appropriately produced, not when it has a particular content. There is a general duty of obedience to the law, but citizens need not regard themselves duty bound because the particular law is, by definition, morally sound. They need only have "insight" into what makes legal order as a whole legitimate—that is, their own rights of potential participation in the production of law, which also secure their opportunity to participate in changing the law. Indeed, Habermas reserves for citizens the right in the last resort to decide whether or not to obey on a purely utilitarian basis. That is, citizens must weigh the moral worth of obedience in general against what they perceive to be the immorality of a particular law.[28]

This distinction between law and morality—one that says that morality provides us with external standards to judge the legitimacy of the positive law—reproduces rather than challenges the positivist separation thesis.[29] If Habermas is to establish an antipositivist position, he must show some other connection between law and morality.

Habermas does not take the Dworkinian route to an antipositivist position, one that looks to judicial reliance on moral principles embedded in the law. Although he is willing to give adjudication an important place in the legal order, he wants to confine the judicial role as far as is possible to the application of the law. For him, the distinction between the justification and the application of the law is central to the legal order and to the separation of powers among the legislature, the judiciary, and the administration.[30] The statute for him is the "hinge" between the legislature and the administration that implements the legislature's decisions.[31] For administrative power to be exercised legitimately, it must be bound to the law, which means to the application of the law. The reason that judges have an important role in the legal order is that the judiciary supplies to *citizens* the mechanisms that ensure that officials will be kept within the bounds of the law.

Habermas does concede that this idea of the separation of powers cannot be institutionalized in watertight compartments. Because of the complexity of the administrative state, statutes must be concretized by both the judiciary and the administration, which means that neither can avoid the task of justification.[32]

His point seems to be that when justification is at issue, when a decision has to be made about the content of a statute, that decision must be made as democratically as possible by allowing for full participation by the parties affected by it. The judge, whether it be the judge of a superior court or of an administrative tribunal, has a special role in this, in that he or she should bring to adjudication an impartial perspective. The judge must reach beyond the parties' immediate articulation of their interests and consider the coherence of the pertinent legal materials as well as the interests of the audience beyond the courtroom.[33]

Habermas explicitly distances himself from what he regards as a misguided positivist quest for certainty through the determinacy of statute law. It is not that he thinks that certainty is without value. But he suggests that his understanding of law achieves certainty in two other respects.[34]

First, even though legal subjects might not have the certainty of knowing the content of the law in advance of an authoritative interpretation, they do have the certainty of knowing that this content will be determined in accordance with the appropriate procedures. Second, there is a certainty that results if we move away from Dworkin's monological or individualistic understanding of interpretation to an understanding of how paradigmatic understandings of law influence judges collectively and stabilize judicial interpretation.

Habermas identifies two main legitimate contenders for such judicial paradigms—the liberal and the welfarist paradigms. Both, he thinks, are legitimate bases for interpreting the law's promise of equality. They are legitimate precisely because they are conceptions of what it takes to be a free and equal citizen of a legal community. But even though both are legitimate bases for interpretation, the liberal and the welfarist paradigms cannot have the exclusive status to which each has historically aspired, for each undermines what it seeks to achieve if it establishes itself as unique.

The liberal paradigm is problematic because in seeking to give private autonomy priority over public autonomy, it tends to understand the equality of law in a way that obscures factual inequalities between individuals. The welfarist paradigm is premised on the legitimacy of the state's delivering factual equality to all legal subjects. But it neglects to take into account the way in which such delivery can destroy private autonomy through the paternalistic creation of clientlike individual dependence on complex bureaucracies.

Habermas does not want to subvert these paradigms, only to challenge any claim by each to being the exclusive paradigm for a democratic society. Like any other substantive set of values concerning how society should be governed, they must be subject to the procedural testing necessary when judges apply statutes to particular contexts. Although the paradigm that should govern is the procedural one, it does not govern substantively, only by putting into play those values that are legitimate candidates for stabilizing judicial interpretation.

It is this procedural paradigm that Habermas believes will ignite the "motor" of legal development—the dialectic between the promise of equality made by the law and the factual equality of its addressees.[35] The law's promise of equality before itself is more than a promise of formal equality. It is a promise of substantive equality for all legal subjects in both the private and the public aspects of their autonomy. The particular contribution of the procedural paradigm is to highlight the way in which that content can be given only by discourse or deliberation.

Habermas's thought seems to be that the procedural paradigm deals with the tension between the liberal and welfarist paradigms by putting that tension into play within the legal order. It also takes account of the fact that our best access to an understanding of that tension is the experience of those directly affected by particular legislation. If we wish to know how a statutory regime that promotes equality affects the freedom of an individual or how a statutory regime that protects individual freedom sustains factual inequality, we must find out from those directly affected.[36]

Just as Habermas wants legislation to reflect a public debate in which participants bring their particular experience to bear on the issue, so he also wants the legislative outcomes of such a debate to be tested by the same kind of debate. Hence we start with a deliberation that happens first in the "weak" public sphere of general public debate and then makes its way into the "strong" public sphere of political parties and the legislature. Once enacted, legislation is then concretized through further debate, initiated in the judicial context, which should keep the legislation constantly responsive to public experience. In the most dramatic cases, the weak public sphere can be directly involved with the question of the legitimacy of particular laws when citizens find themselves driven to civil disobedience after failing to be satisfied by both the judicial and legislative response to their criticism.[37]

It is this emphasis on deliberation and debate that most crucially distinguishes Habermas from the political liberals. Political liberals want a political culture disciplined by public reason and thus by a *culture of neutrality*. Democracy is for them instrumental to this culture. Habermas wants democracy not for instrumental reasons but because it is only democratic institutions that can sustain a *culture of justification*.[38]

We might then say that for Habermas, democracy is instrumental to justification, but in Habermas's case, this is a trite use of the word *instrumental*. There cannot be a set of institutions superior to democracy for realizing a culture of justification, since democracy and justification are internally related. To favor democracy is to think that the way to decide on the terms of collective life is through citizens engaging in a process of justifying to one another what they hold to be right. And to institutionalize a process of mutual justification is to adopt democratic institutions.[39]

Habermas argues that it is appropriate in a culture of justification to entrench rights constitutionally that judges can use both to give content to legislation and to test its validity.[40] In a culture of justification, such rights not only are legitimate but also can be necessary components of the culture. They are legitimate insofar as they express the constitutional responsibilities of legislators to justify their legislation to free and equal citizens. They are necessary if in their absence, citizens do not have the legal mechanisms they need to ensure that the law is indeed justified to them. Thus Habermas takes pains to emphasize that law must be enforceable, which means that his conception of law as the product of deliberation must be enforceable. This requires that all those rights necessary to sustain deliberation be constitutionally entrenched.[41]

It is important to note that Habermas does not want those rights taken off the political agenda in the "once and for all" way that political liberals generally suggest.[42] Those rights are fixed points of reference, but they have a contestable content in the unfinished project that any constitution is.[43] That is, over time, they will be given—or saturated with—content by both legislation and judicial interpretation; their content can and should change in the light of experience.

Habermas also does not think that judicial review can be confined to some pure idea of deliberative democracy, as suggested by John Hart Ely.[44] Ely argues that the essence of democracy—and the proper scope of constitutional concern—is keeping open the channels of political representation and accountability. But as Habermas suggests, the idea of deliberative democracy must be given different concrete expression in different places and at different times in the same place. And it is legitimate for the courts to exercise their powers of review in terms of the current ideas of content, with the proviso that they are open to challenges to that content. Thus Habermas's conception of deliberative democracy is not troubled, as is Ely's, by the obvious fact that constitutional or other legal rights must be given a substantive (and hence controversial) content.[45]

But as we have seen, Habermas contends that the idea of law to which judges should be faithful is the procedural one inherent in a culture of justification, in which the only real certainty is that law will be produced in accordance with deliberative procedures. And as we have also seen, his only other candidates for certainty—the stabilizing paradigms of liberalism and welfarism—must be somewhat destabilized so that they can be judicially tested in the process of interpretation. Thus his position should not permit any strict distinction between justification and application, since application of the law is not application of the content of the law, but of the idea of legality or of procedural law.

Recall that Dworkin's theory of adjudication starts by rejecting the position that the only law that judges have to apply is positive law. Dworkin argues that judges are obligated to apply the content of the wider law, the law that includes certain moral principles. We saw that Dworkin seems to end up with a positivist position, since he claims that the principles of the wider law coincide with the requirements of liberal morality. It follows that the judicial obligation is to apply the principles of political liberalism.

Habermas's legal theory frees judges from this obligation. He might then seem to give judges even more freedom than Dworkin does, thereby placing them firmly at the center of philosophy of law. But by requiring judges to apply a procedural understanding of law, Habermas commits them to try to understand their institutional place as well as the institutional place of others in the legal order. That is, by requiring that judges attend to the institutional structure of their legal order as well as to its substantive moral commitments, Habermas invites them to ask themselves more complex questions in adjudication than does Dworkin. Those questions require judges to think of themselves first and foremost as part of a democratic legal order rather than as the guardians of liberal morality.[46]

In sum, Habermas's route to an antipositivist position is different from Dworkin's in at least three respects. First, his argument for the legitimacy of law does not depend on judicial reliance on suprapositive standards but, rather, on forms of law fundamental to the legal order. Second, in his view, the test of legitimacy is not a coincidence between the substance of positive law and the standards of liberalism. Instead, legitimacy resides in how the forms of law enable the production of moral standards. Third, Habermas gives priority to democracy over liberalism. His argument for the legitimacy of law is that the forms of law fundamental to the legal order are inherently democratic. The rule of law for him is the rule of democratically produced law. It follows for him that judicial fidelity to law must take account of the democratic form of law in a way that demotes the individual conscience of the judge from the central role it has in Dworkin's theory. Habermas's guardian of the law is the individual conscience of the citizen.

THE POLITICS OF JUSTIFICATION

Both the democratic and the liberal sides in the debate about the appropriate vision of political and legal order acknowledge that they share much,[47] and this fact makes it in some respects more difficult—in some, easier—to make progress in the debate between them. It is easier because the common ground offers points of contact on which comparisons can be made. It is more difficult because the differences are highly nuanced, often seeming to amount to a difference in degree of commitment rather than to different commitments.

Consider, for example, the commitment of political liberals to democracy.[48] Fearful of the consequences of too much democracy, they instrumentalize democracy in order to contain it. But I suggest that this tactic creates tension in the universe of political liberalism. Isaiah Berlin remarked in his famous lecture on the liberal conception of liberty, that it is

> principally concerned with the area of control, not with its source. Just as a democracy may, in fact, deprive the individual citizen of a great many liberties that he might have in some other form of society, so it is perfectly conceivable that a liberal-minded despot would allow his subjects a large measure of personal freedom. . . . Freedom in this sense is not, at any rate logically, connected with democracy or self-government.[49]

Implicit in Berlin's remark is a distinction of great significance—the distinction between the citizen and the subject, between the citizen who has the right to participate in political deliberation and decision making on fundamental matters and the passive subject who is content merely to receive his due. If all that matters is the size and stability of the space of liberty, then citizenship is, for political liberals, a purely instrumental good in just the way that democracy is.

But it is also the case that political liberalism has placed much more emphasis on the citizen and on democracy than has the liberalism that Berlin describes. Indeed, sometimes political liberals argue for a reconciliation of liberalism and democracy. They contend that liberal values do not so much impose constraints on democracy as make democracy possible.[50]

The instrumentalist view of democracy and the view that liberalism makes democracy possible are not easily reconciled, and so they seem to express a dilemma in political liberalism, one that it resolves in favor of the instrumental view. Political liberalism, that is, opts for liberalism over democracy. Hence, what might seem to be a difference in degree of commitment between democrats and liberals turns out to be a significant difference regarding the legitimate scope of democratic reason.

At the end of the day, political liberals avoid dealing with this issue because they refrain from offering a full justification for their position, one that makes an argument for its truth. Rather, they simply rest their case on the claim that what democracy means is democracy constrained by an overlapping consensus on liberal political values.

It is because political liberalism declines to offer a full justification for itself that Habermas maintains that it is not ambitious enough. His own remedy is a theory of intersubjective communication in which he claims to have proved that participants in communication are necessarily committed to certain normative principles. A large part of his *Between Facts and Norms* is dedicated to showing how these principles necessarily issue in democratic commitments that are in turn institutionalized in the legal order of the *Rechtsstaat* (state bound by the rule of law).[51]

This kind of move is also an avoidance, however. It is a way of escaping political debate, including the debates of political philosophy. Habermas's theory of communication is complex and philosophically contentious. He thinks that we need a kind of transcendental grounding in morals or politics,[52] that is, that we need a theory that stands outside politics yet provides the basis for politics. Even though *Between Facts and Norms* does not defend the theory so much as it tries to apply it, Habermas's desire for necessity and transcendental presuppositions plagues every step of his attempt to derive the legal institutions of democracy. In particular, the unsatisfactory account of his thesis of the co-originality of public and private autonomy—indeed, his failure to provide an argument for the co-originality thesis—results, I suggest, from his faith that somehow we will just see the necessity of the thesis.

I want to offer an alternative to Habermas's transcendentalism, a democratic account of the legitimacy of law that is thoroughly internal in that it at no time steps outside our political and legal practices. I refer to this alternative as the *internal account.*[53]

Habermas would, of course, reject the internal account as too modest. If we seek to justify our practices by standards internal to them, at best the justification is parochial and at worst circular, but in either case, it leads to quietism and conservatism. We need therefore to find some device to underwrite or legitimize our political traditions from without.

The internal account holds that Habermas's concerns are misplaced. An immanent approach seems too modest only in contrast to a project that is fundamentally misconceived. There is nowhere to go beyond our practices to underwrite them, so any seemingly transcendental justification is really an internalist one that does not understand itself. All the justification we need can be found from within, if only the practice of immanent justification is properly understood and if we are both vigorously critical of our practices and sufficiently imaginative about how they might be transformed. We cannot prove beyond a doubt, with necessity or whatever, that certain norms must govern our practices. What we can do is modify these practices as best we know how, paying careful attention to the requirements of experience and our existing norms.

I do not want to go further here into the philosophical complexity of these debates. Instead, I want to sketch two reasons to prefer the internal account to both Habermas's transcendentalism and political liberalism's stand on an alleged overlapping consensus. The first reason speaks to the point just made, that an internal account can be both an account of our traditions and a resource for their enlightened transformation. This reason then shades into the second, which pertains to positive differences that the account can make in our understanding of politics and in our actual practices and institutions.

The internal account of the Western legal tradition goes roughly like this: Liberals found in law an instrument with the potential to guarantee the rights of the individual against absolutist rulers. The institutional mechanism that law offered was one binding the ruler to the positive law. But if the ruler had unfettered discretion as to the content of the positive law, law would

provide no substantive moral guarantee, so liberals made the
further demand that the law be the product of an assembly whose
legitimacy resided in its representation of the people. The legitimacy of the law, in other words, came to reside in the accountability of legislators to the people.

The liberal demand, one that made a pact with democratic
forces, issued in a successful attempt to shift power from absolutist
rulers to democratically elected assemblies. But then liberals were
faced with the problem that such assemblies might enact policies
that contradicted liberal ideas of what was legitimate.

So liberals tried to find arguments that would show why acting
democratically was necessarily acting in accordance with liberal
standards. Political liberalism can be seen as just the latest in the
line of such attempts, all of which try to limit the development of
democratic responsiveness and accountability to the people. But
these attempts are out of step with the Western legal tradition, if
that tradition is seen as one in which law is primarily the guaran-
tor of political accountability rather than of particular conceptions of individual rights. I want to suggest why it is sound to
adopt this view of the Western legal and political tradition, in part
by revisiting the debate about the legitimacy of law outlined at the
outset of this chapter.

Recall that the liberal antipositivist account of the legitimacy of
law has difficulty coping with the fact of illiberal legal orders.
Indeed, I argued that liberal antipositivists show signs of dropping
their antipositivism in a bid to defend the values of political
liberalism. In contrast, the internal democratic account of the
legitimacy of law can plausibly argue that to the extent that a
society governs itself through the medium of a legal order, we will
find at least traces of the accountability of the ruler to the ruled.
To that extent, the legal order is legitimate.

Such accountability is found in merely the existence of positive
law as the form that political policy must adopt. Positive law is
both highly visible and establishes a standard to which those with
power can be called to account. Even here, we can see that the
existence of positive law is linked to its justification—visibility
plus accountability. These are links that creep into the accounts
of law of even such uncompromising advocates of political abso-
lutism as Thomas Hobbes. As the idea of what ensures account-

ability changes, so will ideas of what legal institutions are required and thus of what the fundamental forms of law are. But such ideas are always linked to the substantive principles that legal forms are meant to serve.

This last claim is, of course, denied by contemporary Anglo-American legal positivists who try, via the separation thesis, to sever moral substance from form. They do so in part because they suggest that the separation thesis has a moral payoff—it enables the individual citizen to decide on the merits of the law free from the constraints of an ideology that holds that law is legitimate. The separation thesis, that is, facilitates conscientious judgment by the good liberal citizen.[54] They also argue for the separation thesis on a theoretical ground: the generality of their legal theory, one capable of understanding the legal order in a way that sheds light on actual legal orders, since the theory does not equate legal order with the instantiation of a particular set of moral values.[55]

In contrast to positivists, the internal account does argue for the legitimacy of law. And in contrast to political liberals such as Dworkin and Rawls, it does not equate the legitimacy of law with the instantiation of any particular set of moral values, although its thesis concerning the legitimacy of law does rest on a connection between law and morality. The moral value that it says law serves is the value of collective self-government—of citizens deciding together on the terms of their common life, subject always to the proviso that the terms will require revision in the light of experience. Different actual legal orders can then be compared on a common measure—the extent to and manner in which they secure, in Lon L. Fuller's words, the "interplay of purposive orientations between citizens and government."[56]

With Habermas, the internal account of the legitimacy of law does not hold that there is an unconditional obligation of obedience to law. The conscientious citizen is the guardian of legitimacy, but the conscientious citizen is first and foremost a democrat, not a liberal.[57] The democratic citizen, faced with a clash between positive law and the dictates of her conscience, accords proper weight to the law in deciding how to resolve the clash. This requires taking into account her democratic responsibilities, including her responsibility to attend to the extent to which the law is the product of a properly functioning democratic legal order. And this brings into question the extent to which the institutions of her legal order are in fact answerable to her in ways that mark her not as a mere addressee of the law—the subject of the law—but as a citizen or author of the law. That is, the internal account brings into question the institutional adequacy of the status quo from the citizen's perspective.

Thus far I have set out the first reason to prefer the internal account—it provides an immanent justification for democratic legal order, one that works entirely in our legal and political traditions. It is at this stage that the first reason starts to shade into a second, which has to do with the way that the account submits itself to politics in a way that makes it very different from political liberalism. At the same time as it makes a stand on its truth, it commits that truth to debate in politics as well as questioning, if need be, the ways in which existing institutions set limits to and structure public reason. If law is to be legitimate, legal institutions must do more than facilitate the debate involving truth claims that political liberalism seeks to screen out through the discipline of public reason. These institutions must be submitted to the kind of questioning from within that can lead to changes in the ways in which the institutions set the limits of public reason.

In taking this last step, the internal account provides a fuller justification than does the one offered by political liberalism. For even though political liberalism declares itself to be political and "not metaphysical,"[58] to offer no arguments other than political ones for its conception of legitimate politics, it does not remain true to that declaration. Rather, it seeks to bury its truth claims, revealing them only when fundamentally challenged. This tells us, as I have suggested, that the declaration requires the impossible. Political liberalism, or any political position, must both make clear its truth claims and be prepared to debate them in politics. Habermas at times seems to want to take the same step as the internal account. But he in effect finds himself in the same position as political liberalism because his theory of communication also amounts to an attempt to shield the truth of his theory from politics.

Consider, for example, debates about limits on freedom of expression in which groups argue for either limits on pornographic expression in the cause of the equality of women or limits on racist expression in the cause of the equality of ethnic minorities.[59] I am not concerned here with the pros and cons of these arguments, only with a feature of the arguments when they are indeed based on equality-seeking grounds rather than on social conservativism or fundamentalism.

I am concerned (at least for the moment) with only those limitations on expression whose justification invokes the following basis: The limitation is necessary to remedy inequalities that restrict the opportunities of those in the groups targeted by the expression to participate as equals in the social and political life of their societies. Political liberals regard such limitations as constitutionally illegitimate, since they allege that a right to complete freedom of expression is one of the values of the overlapping consensus.[60] And they, of course, have the constitutional doctrine of the U.S. Supreme Court on their side in this regard.

As a matter of political argument, however, the exclusion is most arbitrary, if only for the reason that those who find themselves outside this overlapping consensus base their claims on values that the consensus is supposed to secure—the freedom and equality of all citizens. And if constitutional doctrine is uncontroversially on the side of political liberalism in this regard, this positivist "fact of the matter" speaks more to the inadequacy of the doctrine and its institutional backdrop than to the merits of the exclusion. To press things even further, the fact might highlight that arguments about social equality are likely to be given little weight in a political culture that wants to set the limits of public reason by consensus.

In contrast, Canada's Supreme Court has found legitimate the legislative limitations on racist expression[61] and pornographic expression,[62] with a necessary condition of that legitimacy being the limitations' equality-seeking structure. But that could happen in part because in its very first section, the Canadian Charter of Rights and Freedoms expressly permits limits on the rights and freedoms it enumerates when the limits are "reasonable," "prescribed by law," and "can be demonstrably justified in a free and democratic society." In permitting such limits, the Canadian Constitution expands the limits of public reason even as it permits limitations on the freedom of expression. To do this, it opens the determination of the limits of public reason to a process of democratic justification quite alien to political liberalism.[63]

It is no accident that a constitution with this kind of structure was the one adopted in Canada in 1982, since Canada was then socially far to the left of the United States (and remains so despite a recent and sharp swing to the right). In permitting the democratic process to play a role in determining the content of the very rights that a society needs to guarantee if it is to be democratic, the Canadian Constitution accepts controversy as part of the debate even about the most fundamental terms of political life. It is thus closer in spirit to the internal account of the legitimacy of law. Since we can plausibly claim that dissensus, even about fundamentals, is a fact of political life—and a healthy one—here the internal account has the advantage over political liberalism and Habermas, since both make a fetish of consensus.[64]

Political liberalism does so by alleging that we need a consensus only about the basic terms of public debate, one that is suspect because it turns out that the terms are highly exclusionary. Habermas commits the opposite error. He is prepared to call consensual, and thus legitimate, anything that survives the institutional mechanisms of democratic debate.[65]

Notice, however, that the internal account does not conceive of politics as a normative free-for-all. Put differently, it does place limits on public reason. For example, a group that argues on conservative or fundamentalist grounds for limits on the freedom of expression or that seeks to get enacted racist or misogynist policies will not find that the internal account gives the stamp of validity to its legislation merely because that legislation has survived democratic procedures. This legislation will still, assuming a system of constitutional judicial review, have to survive judicial review.[66] And the internal account will say that a court should declare invalid the legislation limiting constitutional rights when the legislation does not meet a necessary condition for legitimacy—that it has what I called an equality-seeking structure.

The internal account must, that is, concede that democracy needs to guarantee individual rights, including the right to participate in politics. It must also concede that these rights are part of the parcel of the individual's rights first identified by liberalism. But it need not concede the correctness of particular liberal positions on the content of those rights. Indeed, a democrat should be committed to making the issue of content—and thus to some extent the issue of what democratic rights are—one that falls within the scope of democratic deliberation. For the internal account, it follows that constitutions that either explicitly or by interpretation do freeze the content of such rights are undemocratic. But as I have suggested, the account is still committed to the view that public reason does set limits.

I believe that the democratic trust in deliberation marks an important difference between the political liberal and the democratic positions. Political liberals are liberal democrats, whereas democrats think that democracy should identify and secure individual rights. Political liberals deal with tensions that arise between liberalism and democracy by alleging the existence of an overlapping consensus, at least on fundamental matters. But because it is the existence of the tensions that makes necessary some strategy for dealing with them, their position is implausible. To the extent that Habermas claims that his theory of communication gets rid of the competition between public and private autonomy, he shares this liberal position.

The internal account, in contrast, responds directly to the issue that makes debate about the legitimacy of law central to political philosophy: the fact that we live in a secular and pluralistic age in which appeals to transcendent moral standards or to tradition are generally regarded with suspicion. The account deals with this fact by seeking to provide more than just the institutions that a plurality of groups can use to debate issues like the delivery of social programs by the state. In this account, law provides the institutional mechanism for dealing with—rather than evading—political tensions. The institutions of legality must make possible in practical politics questions about whether the institutions themselves are adequate to the ideal of law, which is, according to both democrats and political liberals, an ideal of free and equal citizenship.

In a legal order like the Canadian one—one that is arguably closer to the spirit of the internal account—legal mechanisms may exist that allow determined and powerful groups to get their way by legal means on whatever matter they choose. But this is a risk that the internal account cheerfully accepts, for the internal account does not place its faith in the institutions of the legal or political order but in the conscience of the individual democratic citizen.[67] Legal and political institutions should therefore not be designed primarily as bulwarks against the dangerousness of citizens. Rather, the institutions of legality must be first and foremost democratic—they must be answerable to principles of accountability and participation that have always, albeit embryonically, been part of the Western conception of law.

NOTES

I thank David Bakhurst, Patrick Macklem, John McCormick, Cheryl Misak, Bill Scheuerman, and the editors of NOMOS for their comments on drafts of this chapter.

1. Jürgen Habermas, *Between Facts and Norms: Contributions to a Discourse Theory of Law and Democracy,* trans. William Rehg (Cambridge, Mass.: MIT Press, 1996).

2. We can add a requirement for true positivity that positive law is validly enacted law whose content is determinate by virtue of publicly recognized tests for the determination of law. See Joseph Raz, *The Authority of Law: Essays on Law and Morality* (Oxford: Clarendon Press, 1983), esp. chap. 3.

3. H. L. A. Hart, *The Concept of Law* (Oxford: Clarendon Press, 1961).

4. Thomas Hobbes, *Leviathan,* ed. C. B. Macpherson (London: Penguin, 1985); Max Weber, *Economy and Society,* ed. G. Roth and C. Wittich, 2 vols. (Berkeley and Los Angeles: University of California Press, 1978); Hans Kelsen, *Introduction to the Problems of Legal Theory,* trans. B. Litschewski Paulson and S. Paulson (Oxford: Clarendon Press, 1992).

5. Ronald Dworkin, *Law's Empire* (London: Fontana, 1986).

6. In his most recent collection of essays, Dworkin denies the charge that his theory of legal order is designed to produce a match between his own moral views and the content of law on two grounds. He says that his arguments do not always support the positions he approves; for example, his commitment to free speech defends pornographers. Nor, he says, does his position require the "Constitution [of the United States of America] to contain all the important principles of political liberalism." Here he mentions in particular political liberalism's endorsement of the legislative redistribution of wealth at the same time as it precludes a

commitment to this effect from being put into the Constitution. See Ronald Dworkin, *Freedom's Law: The Moral Reading of the American Constitution* (Cambridge, Mass.: Harvard University Press, 1996), 36. But the first ground shows only that one's moral position might have uncomfortable personal consequences, not that there is no match between the moral position and the law. And the preclusion in the second ground, as I again point out later, seems arbitrary.

7. See H. L. A. Hart, *Essays on Bentham* (Oxford: Clarendon Press, 1982), 150–53. I deal with these issues in detail in *Hard Cases in Wicked Legal Systems: South African Law in the Perspective of Legal Philosophy* (Oxford: Clarendon Press, 1991).

8. A rough list includes John Rawls, Ronald Dworkin, Bruce Ackerman, and Charles Larmore.

9. John Rawls, *Political Liberalism* (New York: Columbia University Press, 1993). I discuss Rawls's position in more detail in "Liberalism after the Fall: Schmitt, Rawls, and the Problem of Justification," *Philosophy and Social Criticism* 22 (1996): 9.

10. Rawls, *Political Liberalism*, chap. 4.

11. Ibid., xxiii–xxvi, 13, 154–55.

12. Ibid., xvi–xvii, 191–94.

13. Ibid., 137.

14. See ibid., 11, 147–48.

15. Ibid., esp. 220.

16. Ibid., chap. 6.

17. Charles Larmore, *The Morals of Modernity* (Cambridge: Cambridge University Press, 1996), 182; italics in original. It is worth noting that these remarks are penned in an essay responding to Carl Schmitt's allegation of a contradiction between liberalism and democracy.

18. Rawls, *Political Liberalism*, 232, 152–56.

19. Compare Judith Shklar: "It is . . . fair to say that liberalism is monogamously, faithfully, and permanently married to democracy—but it is a marriage of convenience": Shklar, "The Liberalism of Fear," in N. L. Rosenblum, ed., *Liberalism and the Moral Life* (Cambridge, Mass.: Harvard University Press, 1989), 21, 37.

20. See, for example, Dworkin, *Freedom's Law,* 36 ; Rawls, *Political Liberalism,* 229–30.

21. See Michael Sandel, *Democracy's Discontent: America in Search of a Public Philosophy* (Cambridge, Mass.: Harvard University Press, 1996), esp. chap. 2.

22. It is no surprise that the only truly liberal democratic society turns out to be the United States of America, on a particular understanding of its Constitution. See Dworkin, *Freedom's Law,* esp. 221: "Freedom of

speech, conceived and protected as a fundamental negative liberty, is the core of the choice modern democracies have made."

23. Jürgen Habermas, "Reconciliation through the Public Use of Reason: Remarks on John Rawls's Political Liberalism," *Journal of Philosophy* 92 (1995): 109, 131.

24. Habermas, *Between Facts and Norms,* chap 3, and postscript. I deal with Habermas's position in more detail in "The Legitimacy of Legality," *University of Toronto Law Journal* 129 (1996): 46; and in *Archiv für Rechts- und Sozialphilosophie* 82 (1996): 324. All references to the latter are to the version in *University of Toronto Law Journal.*

25. Habermas, *Between Facts and Norms,* 113ff.

26. Ibid., 122–23.

27. See, for example, ibid., 99–104.

28. Ibid., 120–21.

29. Curiously, this brings Habermas's position very close to the radical democratic theory put forward by Jeremy Bentham, the eminent English positivist and utilitarian. Bentham's motto of the "Good citizen" under a "government of Laws" is "to obey punctually; to censure freely": Bentham, *A Fragment on Government* (Cambridge: Cambridge University Press, 1988) 10. This motto makes sense for Bentham only on the assumption that the laws are produced through the institutions of a radical democracy that also effectively channels criticism or censure of the legislative product into legal reform. For him, as for Habermas, the most important feature of law comes about through its role in a political culture that ensures legislative responsiveness to a critical public. I address the other similarities between Bentham and Habermas and the differences in "The Legitimacy of Legality," 154–65.

30. Here Habermas follows work done by his former student, Klaus Günther, *The Sense of Appropriateness: Application Discourses in Morality and Law* (Albany: State University of New York Press, 1993); also see Habermas, *Between Facts and Norms,* 217 ff.

31. Habermas, *Between Facts and Norms,* 191.

32. Ibid., 194–97.

33. See, for example, ibid., 222–37.

34. What follows summarizes his arguments, ibid., 219–20, and chap. 9.

35. Ibid., 416.

36. Hence Habermas takes very seriously the arguments put forward by feminist philosophers, including Seyla Benhabib, Nancy Fraser, Deborah Rhode, and Iris Marion Young; see ibid., 418–27.

37. Ibid., chap. 8.

38. I owe this term to Etienne Mureinik; see, for example, his "Emerg-

ing from Emergency: Human Rights in South Africa," *Michigan Law Review* 92 (1994): 1977.

39. Compare Bernard Manin, "On Legitimacy and Political Deliberation," *Political Theory* 15 (1987): 338.

40. Appropriateness of entrenchment is, of course, not equivalent to necessity. For some pertinent arguments, see Jeremy Waldron, "A Right-Based Critique of Constitutional Rights," *Oxford Journal of Legal Studies* 13 (1993): 18.

41. Habermas, *Between Facts and Norms,* chap. 6.

42. For this phrase, see Rawls, *Political Liberalism,* 161; and also Dworkin, *Freedom's Law,* 221.

43. Habermas, *Between Facts and Norms,* 128–31.

44. John Hart Ely, *Democracy and Distrust: A Theory of Judicial Review* (Cambridge, Mass.: Harvard University Press, 1980), discussed in Habermas, *Between Facts and Norms,* 264–66.

45. For criticism of Ely on these lines, see Laurence Tribe, "The Puzzling Persistence of Process-Based Constitutional Theories," *Yale Law Journal* 89 (1980): 1063.

46. He thus makes room, for example, for a judicial policy of principled deference to determinations by administrative agencies in a way that Dworkin's one-right-answer thesis excludes. The position sketched in this paragraph is based on remarks by Habermas in *Between Facts and Norms,* 439–46. It is, however, not an unproblematic interpretation of Habermas, as William Scheuerman points out in his "Between Radicalism and Realism: Critical Reflections on Habermas's *Facticity and Validity,*" in P. Dews, ed., *Habermas: A Critical Reader* (Oxford: Blackwell, forthcoming).

47. See Jürgen Habermas, "Reconciliation through the Public Use of Reason," 110, and John Rawls, "Reply to Habermas," both in *Journal of Philosophy* 92 (1995): 132.

48. For an exploration of this issue, see Thomas McCarthy, "Kantian Constructivism and Reconstructivism: Rawls and Habermas in Dialogue," *Ethics* 105 (1994): 44.

49. Isaiah Berlin, "Two Concepts of Liberty," in his *Four Essays on Liberty* (Oxford: Oxford University Press, 1969), 118, 129–30. Berlin brought the political aspect of liberalism to the fore more than thirty years in advance of the current debate, and this explains the recent resurgence of interest in his work, especially in the United States.

50. See Larmore, *The Morals of Modernity,* chaps. 8 and 10; Rawls, "Reply to Habermas." Especially influential in the development of this view are the essays by Stephen Holmes, "Gag Rules or the Politics of Omission" and "Precommitment and the Paradox of Democracy," both

in Jon Elster and Rune Slagstad, eds, *Constitutionalism and Democracy* (Cambridge: Cambridge University Press, 1988), 19, 195.

51. See Habermas, *Between Facts and Norms,* esp. chaps. 1 and 2.

52. See, for instance, Ernst Tugendhat, "Habermas on Communicative Action," in his *Philosophische Aufsätze* (Frankfurt am Main: Suhrkamp Verlag, 1992), 433; and Cheryl Misak, "Pragmatism and the Transcendental Turn in Truth and Ethics," *Transactions of the C.S. Peirce Society* 30 (1994): 739.

53. The internal account is largely inspired by the work of the Weimar public lawyer and political theorist Hermann Heller. See his *Gesammelte Schriften,* 2d ed., 3 vols. (Tübingen: J. C. B. Mohr [Paul Siebeck], 1992). I discuss Heller's work in detail in "Hermann Heller and the Legitimacy of Legality," *Oxford Journal of Legal Studies* 16 (1996): 641; and *Legality and Legitimacy: Carl Schmitt, Hans Kelsen, and Hermann Heller in Weimar* (Oxford: Clarendon Press, 1997).

54. H. L. A. Hart, "Positivism and the Separation of Law and Morals," in Hart, *Essays in Jurisprudence and Philosophy* (Oxford: Clarendon Press, 1983), 53–54, 74–75.

55. See, for example, H. L. A. Hart, "Comment," in R. Gavison, ed., *Issues in Contemporary Legal Philosophy: The Influence of H. L. A. Hart* (Oxford: Clarendon Press, 1989), 35, 36–40.

56. Lon L. Fuller, *The Morality of Law,* rev. ed. (New Haven, Conn.: Yale University Press, 1969), 204. For an attempt of this kind, one much influenced by both Heller and Habermas, see Wolfgang Schluchter, *The Rise of Western Rationalism: Max Weber's Developmental History,* trans. and intro. G. Roth (Berkeley and Los Angeles: University of California Press, 1985).

57. There is, I think, an interesting shift in positivist legal theory between Jeremy Bentham and the present—from Bentham's emphasis on the conscience of the democratic citizen to the contemporary emphasis on the liberal citizen. To emphasize the conscience of the liberal citizen is in effect to put the judge at the center of things, since the guardians of liberal political morality are judges.

58. Rawls, *Political Liberalism,* 10.

59. I rely here on the excellent treatment of this issue by Mayo Moran, "Talking about Hate Speech: A Rhetorical Analysis of American and Canadian Approaches to the Regulation of Hate Speech," *Wisconsin Law Review* 6 (1994): 1425; and on my own work on the freedom of expression: "John Stuart Mill and the Harm of Pornography," *Ethics* 102 (1992): 534; and "Pornography and Public Reason," *Canadian Journal of Law and Jurisprudence* 7 (1994): 261.

60. See Rawls, *Political Liberalism,* 340–56; and Dworkin, *Freedom's Law,*

sec. II: "Speech, Conscience, and Sex." Both Rawls and Dworkin allow for some exceptions, for example, situations of "clear and present danger," which are not relevant here.

61. *R. v. Keegstra* [1990] 3 SCR 697.

62. *R. v. Butler* [1992] 1 SCR 452.

63. Indeed, the Charter of Rights and Freedoms goes even further, since in section 33, it permits both the federal parliament or a provincial legislature to override by legislation various provisions of the charter, including the right to freedom of expression. Such overrides are limited to periods of five years but may be reenacted.

64. Ian Shapiro argues against fetishizing consensus in *Democracy's Place* (Ithaca, N.Y.: Cornell University Press, 1996), 116–22.

65. See Habermas, *Between Facts and Norms,* 308–14.

66. I have argued that legal orders that do not have such a system in place, for example, when judicial review is restricted to the courts' inherent powers at common law, are not as different from constitutionalized legal orders as might ordinarily be supposed. See my *Hard Cases in Wicked Legal Systems.*

67. Indeed, it seems to me to be self-evident that a group that can gather together the political resources to use legal mechanisms to enact, say, racist legislation, will get its way even if it has no such mechanisms available to it. It will simply resort to covert or illegal politics. And institutions designed by the internal account might deal better with this kind of situation, since it seems likely that such a group will first try the path of legality when its aims can be exposed to effective critique.

10

THE INHERENT DECEPTIVENESS OF CONSTITUTIONAL DISCOURSE: A DIAGNOSIS AND PRESCRIPTION

ROGERS M. SMITH

This chapter's discussion of integrity considers judicial decision making. My aim, however, is not to define integrity for judges or to prescribe how judges should decide cases or justify their rulings. Instead, I offer an account of some problematic yet inherent tendencies of judicial constitutional discourse in particular and legal discourse more broadly. I give no advice to judges concerning these matters because if my argument is correct, the problematic tendencies described here cannot be fully eliminated, nor is it clear that they should be. My goal instead is to persuade my fellow public law scholars, especially those in disciplines other than law, and my fellow citizens to think about judicial decision making with these troubling tendencies more fully in view. That perspective may help us better describe, understand, and assess constitutional decision making, American constitutionalism, and good government.

I suggest that we scholars and citizens give greater attention in our thinking about how the legal system actually works, and in our normative evaluations of constitutional decision making, to a central, fundamental, and ineradicable feature of constitutional discourse (and indeed, legal discourse generally, but I focus on constitutional discussions here). This feature is the tendency for constitutional arguments to be unusually deceptive and confusing, in ways that often represent not sophistry but self-deceptions and confusions on the part of the constitutional interpreters. Constitutional discourse is unusually deceptive and confusing, I believe, because constitutional interpreters often feel politically and psychologically impelled to argue simultaneously that the results they prefer are in some sense authorized by the Constitution and that they are the best outcomes, all things considered. The political character of constitutional decision making discourages interpreters from distinguishing these quite different contentions, even in their own minds.

To public law scholars and even many citizens, this claim may instantly appear obvious, and I trust it will seem so to most after a little reflection. Even so, the phenomenon is a vexing one that we tend in one way or another to minimize. Many public law scholars would readily concede that the constitutionality and overall goodness of a decision are two different issues. Most would also concede that judges usually have some concern with both. But in analyzing particular decisions, many behavioral scholars insist that in all significant cases, the judge's view of what is good is decisive. For them, any discussion of a distinct claim of constitutionality is an analysis of a mirage. Many interpretive scholars instead analyze constitutional decisions in ways that stress the question of whether the reasoning meets standards of constitutionality. But they define *constitutionality* and *constitutional authorization* in various ways that all unduly minimize the distinction between what is constitutional and what is good, making identification of the two all too easy.

The result is that both behavioral and interpretive scholars tend to ignore rather than to highlight how often constitutional decision makers conflate these questions, in ways that produce pervasively deceptive and confused constitutional argumentation. This means, I fear, that scholarly literatures do not adequately describe, explain, or normatively evaluate a basic feature of particular decisions and American constitutionalism generally. Citizens' understandings of constitutional decision making fare no better.

We all can think more clearly if in both empirical and interpretive work, we seek to explore more consciously whether such a pervasive tendency to deceptive reasoning exists, whether it is rooted in the political and psychological factors I sketch in the next section of this chapter, and what its consequences are. To undertake such explorations, however, we need an analytical framework that brings into sharper relief the possible differences between constitutionality and overall goodness. Toward that end, I suggest that when scholars and citizens analyze constitutional decisions, they define *constitutionality* in a way that many modern constitutional scholars, particularly liberals like myself, are likely to resist. Hence let me stress again that I propose this definition not as a guide to how judges should decide cases but, rather, as a tool for describing more accurately how they actually do so.

I suggest that for that purpose, we define *constitutionality* as adherence to what seems most likely to have been the meaning or meanings of a provision originally accepted by those who ratified it, stated at the highest level of generality they would have recognized. As many scholars have argued, judging what meanings meet that standard is often terribly difficult to do, and sometimes, at least, it cannot be done at all. When several interpretations of a provision have roughly equal claims to be widely accepted understandings at the time of ratification, we should extend to them all the title of *constitutional* results. If we wish, we can then call the member of that set of results we like best on other grounds the *best* constitutional result, but in so doing we should recognize that it is not "best" because it is "most *constitutional.*" When one reading's claim is plainly historically superior, it ought to be called the *constitutional* meaning, however undesirable it may be. Likewise, when another interpretation is plainly historically inferior, it should be defended in terms other than constitutionality, however desirable it may be. And when no such originally accepted meaning can be discovered, there is no strictly *constitutional* authorization for judicial action at all.

The choice of this definition of constitutionality for the purpose of describing constitutional decisions should not, moreover, be taken to imply that judges should or should not act if they lack "constitutional" authorization or that they should always act on the most defensibly "constitutional" meaning. Instead, this framework is intended to bring precisely those often obscured normative issues to the surface. One chief advantage of this relatively narrow definition of constitutionality is that it enables us to resist the pervasive tendency to identify "legitimate" judicial actions with whatever an analyst defines as "constitutionally authorized" actions. We can then attend more consistently and explicitly to the possibility that an official decision may not in any plausible way be constitutionally authorized and may therefore be to some degree damaging to constitutionalism and yet may be a good thing. This possibility is sometimes rhetorically conceded by scholars, but most try in one way or another to evade or deny it. No one, to my knowledge, argues that any particular decision is not in any defensible sense constitutionally authorized but is still, on balance, good, as I will here.

This point can be dramatized in a table in which the axes are "constitutional/unconstitutional decisions" and "overall good/bad" decisions:

	Good	Bad
con	many	some?
uncon	none	some

Most scholars and citizens assume that many decisions fall in the upper left-hand cell, as both constitutional and good, like *Martin v. Hunter's Lessee,* 1 Wheat. 304 (1816) (supporting the Supreme Court's authority over the state courts on constitutional issues). Most would place some in the bottom right-hand cell, as both unconstitutional and bad, like *Schenck v. U.S.,* 549 U.S. 47 (1919) (sustaining the federal prosecution of politically dissident speech during World War I). Some scholars may say that they have candidates for the upper right-hand cell, decisions that are constitutional but bad, like *Minor v. Happersett,* 21 Wall. 162 (1875) (holding that the post–Civil War amendments did not give women the right to vote).

Yet I doubt they mean that such decisions are bad overall. As Kent Greenawalt commented in regard to this chapter, a judgment of a judicial decision's overall goodness can be conceived as a two-stage process. First, we can assess the goodness of a result on its own merits as well as its constitutionality, defined as distinct from goodness. Then, if our preferred result is not constitution-

ally authorized, we might factor in the costs to the many goods
constitutionalism serves that will occur if that unconstitutional
result is nonetheless reached.

Most analysts imply that even if the constitutional result is
undesirable in itself, it is still in the end better to adhere to it
until it can be altered by constitutional processes. This conclusion
suggests that when we consider the overall benefits of sustaining
constitutionalism—along with the merits and demerits of the
substance of the decision—we should almost always still come out
in favor of the constitutional result. Hence, even decisions initially
termed *constitutional but bad* are ultimately treated as, in one
important sense at least, more good than bad *overall*. And again, I
have not found anyone who believes that any specific decision
belongs in the bottom left cell, as unconstitutional and yet good.
In fact, almost no one gives the possibility any explicit consideration. But as long as we fail to do so, our analytical frameworks
will inevitably tend to conflate constitutionality and goodness.

To fill this void, to provide a concrete example of an unconstitutional but good result (perhaps the only one), I nominate the
specific holding of *Brown v. Board of Education*, 347 U.S. 483
(1954), the ruling that de jure racially "separate but equal" schools
are inherently and always unconstitutional. That holding was certainly a legitimate, good, and right decision—in some ways a
magnificent decision—but not because it was constitutionally authorized. I believe that it would be more accurate for scholars to
depict it as an admirable exercise of what we may term a judicial
version of Locke's "prerogative power." I do not, however, expect
any sitting judges to so describe this or any other decision that
they treat as authoritative, and I am not sure it would be good if
they did so. Disturbing as it may be, some deceptive judicial
rhetoric may still be beneficial overall. We cannot, however, make
that judgment until we see it for what it is.

Let me also stress immediately that this unusual suggestion—
that there can be good but unconstitutional judicial decisions
authorized by nothing except an overriding human prerogative to
do what is beneficial overall—is meant to highlight an important
analytical possibility. It is not meant to encourage unbridled judicial activism, nor should it do so if the extraordinary character of
such decisions is understood. Constitutionalism—adherence to

the rule of fundamental laws—does do a lot of good, and I do not imagine that decisions undermining it are often justified, even if they otherwise appear good on their merits. But the fact that constitutionalism has many benefits, especially in conferring an aura of legitimacy on decisions, leads to undue neglect of the possibility that decisions of the sort I am describing can exist. This neglect, in turn, makes it all too easy for interpretive scholars to fail to distinguish clearly between constitutionality and overall goodness in their own theories and in their accounts of the constitutional reasoning of officials. As a result, the widespread tendencies to conflate these considerations in deceptive ways go unidentified, unexposed, and unevaluated.

The constant practice of conflating constitutionality and goodness, in turn, may well contribute to a public discourse that fails to explore fully the possibilities for good government, because most people equate the question too extensively with what is constitutional. That is an error because the American Constitution, like every human creation, is imperfect in many ways. My aim in trumpeting the possibility that good, unconstitutional decisions can exist, then, is not to urge judges to attempt them. It is to open analytical space for better descriptions, explanations, and normative appraisals of constitutional decision making and of the broader issue of what makes for good—not merely or necessarily constitutional—government.

I. The Root of the Problem

At least since Shakespeare's time ("let's shoot all the lawyers"), and certainly since Dickens's (*Bleak House*), cynicism about legal discourse and lawyers has been part of our culture, and such cynicism flows richly through the social sciences. But our task should not be simply to echo popular cynicism. Rather, we should explain the legal behavior that generates it. Doing so, I think, modifies the cynicism without eliminating it.

Much of the public's cynicism flows from the fact that lawyers are normally hired to represent particular clients. Thus they have an incentive—indeed, they have a duty—to try to interpret the law in ways consistent with their clients' interests. The adversarial system and the role of a judge who is in the pay of neither party to a case are together supposed to ensure that biases in the briefs cancel out each other and that the law as construed by the judges is not unduly weighted toward any party's cause. No system is perfect, but this arrangement clearly makes much sense. Why, then, should the legal reasoning of judges, and constitutional commentators imagining themselves to be judges, still tend to be deceptive and confusing?

The short answer is that judges, and all constitutional interpreters, do have clients. As most public law scholars recognize, judges normally feel compelled to justify their decisions to both themselves and the general political community whose good they are supposed to serve, to say nothing of more specialized constituencies like the other members of the judicial system, the political leaders with whom they may have long been allied, and the legal commentators who parse their work most closely.[1] Although the interests of those constituencies are not identical to one another or to what is good purely and simply, they all are capable of bringing various sorts of pressures to bear if a relevant constitutional decision is not good by their lights. They can criticize, they can delay or outright refuse to comply, and they can support contrary laws, among other means.

Hence, judges want to be able to tell these groups as well as themselves that their decisions are both constitutional and good. Although better evidence should ultimately be provided in ways that go beyond my aims here, I do not think it much of a stretch to postulate that in consequence, judges often generate constitutional arguments that are deceptive and confusing. The psychological and political pressures responsible for these tendencies are not ones we can lightly disregard, nor can identification or criticism of them make them go away. These facts make it all the more important for us to be conscious of their presence and effects.

I might illustrate the workings of these political and psychological needs and pressures by picking apart various famous constitutional decisions to show how they conflate claims about what is constitutional with claims about what is good; and I applaud teaching, scholarship, and civic discourse that do just that. But I fear that such an effort would read too much like traditional interpretive criticism that tries to show when reasoning departs from what the critic believes to be the correct constitutional path, and again, I am not trying to prescribe the right way for judges to reach or defend their rulings. Let me therefore make the case for the sources of the tendency to conflate the good and the constitutional by appealing to experiences that will, I believe, be quickly recognizable to most public law scholars.

Anyone who teaches an introductory constitutional law course can see how rapidly students begin discussing constitutional issues in the ways I am describing. They come in knowing little about the Constitution's text, its origins, or its previous interpretations. Yet when they read a constitutional provision, many instantly assume that it must have been intended to mean what they think it would be good for it to mean. Conversely, when they read about a constitutional controversy, they intuit the result that seems good to them, and they assume that it is not only appropriate but also constitutionally necessary to reach that result. They begin explaining how that result is what "the founders"—only a few of whom they can name—really wanted.

I doubt anyone will deny that this is a normal form of human behavior, and we all also can easily see why it exists. Everyone rapidly picks up on the fact that American constitutional discourse treats the Constitution and the rule of law as in some sense the founts of legitimate authority for all American governmental actors and especially for the Supreme Court's self-proclaimed power to declare the actions of others to be unconstitutional. But everyone also soon sees that the Court's decisions affect many things that are important to them for other reasons. The decisions implicate values they possess that often have little direct connection to constitutional texts or principles. And everyone then wants to find and to prove that they can legitimately get all they want in terms of both sorts of standards. This desire is not sheer self-indulgence. Many students work hard to understand the Constitution as authorizing results that are consistent with its text and also with everything else they value. They strain to avoid concluding that what the Constitution implies about a controversy and what they think the result should be are different things.

These efforts can be self-consciously casuistic, but often even the most transparent projections of a student's own values to "the framers" are touchingly sincere. Many students find it hard to conceive that what is ultimately authoritative in their nation's

legal and political systems might be, at the deepest level, opposed
to what they regard as legitimate values. If they identify with their
political community at all, that can be a very threatening, indeed
agonizing, possibility. Thus, beneath a superficial air of worldly
sophistication, many students truly believe that the great and
powerful framers and the ratifying American people must have
been at some level wise, kind, and good and aiming to provide
what the students want to have.

Bright gay students, for example, are sometimes shocked at the
overwhelmingly likely suggestion that the Constitution's framers
and ratifiers might not at bottom have wished to protect gay
rights, however much some of us today may believe that the things
to which they were consciously committed logically imply such
protection. In a classroom, the crude efforts of students to read
the Constitution in light of what they think is good and right
can, however, be costly. They often produce arguments that are
transparently contradictory and false, twisting the constitutional
text beyond any recognition. These arguments usually get low
marks, especially if they depart drastically from the teacher's views.

But the pressures to interpret the Constitution in these wishful
ways are vastly more powerful, not less, out in the "real world"
of law and politics. There are undoubtedly tendencies toward
confusion and deception, to project what we want into whatever
we are reading, in all acts of interpretation. These tendencies are
certainly present when any authoritative legal text is interpreted.
But the pressures on government officeholders to interpret the
Constitution in ways that accord with their notions of the good
are unusually high. The Constitution is supposed to be the most
fundamental American law. When interpreting it, judges and
other officials often decide painful controversies deeply affecting
the lives of large numbers of individuals and groups, in ways so
vital that often many people will not follow the decision without
coercion. Many officials take that power seriously. For them, the
impact of a decision on other people and on their own sense of
worth raises the cost of not reaching a result that seems good very
high, perhaps too high to pay. Many are also, again despite an air
of sophistication, patriots who believe the Constitution is directed
at achieving what is, in the last analysis, good and right.

Judges are, of course, vividly aware that most participants in constitutional discourse tend to equate what is constitutional with what they think is good or at least in their interests. They also know that in the "real world," there are many professional interpreters who are enormously skilled at conflating those things in persuasive but misleading ways. That awareness, no doubt, produces skepticism about any particular argument judges hear. Yet this approach is, I submit, also compatible with permitting oneself to believe that among all these truly clever arguments connecting what is truly constitutional with what is truly good, many are phony but one must be right. Hence, a judge can have, and I believe many do have, a more sophisticated version of the students' faith that doing what is constitutionally required, doing what will benefit their allies, doing what expresses their own values, and doing what is good all are ultimately the same. One answer can be found that will in the end satisfy all those criteria better than any other can.

Note that I am not suggesting that when judges and other officials give weight to their concerns that decisions unpopular in the wrong quarters will endanger their personal and institutional prestige, they are introducing considerations extrinsic to proper normative judgments. I accept that these factors are part of what judges must consider when they ponder what results would be "on balance" most beneficial by their lights. It is not unreasonable for them to think that results so unpopular that they threaten the power of both individual judges and the judiciary more broadly are too harmful to constitutionalism and good government to be constitutionally required. Yet even if sensible, such beliefs still militate against decision making that clearly distinguishes "constitutional" factors from considerations of "goodness" and honestly assesses both.

In writing justifications for their results, moreover, adjudicators must also factor in how they can best persuade or mollify whatever people will be made disgruntled losers by a decision. They hope to find a way of presenting the result as, if not best from the losers' points of view, at least legitimate. Those considerations lead them away from appealing primarily to the overall goodness of their decisions, however much such considerations may in fact determine their judgments. American judges are almost irresistibly impelled to justify their results publicly as mandates of authoritative legal sources, especially the Constitution, rather than as products of a calculus of overall benefit. For many generations, judges and most other participants in America's political culture and its European forebears have understood legitimate judicial power to rest on the application of properly established laws to particular cases or controversies. In the United States, most people have accepted the Constitution to be what it claims to be, the supreme law of the land.

Those well-established political and legal traditions are, moreover, not accidental. Although I am stressing here political and psychological factors in decision making, I do not mean to deny that claims that legitimate decisions are and must be in accord with the original meaning of the Constitution are rooted in the logic of constitutionalism itself. Such decisions seem particularly requisite when a constitutional system rests on a written constitution, as in America. Even the most expansive constitutional interpreters acknowledge that if the enterprise of having a written constitution makes any sense at all, the written constitution must be understood as in some way defining limits on what officials can legitimately do that are both reasonably ascertainable and enduring. If we are to say that it is the Constitution that constrains judicial results, moreover, it is logical to contend that those ascertainable, enduring limits must in some fairly determinate way trace back to what was meant by those who authorized the Constitution, even if multiple readings of those meanings are inescapable. Nonoriginalists often resist this last point, but it is hard otherwise to understand why we might want to have a written constitution at all.

Many scholars, to be sure, deny that the enterprise of written constitutionalism makes sense on its own terms or that its terms are practicable. Far from dismissing those claims, I am urging attention to the distinction between constitutionality and goodness in part because it can help us assess them better. But all those who think that constitutionalism does make sense on its own terms necessarily also think the range of legitimate constitutional interpretations is finite. In political science, some of the most prominent and sophisticated arguments for constitutional interpretations that go beyond narrow readings of the framers' "original intent" have come from the so-called Princeton school of scholars influenced by Walter Murphy. But its members all accept that—as Sotirios Barber said more than a decade ago—"a plastic constitution cannot be a real constitution." If "the Constitution can be anything it has to be," if it is so indeterminate that there is no serious chance that what is constitutional and what is good are two different things, then we "cannot perceive the Constitution as law," as something limiting conduct in certain recognizable ways.[2] Will Harris also contends that the enterprise of constitutional interpretation must be "bounded," with "sustainable principles of exclusion and inclusion" for imaginable results, an approach that for Harris more than Barber permits attending to only "that portion of natural law subsumed by the logic of the political form" that the Constitution creates.[3] Graham Walker insists that "a constitution cannot be equated with full and real justice or with the true good," although it should have some sort of partly institutionalized "umbilical cord" to the good.[4]

How should we understand the "bounds" of the Constitution? There are many responses, but they all recognize that the most familiar answer, defined by both the logic of written constitutionalism and our legal traditions, is that the Constitution can be understood to impose fixed limits from the outset only if those limits are indeed interpreted in accordance with meanings that the Constitution's framers and ratifiers would have recognized, as far as those can be ascertained. Contemporary scholars often treat this position as something to be transcended, but all understand its political force, and some believe that we should adhere to it.

My own students have been arguing forcibly in recent years— against me, among others—that constitutionalism makes little intrinsic sense if the sometimes ill-advised limits that its ratifiers understood it to impose on conduct are ignored.[5] Thus our task is said to be to read the Constitution not as a blueprint for the best society but as a set of identifiable compromises that we should adhere to as long as the results are not so intolerable that we clearly could do better by moving to a new constitution.[6] Even a Critical Legal Scholar like Mark Tushnet, who denies that we can ultimately distinguish interpretively between originally authorized, legitimate and unauthorized, illegitimate constitutional results, affirms the practical power of the widespread belief that constitutionalism requires judges to adhere to originally ratified meanings. He says he would and could, if on a judicial bench, proclaim that his political preferences are instead actually mandates of the Constitution.[7] If Tushnet would do that, we cannot realistically expect actual judges to stop doing it.

Thus the logic of interpreting a written constitution and the political task of justifying readings of such a document to the general public create additional pressures for judges (far more than scholars) to produce interpretations that treat the Constitution's meaning as bounded and properly interpretable through some form of "originalism." Even so, they still also feel impelled to reach what they regard as the overall best outcomes. The result is that the pressures judges and lawyers face, to claim and to believe that their preferred results are simultaneously justified by both constitutionality and overall goodness, are so overwhelming as to be inescapable.

II. The Costs of the Problem

So what? we might ask. Since most citizens probably want decisions that are both as constitutional as possible and as good as possible, what is the harm in constantly reasoning with a view to both? We might answer that judges would do a better job of reasoning with a view to both standards if they did not mistakenly treat them as the same. But even though individual judges might think more clearly by keeping this distinction in view, my argument is that few will ever be able to resist conflating the two criteria, even in their own minds.

It is still reasonable, however, to think that this framework can assist scholars studying law and, through them perhaps, citizens more generally. We scholars without official governmental responsibilities are somewhat better positioned to keep constitutionality and goodness analytically distinct. And if we do so, we should better be able to grasp and explain a behavioral and discursive tendency toward confused and deceptive reasoning that is a central, often frustrating part of the experience of our legal system for all concerned. If we simply dismiss these patterns of reasoning and arguing as mistakes or hoaxes without analyzing their sources and frequency and assessing their costs, we are not likely to produce accounts that ring true to most of the system's participants.

We also will not get on the table the questions of the ultimate goodness of a particular decision, a particular constitution, or constitutionalism itself if we do not recognize that constitutionalism's worth is only a part of the judgment of overall beneficiality.

In both scholarly work and broader political discourse, important alternatives and reforms are easily neglected if we generally assume that constitutionality—especially as specified in current constitutional arrangements—and good government are roughly the same. It is possible, though, that emphasizing the distinction between constitutionality and goodness may do harm, corroding faith in the legitimacy of desirable decisions and broader political processes and institutions. But we scholars cannot in good conscience simply presume that these possible harms are decisive. We must take the risks attendant on making that possibility a matter of explicit inquiry.

It is plausible, then, to think that it would be useful to pay more attention to the distinction between constitutionality and goodness and the tendencies of courts to blur these criteria. Most public law scholars may respond, however, that their particular approaches actually capture quite well this distinction and the relationship of constitutionality to overall goodness. I think instead that most of us evade much explicit attention to these topics, for inadequate reasons, but I cannot make that case fully here. I will, however, identify some leading accounts of the relationship of constitutionality to goodness that I think amount to unpersuasive evasions or denials of the distinction.

III. Influential Evasions of the Problem

Some scholars endorse the evasion of this vexing distinction that is characteristic of sitting judges. In countless opinions, judges have asserted, sometimes heatedly, sometimes regretfully, that the question of a decision's ultimate goodness is just not part of their job.[8] They accept the Constitution as authoritative for them, and they understand it or its authorizers to make the judgment that the summum bonum will best be advanced if judges keep their eyes and mitts off that grandiose topic and stick to applying the law. This claim is far from silly. Indeed, part of my objective here is to help us consider whether it is better when judges do or do not stick to considerations of constitutionality alone, defined in the more narrowly bounded way that I am proposing.

It is likely that judges cannot, and it is certain that they do not, make good on their claim to adhere strictly to the law's clearly ascertainable original meanings, but those points do not refute the notion that judges should think they ought to try to do so. That belief might still produce judging that is overall better and more responsible than any alternative jurisprudence. But whatever the merits of the sitting judges' argument for their own responsibilities, scholars cannot invoke their view of proper judging to define our research responsibilities. Our mandate is not to judge according to the law but to describe, explain, and evaluate human conduct in as illuminating a fashion as possible. Thus we must treat the claim that judges always do the most good if they try to do only what the Constitution can be fairly seen as originally authorizing them to do as a hypothesis to be examined, not as a postulate to be applied.

To answer yes, to say that judges should try to consider only constitutionality thus understood, and not overall benefit, is to presume that as Alexander Bickel argued, constitutionalism and the rule of law do comprise "the value of values," that the "highest morality . . . is the morality of process," adhering to lawfully established processes of decision making. But I know of no one who is willing to defend that view. Even the more conservative "late Bickel" said only that such morality is "almost always" the highest.[9] Even for him, constitutionalism was an instrument of, not a synonym for, good government.

Yet more strikingly, Justice Antonin Scalia has also conceded that "originalism is strong medicine . . . one cannot realistically expect judges (probably myself included) to apply it without a trace of constitutional perfectionism," without occasional modification to produce results that conform to a judge's standards of overall goodness.[10] However rare, Scalia's willingness to make such modifications amounts to a concession that a decision may be, on balance, good even if it works real harm to the good that constitutionalism does.

Such decisions may indeed be rare, since the contributions of constitutionalism to good government on almost any conception of that term are many. If adhered to, constitutional procedures usually reduce the scope for arbitrary decision making by creating many motions that must be gone through before decisions are made and enforced and by authorizing potential points of resistance among the many officials who must agree on a course of action. Constitutionalism, especially with a written constitution, can also help preserve whatever wisdom the original lawmakers may have had, which is considerable in the American case. And in many cases, constitutionalism also includes important substantive checks on governmental tyranny. Furthermore, by making rapid change more difficult, constitutionalism can promote stability, which makes it easier for people to plan their lives securely. By establishing stable patterns of decision making that grow venerable with time, constitutionalism can also foster a sense of common memory and common cooperative endeavor among a political people that may promote both unity and belief in the system's legitimacy. All these and others are advantages not to be foregone lightly.

Yet all those virtues have their attendant vices.[11] Constitutional procedures may be unduly cumbersome in responding to national emergencies, notoriously so in wartime, but in other sorts of economic and social disasters as well. If a written constitution helps preserve the wisdom of its framers, so too it helps preserve their follies, their undue compromises of principle, their injustices. And in the very ways it contributes to stability, constitutionalism can help shelter unfair, exploitative status quo arrangements against necessary reforms. Insofar as it does so, it may provoke not gradual, orderly change with security but violent uprisings. For those who find their Constitution a major obstacle to the advancement of the human good, as William Lloyd Garrison and many Progressives did, constitutionalism thus does not foster unity and legitimacy. It is, rather, a symbol of the system's incorrigibility and evil. Constitutionalism, then—like anything except perhaps the idea of the good itself—can be good or bad. Whether or not a decision conforms to it and preserves it is thus only part of the question of whether that decision is good or bad.

What about the opposing view, visible in much empirical work on judicial decision making, that constitutionalism never matters much, at least in significant cases, precisely because constitutional discourse is pervasively deceptive, serving often to "cloak the real-

ity of the Court's decision-making process," as, for example, Jeff
Segal and Harold Spaeth argue? My quarrel with many such scholars is that they then proceed as if this phenomenon of deceptive
and confusing reasoning is not worth much attention in its own
right. Segal and Spaeth take the view, not far removed from Mark
Tushnet's, that although the meaning of some legal texts may be
"indisputably" clear, and there may be some "meritless cases that
no self-respecting judge would decide solely on the basis of his or
her policy preferences," most cases considered by the Supreme
Court, at least, have "plausible legal arguments on both sides."
These cases are then decided according to prevailing judicial
"attitudes," the judges' own beliefs about what is ultimately good.
Since that is so, there is little point in focusing on the deceptions
of judicial discourse. Their pervasiveness is taken for granted.[12]

This stance is so sweepingly dismissive of the intrinsic meaning-
fulness of constitutional discourse that it militates against making
more nuanced identifications of just how deceptive particular
decisions are. It thereby prevents recognizing that such deceptiveness is not only chronic but also, in some cases, acute. It does so,
moreover, by neglecting an important distinction. It may well be
true that there are plausible legal arguments on both sides of
Supreme Court cases, but it is less likely that there are always on
both sides arguments of equal plausibility from the standpoint of
any jurisprudence focused on the original meanings of constitutional provisions.

Segal and Spaeth themselves deride the arguments used by
justices in some decisions as obviously weak and strained from an
originalist standpoint.[13] The results favored in those opinions
might still be defensible from various moral and philosophical
perspectives. But the fact that we can and do judge them to be
less rather than more plausible exegeses of the original meaning
of the written constitution is significant: it means that we can
reasonably attribute to them a specific cost to the enterprise of
constitutionalism that another decision would not exact. They
strain the credibility of courts and constitutional governance
more, at least in one regard. This is a fact about a decision worth
knowing, and it cannot be known if we evade the distinction
between constitutionality and goodness by claiming that all deci-

sions turn equally on the judge's view of the latter and that all opinions suggesting otherwise are equally deceptive.

The latter claim has, moreover, more the air of a first principle than an empirical finding. It does more to communicate to us that political scientists like Segal and Spaeth do not take constitutional discourse on its own terms very seriously than it does to show us that as an empirical reality the tendency to deceptive or confused reasoning is widespread and uniform. To undertake studies that might show this, we need to believe that it is possible to identify both reasoning that plausibly discerns and applies originally accepted constitutional standards and reasoning that is deceptive about doing so. By seeming to dismiss the possibility of such identifications, Segal and Spaeth and like-minded public law scholars deny an experience that most readers of legal opinions frequently have. If accepted, that denial discourages us from analyzing the extent and sources of deceptive discourse. It is, in fact, such a broad dismissal of analyzing judicial discourse interpretively that it can generate its opposite. Many scholars may wrongly dismiss Segal and Spaeth's view and fall back into denying that deception and confusion are both rife and inescapable in important constitutional opinions (as well as lots of other legal decisions). Exaggerated cynicism can boomerang, producing undue respect for the object of cynical acid. Thus it would be better if the reasons that judges tend to go beyond originalist interpretations and grant constitutional status to their standards of good were explored and the pervasiveness of this tendency were concretely shown instead of simply asserting that the substance of legal reasoning is too myth ridden to be worth discussing.

Most public law scholars do analyze legal reasoning, perhaps ad nauseum, in ways that use different evasions of the distinction between constitutionality and goodness. Some assume, as Bickel almost argued, that judges conform to the "highest morality" when they attend only to standards of constitutionality, defined in terms of the ratifiers' intentions. But the most widely discussed recent statement of that view, by Robert Bork, ultimately appeals not to the desirability of the American Constitution or constitutionalism per se but to what is "democratically legitimate." It is because the Constitution represents the democratically alterable will of the American people and because the alternative to adhering to it is, in Bork's view, "authoritarian judicial oligarchy" that he thinks constitutionality defined as original intent should be all that judges consider. Rather than look to any other standard, they should refrain from judicial review of constitutionality altogether.[14]

All this is only a way of arguing that for Bork, there is no real distinction between adhering to constitutionality and achieving overall goodness. His view simply specifies that what is "democratically legitimate" is good, and he argues that this good requires defining *constitutionality* in terms of original intent. His equation of the good with what is democratically approved and his belief that democratic legitimacy demands a jurisprudence of original intent have won Bork widespread criticism as a relativist and reactionary.[15] Although he announces his positions firmly; moreover, it is not clear that even he strictly adheres to them. He also contends, somewhat as Bickel did, that sometimes a decision may be "clearly wrong" in terms of the original intent of the Constitution, yet "so thoroughly embedded in our national life that it should not be overruled." That language suggests Bork acknowledges that an "incorrect" decision may, at least after a time, be regarded as overall more beneficial than any reversal of it.

But even in making this concession, Bork cannot go quite so far as to say explicitly that the decision is or becomes good and that it remains unconstitutional. He insists that the judgment to continue to uphold the erroneous result is a "valid" one, an ambiguous term suggesting that the result may be "constitutional" after all. In any case, Bork recommends pruning back the reach of such decisions, and he probably would not urge that a decision that is "incorrect" from the standpoint of original intent be made in the first place (*Brown* might have been the exception). It is apparently only after such rulings become inextricably "embedded" in our national life that they become "valid."[16]

The overwhelming thrust of Bork's position, then, is to suggest that there is no need to distinguish between constitutionality and overall goodness, because democratic legitimacy defines overall goodness and it is always best preserved by constitutionality defined in terms of original intent or by abdication of judicial review of constitutionality altogether. Yet since even Bork ends up departing from these claims, the contention that constitutionality understood as conformity to original intent always promotes over-all goodness, understood as democratic legitimacy, seems a decep-tive preempting of difficult questions that we should consider more explicitly and clearly.

In political science, Christopher Wolfe has made the most fully developed recent argument for confining judges to judgments of constitutionality defined in terms of original intent. He also does so because he feels these practices promote overall goodness, defined by a standard that goes beyond esteem for the original Constitution or constitutionalism. His deepest allegiance is to particular versions of "preliberal" philosophic traditions of "natu-ral right and natural law" and especially "Christianity." He values the Constitution because in it and in the thought of the framing, these elements provided "balance in the principles of our political community" in ways that are now in "great danger." Wolfe ac-knowledges that his defense of a jurisprudence focusing on consti-tutionality defined in originalist terms alone is not due simply to a belief in " 'procedural' political principles" such as constitution-alism and the rule of law. It is instead an effort to ensure that these "preliberal" elements remain important to determining "the substantive goals of American political life." [17]

Again, these arguments imply that overall goodness, under-stood by Wolfe in these "preliberal" terms, is not simply identical to constitutionality. It therefore is in principle an open question whether particular "originalist" decisions or broader interpretive practices of adhering to constitutionality defined in originalist terms advance his overall good as much as do alternative ap-proaches and results. But Wolfe's claim that originalism is always the best way to approximate overall goodness again operates as a limiting assumption that leads us to minimize rather than pursue the distinction between constitutionality thus understood and overall goodness, however understood.

The most celebrated nonoriginalist account of constitutional interpretation, by Ronald Dworkin, makes the opposite move to evade any clear distinction between constitutionality and good-ness. Instead of holding that adherence to constitutionality, un-derstood as conformity to original intent, is the best way to achieve overall goodness or rightness, Dworkin offers a different, and influential, definition of constitutionality. He argues that judgments of constitutionality properly hinge on judgments of the overall best result, at least in hard cases.[18] Somewhat like Segal and Spaeth, Dworkin argues that this reliance on the judge's own standards of goodness is inevitable, but for Dworkin this result does not show judicial reasoning to be mere mystification. It is, instead, the appropriate result of excellent judging.

This reliance is inevitable because, Dworkin argues, everyone who treats the Constitution as at all authoritative must have an account of why it is authoritative. This account cannot simply be that the Constitution is authoritative because it says it is. Such an answer would "beg the question" of why we should accept its claims. Every interpreter thus relies at least implicitly on an extrinsic "political theory showing why the Constitution should be treated" as authoritative law, and this theory inevitably shapes how the interpreter understands the Constitution; that is, what parts of it are regarded as most central and decisive and what parts are given only limited importance.[19]

If constitutional interpreters are to reason coherently, they must ensure that their constitutional decisions fit with their broader theories of why the Constitution legitimately governs, a theory that relies ultimately on the interpreters' own judgments about what the standards for good and just government are. Bork's appeals to what is "democratically legitimate" and Wolfe's to the desirability of "preliberal" natural law and Christian traditions may be taken as evidence that some such broader political theory indeed undergirds even positions urging adherence to constitutionality understood as original intent.

But if this is so, if the ways and degrees to which interpreters accord authority to the Constitution depend on their extrinsic theories of good government, then judgments of what is constitutional and what is overall good are not ultimately different. And Dworkin has long urged that in hard cases, judges do and should rely most on their own views of "sound" political morality. He does maintain that a judge's interpretation should have an "adequate fit" with the ascertainable original understanding of the constitutional text, but he has never said much about that rather pro forma criterion. He contends that judges need only interpret the more general "concepts," not the more specific "conceptions" expressed in the constitutional text, and he stresses that many results meet this rather minimal "adequate fit" standard of conformity to constitutional "concepts." Therefore, this standard rarely determines specific outcomes.

Dworkin also argues that a judge can and should choose a result that has less "fit" with originalist understandings of a constitutional "concept" than another does if the judge's preferred result is more morally "compelling" and its "fit" is at least "adequate." Even in his writings urging a jurisprudence of "integrity," a norm that requires judges to treat current law as "expressing and respecting a coherent set of principles," Dworkin has continued to indicate that if the law, construed coherently, works injustice, a judge may disregard it. And although he terms that disregard a "lie" about what the law is, he also gives judges permission to render the law "coherent" by giving more "fidelity" to immanent principles that they find compelling than to "past decisions" that seem unjust. Aided by that discretion, they should not need to "lie" often.[20]

I have long regarded as irrefutable Dworkin's argument that all interpreters must rely on an implicit or explicit political theory in their approaches to constitutional interpretation, and I still do. Why, then, have I come to think that scholars and citizens should give more weight than Dworkin does to the distinction between constitutionality understood as "fitting" with the language and original understandings of the document, and overall goodness? Note first that even though Dworkin argues reasonably that we often cannot discover any single "original intent" among the Constitution's many framers and ratifiers, his own account indicates that he still regards conformity with the language and early understandings of the Constitution as a distinguishable and meaningful standard for decision making, apart from substantive desirability. Many results may have adequate fit, but not all do. Dworkin nonetheless advances an approach that makes a judge's own view of a decision's overall political and moral rightness and goodness far more definitive of constitutionality than fit is. I therefore think that his position again encourages us to evade the distinction between constitutionality and goodness in scholarly analysis as well as in judging.

This distinction could have real bite for Dworkin only if the best result in his eyes did not have even the most minimal fit with original intent, and those occasions can be expected to be few. Again, like Segal and Spaeth, he would have us act as if there is no important difference in how well possible results fit with the constitutional language and original understandings, as long as their fit can be deemed "plausible" or "adequate." But this makes the test of fit trivial when most constitutional discourse presents it as central, however misleadingly. It also leaves us ill equipped to judge the costs of choosing results that clearly have less fit than others do. The others are, after all, still said to be the "constitutional" ones if they seem better overall. If instead of trying to find a way to bestow the title of "constitutionality" on decisions we like, we want to capture more accurately what is being explicitly claimed in much judicial discourse, and if we wish to appraise the costs and benefits of decisions that treat constitutionality in ways that conflate fit and goodness, we need a different framework. We must instead say that if result A clearly has a better fit with discoverable original understandings than result B does, A is the "constitutional" result, even if B may seem to be the best result.

We would then still be left wondering how to characterize the choices that judges face when the test of fitness leaves a range of possible results, at least some with claims of fit that seem roughly equal in force. A pure originalist like Bork would say that under those circumstances, the courts have no determinate standard and so should let electoral officials decide which of these equally plausible meanings should prevail. Deference, then, is the only course that should be deemed "constitutional." My proposed "qualified originalist" definition of constitutionality holds instead that if several results are equally plausible on originalist grounds, scholars should call all of them equally constitutional, even if the judge has clearly chosen among them on the basis of what she regards as sound morality. The deference under these circumstances that strict originalists urge has an equal, but not a superior, claim to the title of "constitutional" result, for such deference does not itself fit better with the text's ascertainable original meaning. It merely reflects a broader theory about how to respond to the text's indeterminacies. Hence it blurs rather than clarifies my proposed scholarly distinction between constitutionality and goodness to accord deference sole rights to the label of constitutional holding.

In light of the difficulties of defining precisely how a provision may have been originally understood, the proposed framework would not only allow but also require scholars to view a wide range of decisions as constitutional, far more than Bork would do. But again, if one outcome is admitted to have a better fit than others, even if it is not the only one with a fit that Dworkin would term "adequate" or Segal and Spaeth would term "equally plausible," then scholars would have to designate that best fitting result as the one dictated by standards of constitutionality. We scholars and citizens might still prefer that judges reach a different result, but if we do, we should say it is because we regard that result as better overall, not better in terms of constitutionality, to which it will in fact inflict some harm. How judges should themselves describe their results remains a different question.

If we reserve the term *constitutional* for results that have unsurpassed fit with what we can discover about the original meaning of a constitutional provision, it should not only be harder to forget that considerations of goodness and constitutionality are not simply identical and to neglect the costs of choosing decisions with lesser fit. It should also be harder to claim that decisions that have the best fit are the best overall simply because they do display such fit. Compared with Dworkin, scholars and citizens may then be less likely to assume that good government is always compatible with, much less defined by, the properly interpreted substance of the American Constitution. That caution is, I think, all to the good.

Given the political, psychological, and logical pressures to defend constitutional decisions in terms of originalist standards, it is likely that the framework I suggest would make it harder even for many scholars, much less judges, to defend decisions that are admitted not to be most "constitutional" in these terms. I suspect that is why Dworkin, a champion of liberal judicial activism, insists that we define constitutionality largely in terms of a decision's substantive desirability according to the most defensible political theory of our system that we can find. I am skeptical about whether we commentators should supply misleading legitimating wrapping for such judicial decision making, preferring instead to bring out in the open issues of whether constitution-bound adjudication and our constitutional provisions themselves are good. At the same time, I maintain that we can descriptively equate constitutionality with equal or superior historical fit and still defend normatively some decisions, though not many, that do not have superior or even adequate fit.[21]

IV. RECOGNIZING A PREROGATIVE TO DO UNCONSTITUTIONAL GOOD: THE CASE OF *BROWN*

As advertised, my example here is *Brown v. Board of Education.* Without rehearsing the vast literature on that case, suffice it to say that as Michael McConnell argues in a major recent article, even most of its admirers do not regard the decision as well grounded in terms of the original intent of the Fourteenth Amendment.[22] Let me repeat that what is not well grounded is the specific ruling in *Brown,* that racially separated educational facilities "are inherently unequal."[23] The result in *Brown,* as distinct from that holding, seems to me unquestionably constitutionally well founded.

Because Jim Crow segregation in America was always part of a caste system of white supremacy that included largely successful efforts to exclude blacks from voting booths and juries and because the schools provided to blacks were themselves usually inferior to those supplied to whites, school segregation as it existed in 1954 clearly did not represent "equal protection of the laws." But as is well known, the lawyers challenging school segregation wished to avoid having to prove in every Jim Crow school district that separate was not equal there. They also wanted to forestall renewed efforts by southern whites to provide more "equal" segregated schools, as South Carolina was then doing. Hence they sought a broad ruling that segregation was unconstitutional per se, that as the NAACP Legal Defense Fund brief put it, there "never was and never will be any separate equality."[24]

The problems with claiming that the Fourteenth Amendment's framers shared that view are well known. The same Congress that passed the Fourteenth Amendment also funded segregated public schools in the District of Columbia. Although most Republicans accepted, following Abraham Lincoln, that African Americans were equally entitled with whites to the basic rights of the Declaration of Independence, including the rights of free labor, many nonetheless thought of blacks as a distinct and, in many respects, inferior race, whether for environmental, historical, or biological reasons. Thus few were prepared to accept the full social equality and intermixing of the races. Many Republicans therefore saw no harm in segregation so long as the schools were equal, and by that, many meant equally appropriate to their particular students, which often amounted to vocational training for blacks and preparation for higher education for whites.[25] To be sure, other Republicans like Charles Sumner consistently opposed racial segregation, especially school segregation. But Sumner did so both before and after the Fourteenth Amendment, all the while proclaiming that segregation was unconstitutional, and all his efforts to win a congressional ban on school segregation failed.

McConnell's article is an impassioned effort to justify *Brown's* ban on all forms of state-imposed segregation in terms of original intent, despite these facts. It is the most important such effort in many years, but in my reading, it breaks down under the weight of its own evidence. Instead, it provides another instance of the tendency to say self-deceptively that what is constitutional and what is good must somehow ultimately be the same. The only pertinent statement in regard to school segregation that McConnell can find by a supporter of the Fourteenth Amendment indicates that such segregation was not banned by Reconstruction measures.[26]

McConnell finds five state decisions prohibiting school segregation in the wake of the Fourteenth Amendment, but unfortunately, they all rely on state constitutional provisions. The four that look to the Fourteenth Amendment instead sustain segregation. McConnell tries to write off the segregation in the D.C. schools by saying, correctly, that the Fourteenth Amendment did not apply to them and that the amendment's framers only appropriated funds to segregated schools instead of actively endorsing them.[27] But appropriations *are* active endorsements, as was the rejection in 1870–71 of Charles Sumner's effort to win repeal of school segregation in the District, however equivocally that rejection was defended. And however much Congress may in modern times have exempted itself from laws it applied to others, McConnell provides no evidence that it claimed it did not need to abide by the principles of the Fourteenth Amendment. All his evidence supports the view that Congress thought those principles binding on it and indeed that many thought them binding even without the Fourteenth Amendment.[28]

McConnell's defense of *Brown* as a matter of "original intent" relies almost exclusively on what congressmen said *after 1870* in pushing for forerunners of what became the 1875 Civil Rights Act. Many then claimed that the "spirit," and some said the letter, of the Fourteenth Amendment was indeed hostile to school segregation and that Congress should ban it. But McConnell supplies no evidence that any of these legislators explicitly contended that by itself, the Fourteenth Amendment empowered the *courts* to overturn state school segregation. Many of its supporters are shown to be distrustful of courts, and they discussed the decision to ban segregation exclusively as a legislative one. McConnell is right to say that even so, it is likely that some independent enforcement by the courts of rights under the Fourteenth Amendment was surely contemplated.[29]

It is not, however, so persuasive to claim for the judiciary a power to enforce rights that none of the amendment's framers or ratifiers said it included. This was an era when many Republican congressmen claimed that Congress was the preeminent institution in America's republican government, with both the executive and judicial branches subordinate to it.[30] We ought therefore to be careful about attributing to them assumptions of fully equal and independent judicial power.

Although McConnell shows that majorities in each house voted for banning school segregation at various preliminary points, moreover, the fact is that the 1875 Civil Rights Act was passed only after those provisions were removed.[31] Furthermore, even if it is plausible to say that what Republican legislators (and not the courts) said in the early 1870s is the best available evidence of the intent of the Fourteenth Amendment, their speeches remain political discourse in a different context. Perhaps it is the perspective of a political scientist rather than a lawyer, but to me it is pertinent that they were trying to validate controversial legislation. Hence they were likely to define their constitutional authorization as expansively as they could. They were certainly not likely to suggest the Constitution did not authorize the bans on segregation they now wished to pass.

But their politically strategic claims are uncertain evidence of how the measure was understood years earlier by those who ratified it without ever hearing those arguments (and in Madisonian constitutional theory, at least, it is the ratifiers' understanding that is most decisive). I regard the fact that the Americans who ratified the Fourteenth Amendment overwhelmingly continued to create segregated schools as better evidence of how they read the amendment than any later claims are. In any case, from any originalist standpoint, the terms *best available* evidence and *sufficient* evidence cannot be synonymous. The political context of the 1870s makes McConnell's evidence too shaky to carry the heavy load he assigns to it.

Thus, if his case is in fact the best that can be made for the precise *Brown* holding as a matter of original intent, as I believe it is, then the most charitable thing that can be said is that the argument that the Fourteenth Amendment was intended to empower the courts to ban school segregation is inconclusive. That fact is enough to require strict originalists like Bork to conclude, if they are consistent, that the proper response is not judicial intervention but judicial restraint, as McConnell recognizes in criticizing Bork. By Bork's originalist canons, if segregation cannot be clearly shown to have been constitutionally banned in a way enforceable by the courts, then the courts should not enforce such a ban. The issue should be left to Congress, and in the years on which McConnell concentrates, congressmen certainly acted as if they thought enforcing any such ban was their job.[32]

My own view is different. Although the issue requires more discussion than is appropriate here, I currently conclude that the case that the Fourteenth Amendment was intended to ban school segregation is not strong enough to claim the title of "constitutional" for the *Brown* holding. The evidence better supports either the conclusion that no widely shared original understanding can be found in this regard at all or the conclusion that "separate but equal" segregation was generally expected to be permitted.

I am reinforced in that belief by the fact that almost none of the champions of *Brown* defend it simply because they think it is what the ratifiers of the Fourteenth Amendment anticipated. They defend it because they know Jim Crow was an evil system and they want to be able to say that it is also unconstitutional. Thus they try very hard to read the Fourteenth Amendment as banning it, exactly as do the introductory course students I referred to earlier. I think this is also what McConnell is trying to do. He does it well, and because his argument is so much what so many people want to believe, I expect it will win much acclaim and acceptance. But if we are truthful, we must admit that his effort, like so many others, emits what Robert McCloskey called "the smell of the lamp."

If judges and litigating lawyers, as McConnell often is, cannot escape that odor, pure scholars should try. I therefore suggest that we who do not sit in official chairs should explore another, less wishful defense of the *Brown* holding. Acknowledging that the specific ruling that legally segregated schools are everywhere and always "inherently unequal" probably went beyond what the Fourteenth Amendment was originally understood to forbid, we should admit that *Brown* was therefore in all likelihood harmful to some degree to many of the values that constitutionalism serves. It is also plausible to think that some of those harms have grown over the years, as *Brown* has been followed by more decisions that few believe to be closely tethered to the text and as those rulings have been defended by arguments on and off the bench that often fall into visible contradictions and interpretive knots.

Yet granting all this and before a more careful accounting, I think it is reasonable to say that the decision still was good because the evil it repudiated was so great and that its goodness legitimates it. I know that it certainly did not end the great evils of racial segregation and inequality. Its direct consequences are meager, and its indirect ones are difficult to assess and to show to be great, as Gerry Rosenberg has demonstrated.[33]

But *Brown* nonetheless removed the official sanction of the Supreme Court from the great evil of segregation. If it had done so more equivocally, if it had said that racially segregated schools could be constitutional if they were made sufficiently equal, it would not have succeeded in repudiating the legitimacy of Jim Crow. And to me, the fact that in pure positive law terms, there seemed no way to repudiate Jim Crow emphatically without cost to the values of constitutionalism only affirms that constitutionality is not goodness and that there is sometimes a higher morality than the morality of process. The aspects of American constitutionalism that permitted Jim Crow in principle, and therefore validated racial hierarchy in practice, deserved to be repudiated, if not by any means necessary, then certainly by this highly pacific and moral means. And for all the troubles that have ensued, I believe the American political system is better today and clearly more morally defensible because of the result the Court reached.

But it obscures the costs of the decision and makes that conclusion too easy, I think, if we call *Brown* a "valid" finding of "constitutionality" either as a matter of "original intent" or according to some other jurisprudence that defines constitutionality as largely identical to goodness. I believe it would be more accurate and more beneficial to term *Brown* an exercise of a judicial version of Locke's "prerogative power." Locke defined that power not as a constitutional device but as a "power to act according to discretion, for the public good, without the precept of the law, and sometimes even against it." The reason that executives (and for Locke, judges were part of the executive branch) could sometimes do "things of their own free choice, where the law was silent, and sometimes too against the direct letter of the law, for the publick good" was because adherence to rules was sometimes insufficient to accomplish such good. Locke argued that if these claimed prerogatives were used for evil, the people could be expected to resist. He suggested, therefore, that prerogative is properly "largest in the hands of our wisest and best" governors, whom the public sees to be doing good.[34]

I think those premises make a good case for *Brown*'s holding.[35] It went beyond, probably even against, the Court's constitutional authority, but it did so to proclaim the illegitimacy of a vile institution so deeply and strategically entrenched that most elected politicians were reluctant to take it on and not likely to succeed if they did. And even though the Court did not succeed in eliminating segregation, even though segregation is in some ways deepening again today, and even though many of the civil rights movement's legacies have become unpopular and separatism is increasingly endorsed by both blacks and whites, still virtually no one openly advocates overturning *Brown* and bringing back official Jim Crow laws. Instead, I think most Americans believe that banning those laws was a good result, even if many might wish that it could have been done by a different route. Hence I think it is realistically seen as an exercise of Lockean prerogative power and, on the whole, a successful, popularly accepted exercise. In my admittedly intuitive weighing, that success overbalances its costs to constitutionalism.

Even so, it is not at all clear to me that the Warren Court should have announced that the *Brown* decision was unconstitutional but good, adding further fuel to the already intense flames of controversy that the decision stirred. Certainly no court is ever likely to do so in any case. Again, my praise for *Brown* should also not be mistaken for a general celebration of untethered judicial innovations as happy exercises of prerogative powers.

But if no court will ever announce that it is doing what I think courts are sometimes doing, doubts may again arise. What is the point of urging that commentators describe *Brown* in this way? I think if we as scholars talked about *Brown* as a prerogative power decision, we would, first, be telling the truth, which is very good if not the summum bonum, according to my lights. We would also thereby relieve many scholars and citizens, although not the courts, of the strain of endlessly insisting that the *Brown* result was in fact originally intended, because we believe the result was too good for it to be otherwise.

We could also begin to assess different judicial rationales for the result, not in terms of whether they "solve" the unsolvable problem of proving that *Brown* was originally intended but, rather, in terms of how they cope with the real difficulty: how to execute a prerogative decision without harming the values of constitutionalism too much. We might end up defending the *Brown* decision's justificatory language or McConnell's alternative defense or something else as the best way to minimize the decision's harms to constitutionality while reaching the overall good result. We would do so, however, not because those defenses are simply right on the merits but because we recognize soberly, and I trust cautiously, that some mystification may sometimes serve the cause of good government. This understanding would undoubtedly lead us to new and, I think, richer and wiser assessments of the relevance of *Brown* to broader debates over the powers appropriate to judges and other officials in a constitutional system and of the value of constitutionalism in general.

In so contending, I recognize that commentary terming *Brown* a prerogative decision might well make both commentators and courts somewhat less likely to craft rationales for further judicial activism building on *Brown*-like reasoning. They would have a deeper awareness that to do so is to carry further those jurisprudential moves that are in important respects deceptive and harmful to central constitutional values. If so, that seems to me largely a beneficial consequence and not only because the liberal Warren Court is gone and conservatives with whom I disagree now grip most of the levers of judicial power. It is also because the critics of the Constitution's ultimate adequacy, and the defenders of the superior legitimacy of democratic decision making, have some strong points that we can address better if we admit that *Brown* was unconstitutional. That recognition heightens our awareness of what the abolitionists and many Progressives realized, but too few commentators now acknowledge: that the Constitution is an impressive but flawed document, and it is unwise to premise most political discussion on the assumption that adhering to it is the right thing to do.

But true as I think that point is, I want to rest my case for emphasizing the distinction between constitutionality and goodness, and for recognizing the possibility of judicial "prerogative power" decisions, on the less political argument that such a framework would help us see, describe, explain, and evaluate better what is going on in a lot of constitutional decision making. If judges have the privilege and duty of exercising power responsibly in ways that we do not, we should be sure to exercise our privilege and duty to think and speak honestly and clearly about politics and law in ways that they do not. Fidelity to legal principle may be what "integrity" means for judges, as Ronald Dworkin says, but fidelity to truth is what integrity must mean for scholars.

NOTES

1. Martin Shapiro argues forcefully that whenever disputes are taken to an official third party, at least one more interest is introduced, that of

the "regime" the official represents. If that regime is complexly constituted, as the U.S. government is, it will usually bring a variety of interests
to bear on the official decision maker. Martin M. Shapiro, *Courts: A
Comparative and Political Analysis* (Chicago: University of Chicago Press,
1981), 8–32.

2. Sotirios A. Barber, *On What the Constitution Means* (Baltimore:
Johns Hopkins University Press, 1984), 49–51, 59–61, 191; Sotirios A.
Barber, *The Constitution of Judicial Power* (Baltimore: Johns Hopkins Uni-
versity Press, 1993), 45–48.

3. William F. Harris II, *The Interpretable Constitution* (Baltimore: Johns
Hopkins University Press, 1993), 32, 159.

4. Graham Walker, "The Constitutional Good: Constitutionalism's
Equivocal Moral Imperative," *Polity* 26 (1993): 91–111, 99, 110–11.

5. Keith Whittington, "Constitutional Construction: Divided Powers
and Constitutional Meaning" (Ph.D. diss., Yale University, 1995).

6. Mark A. Graber, "Our (Im)perfect Constitution," *Review of Politics*
51 (1989): 86–107; Mark A. Graber, "Why Interpret? Political Justification
and American Constitutionalism," *Review of Politics* 56 (1994): 415–40. I
think that logically Graber's distinction between reading the Constitution
as a blueprint for the philosophically best society and as a compromise
arrangement we sustain as long as it is not intolerable amounts to less
than meets the eye. Both approaches, and a third Graber discusses, all
ultimately point us to interpreting the Constitution in ways conducive to
the best possible results, given all existing political realities. Even so, I
accept that even if the approaches fully executed did converge in this
way, in practice they would represent different interpretive mind-sets
likely to produce different sorts of opinions. When Graber suggests that
judges might regard "provisions in the text that are unacceptable to
substantial or powerful groups ... as excretions that are in some important sense not really part of the Constitution," however, he is replicating the recurring tactic of minimizing the possibility that what is constitutional and what is best may be two different things (Graber, "Why
Interpret?" 438).

7. Mark Tushnet, "The Dilemmas of Legal Constitutionalism," *Ohio
State Law Journal* 42 (1981): 411–26, 424–26; Mark Tushnet, *Red, White,
and Blue: A Critical Analysis of Constitutional Law* (Cambridge, Mass.: Harvard University Press, 1988), 137–46, 317–18. Martin Shapiro made the
same argument at an APSA panel several years ago, although as far as I
know, he has not been incautious enough to put it into print.

8. For examples of this position in the context of judicial decisions
involving slavery, see Robert M. Cover, *Justice Accused: Antislavery and the
Judicial Process* (New Haven, Conn.: Yale University Press, 1975).

9. Alexander Bickel, *The Morality of Consent* (New Haven, Conn.: Yale University Press, 1975), 5, 123.

10. Antonin Scalia, "Originalism: The Lesser Evil," *University of Cincinnati Law Review* 57 (1989): 863.

11. Sanford Levinson, *Constitutional Faith* (Princeton, N.J.: Princeton University Press, 1988), 10, 17.

12. Jeffrey A. Segal and Harold J. Spaeth, *The Supreme Court and the Attitudinal Model* (Cambridge: Cambridge University Press, 1993), 3, 34, 70.

13. Ibid., 42–43.

14. Robert H. Bork, *The Tempting of America: The Political Seduction of the Law* (New York: Free Press, 1990), 160, 174.

15. For example, Barber, *The Constitution of Judicial Power,* 2–10.

16. Bork, *The Tempting of America,* 158–59.

17. Christopher Wolfe, *The Rise of Modern Judicial Review: From Constitutional Interpretation to Judge-Made Law,* rev. ed. (Lanham, Md.: Rowman and Littlefield, 1994), 400–1.

18. Most, though not all, advocates of natural law or moral realist jurisprudence make a similar move, claiming that hard cases should be decided by appeal to these transcendent standards. Although many nonetheless insist that constitutionality and goodness are distinct, as Barber and Walker do in the quotations cited earlier, it is exceedingly rare for them to argue that a particular decision is unconstitutional but good, or even constitutional but bad.

19. Ronald Dworkin, "The Forum of Principle," *New York University Law Review* 56 (1981): 469–518, 473–74.

20. Ronald Dworkin, *Taking Rights Seriously* (Cambridge, Mass.: Harvard University Press, 1978), 106–7, 117, 127–28, 134–36, 340–42; Ronald Dworkin, *Law's Empire* (Cambridge, Mass.: Belknap Press, 1986), 65–68, 87–88, 217–24, 387–92.

21. Kent Greenawalt and others have suggested that, as Dworkin believes, conformity to precedents should also count as part of the test of fit because the Constitution is a set of ongoing understandings, not just the original text, and because constitutionalist values of stability and predictability are served by honoring *stare decisis.* I think that counting precedents as part of the meaning of the Constitution defines the Constitution too much in terms of what courts have said, not what the people's elected representatives have ratified, in contradiction to the Constitution's professed source of authority. I agree that conformity to precedent often serves values that constitutionalism aims to realize, but so does much legislation to which we would not accord constitutional status. I therefore think that we should count conformity to precedent as a factor

in assessing the decision's overall goodness, not its constitutionality. It is true, nonetheless, that early precedents, in particular, may be helpful in ascertaining the understandings of a constitutional provision held by its ratifiers.

22. Michael W. McConnell, "Originalism and the Desegregation Decisions," *Virginia Law Review* 81 (1995): 947–1140, 950–51.

23. *Brown v. Board of Education*, 347 U.S. 496 (1954).

24. Richard Kluger, *Simple Justice: The History of Brown v. Board of Education and Black America's Struggle for Equality* (New York: Random House, 1975), 334–35, 620–46.

25. There is little dispute that although many reformers of the mid-1860s favored integrated schooling as an ideal, many others thought racial differences needed to be taken into account in education. Even the New England Freedmen's Aid Society said in 1865 that "while we do not admit the absolute inferiority of any race . . . there can yet be no question that races, like nations and individuals, have their peculiarities. All elements are present, but they are blended in various proportions. In the negro race we believe the poetic and emotional qualities predominate, rather than the prosaic, mechanical, and merely intellectual powers." Cited in Robert C. Morris, *Reading, 'Riting, and Reconstruction: The Education of Freedmen in the South, 1861–1870* (Chicago: University of Chicago Press, 1981), 167; compare Leon F. Litwack, *Been in the Storm So Long: The Aftermath of Slavery* (New York: Vintage Books, 1979), 489–90; and Joe M. Richardson, *Christian Reconstruction: The American Missionary Association and Southern Blacks, 1861–1870* (Athens: University of Georgia Press, 1986), 185.

26. The statement is by James Wilson, the chair of the House Judiciary Committee, and it actually is a denial that a broad provision for protection of civil rights and immunities in an earlier version of the 1866 Civil Rights Act would ban school segregation. Wilson nonetheless withdrew the language, in part because critics said it could be so interpreted. The Fourteenth Amendment, which many understood to be an effort to guarantee the 1866 Civil Rights Act's constitutionality, restored a version of Wilson's language in its "privilege and immunities" clause. McConnell suggests that this restoration can be interpreted as including in the amendment a ban on school segregation that he agrees was not included in the act, and he cites a number of legislators so arguing from 1870 to 1873, when the Supreme Court gutted the privilege and immunities clause. But the restoration of language that was explicitly described by its proponent as not banning school segregation is hardly decisive evidence that the language did ban school segregation, regardless of what others said later. And as noted later, none of those legislators said that the

clause enabled courts to overturn school segregation. See McConnell, "Originalism and the Desegregation Decisions," 960, 997–98.

27. Ibid.,, 969–71, 977–80.

28. More evidence for this latter point is provided by Mark A. Graber, "A Constitutional Conspiracy Unmasked: Why 'No State' Does Not Mean 'No State,' " *Constitutional Commentary* 10 (1993): 87–92.

29. McConnell, "Originalism and the Desegregation Decisions," 991, n. 194. In fairness, McConnell does not take full advantage of an argument that works in his behalf. In 1866, many radical Republicans argued that the Thirteenth Amendment's enforcement section gave Congress broad power to address evils beyond the ban on chattel slavery that the first section of the amendment imposed. But the view that the enforcement section empowered Congress only to specify the remedies and penalties for the judicially cognizable ban was widespread, which was why many people thought the 1866 Civil Rights Act needed to be constitutionalized by a further amendment, as it then was. If we take the narrower view as having prevailed, then the enforcement power under the Fourteenth Amendment, when invoked on behalf of a school segregation ban in the 1870s, might well have been understood as an effort to provide further means of remedying and penalizing a practice already constitutionally banned in a way that was judicially cognizable. But since congressional views of the scope of such enforcement powers were divided, McConnell cannot claim that every vote for such a bill reflected a belief that segregation was constitutionally banned in a judicially enforceable fashion. Whether a majority had the view he claims thus remains unproven. For discussions of the enforcement power issue, see, for example, Harold M. Hyman and William M. Wiecek, *Equal Justice under Law: Constitutional Development, 1835–1875* (New York: Harper & Row, 1982), 386–406.

30. Whittington, "Constitutional Construction," 426–41.

31. McConnell, "Originalism and the Desegregation Decisions," 1080–86. In a couple of places, McConnell responds to the Republicans' abandonment of their quest to ban school segregation by quoting a desegregation supporter, James Monroe of Ohio, as saying that blacks in the South thought at that point that their "chances for good schools will be better under the Constitution with the protection of the courts" (1086, 1114). It is surely a sign of desperation when an effort to discern the intent of a majority of the overwhelmingly white framers and ratifiers in 1868 ends up appealing to the hopes of southern blacks in 1875. I fully accept those statements as better guides to justice and goodness, but not original intent.

32. Ibid., 951, n. 11, 1112–14.

33. Gerald N. Rosenberg, *The Hollow Hope: Can Courts Bring about Social Change?* (Chicago: University of Chicago Press, 1991).

34. John Locke, *Two Treatises of Government,* ed. Peter Laslett (Cambridge: Cambridge University Press, 1960), 421–22, 424.

35. I also think these Lockean premises make a strong case for granting to the wise and good Warren Court more prerogative power than to the current Rehnquist Court, but I will not risk arguing that here.

11

CONSTITUTIONAL DISCOURSE AND THE DECEPTIVE ATTRACTIVENESS OF SHARP DICHOTOMIES

KENT GREENAWALT

If I had to answer true or false to Rogers Smith's thesis about the need to clarify the distinction between constitutional legality and overall goodness, I would answer true, but I would complain that the stark simplicity with which he poses his thesis is misleading. What follows is my complaint and the sketch of a more productive way to pose the fundamental issues that concern Smith in his interesting and provocative chapter.

The summary of my complaint is this. (1) The stages at which constitutionality may conflict with goodness need to be clarified. (2) If the main values of constitutionality are consequential, those values are less weighty when the constitutional arguments each way are closely balanced. (3) The basic problems of self-consciousness and candor that Smith identifies concerning *constitutional* decision are pervasive in law. (4) Smith's originalist version of constitutionality adopts, without defense, a debatable emphasis on intent regarding particular practices. (5) His account understates the significance of the body of constitutional decisions, with the result that in his either–or categorization, adherence to precedent is an aspect of goodness rather than constitutionality. (6) Much of his own justification for adhering to constitutionality misfits his version of constitutionality. (7) The conflict he poses does exist, but it is much more blurred than he recognizes. The first three items in this summary are in the realm of clarification; the last four represent at least a partial disagreement with Smith.

I. Truth and Scholarship

As a preliminary, I raise a question about how a scholar should respond to the difference between the *discourse* of judges and the *bases* for their decisions if the scholar perceives such a difference. In one passage, Smith notes that "emphasizing the distinction between constitutionality and goodness may do harm, corroding faith in the legitimacy of desirable decisions and broader political processes and institutions." But, Smith continues, "scholars cannot in good conscience simply presume that these possible harms are decisive. We must take the risks attendant on making that possibility a matter of explicit inquiry."[1] No doubt, scholars should not presume that telling the truth as they see it will be harmful as soon as anyone raises the caution flag of plausible negative consequences. But what should scholars do if their pursuing a course of research and publishing the results seem reasonably likely to produce an overall negative balance of consequences?[2]

Among the possible approaches are these: (1) scholars might carefully evaluate the likely consequences and go forward only if they believe that the balance (taking into account the probabilities and magnitude) is apt to be positive; (2) they might consider the likely consequences and go forward unless the balance is apt to be both negative and substantial; and (3) they might speak the truth unless horrible negative consequences stand up and slap them in the face. Since scholars in the social sciences are not adept at estimating the likely effects of their research, I believe that they should not spend much time worrying about them. They should tell the truth unless they perceive an overwhelming likelihood of some very bad effects. I think this is close to Smith's own position, which he reveals at the end of his chapter with the comment that "fidelity to truth is what integrity must mean for scholars."[3]

II. Conflicts of Constitutionality and Goodness

I turn now to the substance of Smith's discussion, beginning with clarifications. Notice, first, that at least two conflicts between constitutionality and goodness may arise. At what we might call stage 1, the judge could line up the constitutional arguments for a particular result, putting aside his own view of desirable consequences.[4] He could then evaluate which result would be better, assuming for the moment that the constitutional arguments are in equipoise. The judge might find that the legal arguments frequently point one way and good results the other. Since the result that Smith conceives in *Brown v. Board of Education*[5] is a legal rule covering many situations, not just the outcome of a particular dispute between parties, goodness includes a component of legality, even at stage 1. The "result" is a decision based on a holding that will control a vast number of other actual and potential disputes.

If the judge discerns a conflict at stage 1, he might adopt different strategies at stage 2. One strategy is to adhere to constitutionality, no matter what the outcome. (Of course, judges knowing that they were going to follow this strategy would probably not attend self-consciously to goodness at stage 1.) A second strategy is to weigh the goodness of adhering to constitutionality against the goodness of reaching the better result, deciding in the way that would best achieve goodness overall. A third strategy (or a variation of the second) is to give extra weight to adhering to constitutionality, deviating from that only if considerations of overall good are strongly in the opposite direction.[6]

These relations between stages reveal two obvious points. The first is that the number of conflicts at stage 1 is greater than the number of conflicts at stage 2. If constitutionality conforms with goodness at stage 1, the decision is simple. If they are in conflict but the value of adhering to constitutionality is great, judges usually decide according to constitutionality even when goodness at stage 1 opposes that result. In those instances, constitutionality is not opposed to stage 2 goodness.

The second point is that for a strategy that assigns some weight to stage 1 goodness, the questions of judicial self-understanding and candor arise. Even when resolution is achieved in stage 2, because the goodness of adhering to constitutionality outweighs the goodness of a contrary result, a self-conscious, candid judge would explain that the right result constitutionally is not overridden by stage 1 goodness that points in the contrary direction. Even if judges do not explain decisions in this way, astute social scientists might do so.

What Smith says is consistent with these observations, but it does not always come through clearly. When he is explicit, it is the conflict at stage 2 that interests him, that is, when ultimate goodness—including the value of adhering to constitutionality— is opposed to adhering to constitutionality (because other goodness values weigh so strongly in the opposite direction). He does not emphasize that this conflict may arise in very few cases if the values of constitutionality are themselves large, and he seems not to notice that the problem of candor in explanation arises for a much broader range of cases than those of ultimate conflict between constitutionality and goodness.

III. THE VALUES OF CONSTITUTIONALITY AND THEIR WEIGHT

What is the value of adhering to constitutionality? Very roughly, perhaps judges should adhere to it for deontological reasons— such as promising to defend the Constitution when they take their oaths of office—or for consequential reasons—such as the undesirability of people believing that judges are exercising naked power. Even if the primary reasons for deciding in accord with constitutionality are deontological, decisions against constitutionality and in favor of ultimate goodness can still be justified. After all, if the consequences of breaking a promise or lying are beneficial enough, one should break the promise or lie.

Interestingly, the nature of the values of constitutionality may influence the calculations at stage 2. Imagine two cases. In the first, a judge thinks the arguments about constitutionality are strongly on one side, and she knows that others will see them similarly; stage 1 goodness suggests the opposite result. In the second case, the arguments are finely balanced, with the opinions of relevant scholars, lawyers, and other judges about evenly divided; after hard work the judge develops a conviction about constitutionality that happens to oppose her beliefs about stage 1 goodness. For stage 2, what weight does constitutionality have in the balance of overall goodness in the two cases?

If the reasons to adhere to constitutionality are mainly deontological, the apparent decisiveness of legal arguments may not matter too much. There may be strong deontological reasons to follow one's view of what is right even if one's judgment is uncertain. If the reasons to adhere to constitutionality are overwhelmingly consequential, apparent decisiveness will make a tremendous difference. If everyone sees that a decision flaunts constitutionality, as in the first case, that may create a serious disturbance. But if, as in the second case, a result either way would be accepted by many as legitimate and attacked by many as a usurpation, the effect on stability and public legitimacy may be similar, however the court decides. These consequential considerations connected to constitutionality will not count for much against stage 1 goodness that points in the opposite direction.

What is Smith's view of this? He says that he is not concerned about the influence of his thesis on judicial behavior, but many readers are interested in the implications of what he writes for judges. When he addresses the values of constitutionality, Smith uses such phrases as "works real harm to the good that constitutionalism does."[7] His partially expressed theory is that the values of constitutionalism are consequential. But he does not address a corollary of this approach: that when the constitutional result is highly debatable, those values have comparatively little weight— as long as judges write opinions that make the results seem about as plausible as their competitors.[8]

IV. THE BREADTH OF THE PROBLEM

I turn now to my objections to the manner in which Smith poses his problem. In his chapter, he treats constitutionality and the Supreme Court as if they are discrete, isolable aspects of the U.S. legal system, rather than parts of a much larger set of rules, principles, and institutions. Much more troubling for his thesis is that his standard of constitutionality is absurd—not remotely close to what the standard of constitutionality is, and should be, for most of the cases in the U.S. constitutional order. Perhaps the root of these problems is the tendency of courses in public law to focus on innovative, blockbuster Supreme Court decisions. I next show briefly that something like the problems Smith identifies are universal for U.S. law (and perhaps all highly developed law) and that the problems are usually much more subtle and complex than he suggests.

U.S. law consists of statutes and their interpretations and a common law developed by judicial decisions, as well as constitutional law. (I put aside here the further complexity that the U.S. system contains state constitutions and statutes as well as federal ones. Since state constitutions are often more detailed, more easily amended, and less important symbolically than the federal Constitution, the mode of their interpretation may be somewhat different.) The Supreme Court sits atop a hierarchy of federal and state courts, all of which engage in statutory interpretation, common law decision,[9] and interpretation of the federal Constitution.

Statutory interpretation raises a problem just like the one that concerns Smith. Judges may decide that relevant legal criteria, whatever these may be, point toward one result, whereas stage 1 goodness points in the opposite direction. In stage 2, a judge needs to achieve resolution. One possibility is that the value of adhering to the authority of the enacting Congress lessens as the date of a statute recedes in time. That is, what Congress wanted in 1995 perhaps should carry more weight now than what Congress wanted in 1872.

Common law development is a bit more mysterious, and the line between legality and goodness is less distinct. Courts pay attention to the language of earlier opinions, but they often try to discern a convincing logic of decisions not found in any particular language. When new cases differ significantly from their predecessors, courts often reason by analogy. To decide what factors are significant, they draw on community notions of right and good or their own notions of right and good, or both.[10] In the common law, one cannot wholly distinguish legality considerations from goodness considerations.

The problems of self-consciousness and candor in statutory interpretation are virtually identical to those posed by constitutional interpretation. The problems in common law development are similar: Should judges recognize and acknowledge how far their drawing on common law sources depends on modern conceptions of good and right, as opposed to the authority of what earlier cases decide and say? The practical problems with constitutional decision are not unique (though they may have special ramifications); the difficulties are endemic to our law. In every branch, judges pervasively understate the influence of considerations of (nonlegal) right and good. Opinions make decisions sound as if they flow more easily from authoritative legal sources than they actually do.

What is the explanation? Part lies in self-consciousness. Smith sharply depicts students who honestly strain to discover that constitutionality tracks their ideas of good and right. This phenomenon is so widespread that it must be rooted in the human psyche. How often do people say that our participation in a war is good for us but bad for the host country, or vice versa? Ordinary people, as well as politicians, want to believe that what is good for us coincides with what is good for those we assist. Parents disinclined to finance children approaching maturity usually are convinced that financial independence will teach them responsibility. In general, people strongly desire to make relevant considerations line up on the same side.

Judges are no different. Despite their legal training, they are disinclined at stage 1 to discover that legality points one way and goodness the other. If they do see a conflict, they are reluctant to decide at stage 2 that goodness considerations are strong enough to support a decision that would be legally inappropriate. (This problem is lessened for common law decisions because it is recognized that when an established rule is highly unwise or unjust, that is a reason to abandon it.)

As we move from self-consciousness to candor, special considerations about the law become more significant. One factor is that most decisions are made by lower courts on subjects that higher courts have already addressed. According to conventions in common law systems, lower courts are bound to follow higher courts. A second factor is that the decisions of appellate courts are typically supported by the opinions of a majority. Judges must agree on language. A third factor is that legal considerations, such as the force of statutory language, may appear more objective than ideas of right and good. None of these factors compels judges to underplay the role of their judgments about good, but each factor inclines judges in that direction. In these respects, judges in constitutional cases act very much like judges in other cases.

V. Standards of Constitutionality

If scholars are able to differentiate constitutionality from goodness, how are they to understand constitutionality? Smith offers an originalist answer, which takes slightly different forms at various points in his chapter. Representative is his suggestion to "reserve the term *constitutional* for results that have unsurpassed fit with what we can discover about the original meaning of a constitutional provision." This approach, he indicates earlier, has to do with "the logic of written constitutionalism and our legal traditions."[11] Smith means not only that "constitutionality" may not fly in the face of the original meaning but also that it is determined by this meaning to the degree that judges can discern it.

I raise a modest quibble about Smith's standard before discussing a much more telling difficulty. I then proceed to the standard's most serious defect.

The modest quibble is that Smith seems to assume that the right originalism concerns what the framers and ratifiers had in mind. That is by no means obvious. A strong argument can be made that how reasonable readers then understood the language is as, or more, important. This difference is not significant for Smith's thesis. In any real case involving what people thought more than a century ago, distinguishing the content of the participants' intent from the assumptions of reasonable (legal or general) readers is virtually impossible. A shift in emphasis on whose original understanding matters would not affect Smith's major claims.

Another aspect of Smith's version of originalism is more troublesome. Much has been written in the last two decades about various kinds of intentions. From his discussion of *Brown v. Board of Education* and other passages, Smith seems to assume that constitutionality depends mainly on specific intentions concerning particular practices.

Let me illustrate the problem with this with a constitutional issue Smith does not discuss. When the Bill of Rights and Fourteenth Amendment were adopted, the country was overwhelmingly Christian, and atheists and agnostics were few and far between. The framers and ratifiers, let us suppose, thought that nonpreferential aid to Christianity was permitted under the religion clauses and (later) the Fourteenth Amendment. They did not foresee a country in which atheism and agnosticism are more common and in which immigration policies bring to our shores a steadily increasing percentage of persons who are not Christian (or Jewish). Should the adopters' intent be determined by their specific views of nonpreferential aid or by their general sense of the place of religion, as applied to modern conditions? Is not the latter intent the more important to interpreting a document written in highly general language, especially in light of evidence that the framers themselves did not suppose that the interpretation of statutory language should be guided by the narrow, specific intent of the legislators?

Although this is complicated, two points emerge with crystal clarity. First, it is far from obvious that the intent that should count the most is the narrow one regarding the validity of a particular practice. Second, the more that the general intent counts, the harder that it will be for the modern judge to draw a distinction between what the framers would have wanted if their broad understandings had been applied to our social conditions and the judge's own appraisal of the most desirable present application of general language.

This discussion has a straightforward relevance to Smith's discussion of *Brown*. Even if all he says is accurate, constitutionality becomes more debatable if we shift to the more general intentions of the adopters of the Fourteenth Amendment.

The gravest defect in Smith's version of constitutionality is the omission of intervening case law. Most constitutional issues are variations on decisions that the courts have previously rendered. Lower courts mainly concentrate on being faithful to what has previously been decided by Supreme Court justices and other judges, not on original intent. The Supreme Court has more flexibility to swerve from the path of preceding decisions, but it, too, tries to develop consistent principles for adjudication in various areas. The main body of opinions is often tied to earlier cases.

Why does Smith disregard prevailing case law as directly relevant to constitutionality? This is puzzling but perhaps not inexplicable. Smith cites Ronald Dworkin's well-known distinction between legal fit and considerations of morality. Smith tells us that for Dworkin, constitutional fit is a matter of conformity with original intention, but Dworkin is not so narrow; he counts the existing body of constitutional doctrine and decisions as part of fit.[12] Smith, of course, is free to be more of a purist than this, but the inevitable result is to line up all considerations of following precedent on the goodness side for stage 1: *A judge who follows precedent according to standard legal conventions is thus favoring goodness over constitutionality.* This is a strange and confusing way to speak. Is Smith so oblivious to the centrality of precedent because public law teachers focus on major Supreme Court cases for which precedent is not controlling and because Smith's special interest is in decisions that are not strongly supported by precedents? *Brown, Roe v. Wade,*[13] *Reynolds v. Sims,*[14] and *Miranda v. Arizona*[15] all fall into this category.

Once we pay attention to the importance of earlier judicial decisions in the general run of constitutional issues, some other truths emerge. The question of whether constitutional results are frequently clear takes on a different dimension. According to actual standards of interpretation, many constitutional issues raised by clients, and even many argued by lawyers in lower courts, have clear answers. The Supreme Court usually chooses among the most difficult issues to decide. That its decisions can usually be challenged does not mean that the same is true about constitutional judgments by lawyers[16] and judges in general.

Under the conventions of the U.S. system, lower courts generally try to follow the principles established by higher courts. They must pay a lot of attention to Supreme Court precedents. This, of course, does not mean that the Supreme Court must do the same. It could say, "You have done a fine job. You decided correctly from your point of view. We, however, are bound to reach behind precedents to original intent (and perhaps to goodness). So we are reversing you." On some occasions, the Supreme Court does say something like this, and it has indicated clearly that other courts should not disregard earlier Supreme Court decisions, even when they expect them to be overruled.[17] But it is easy to understand that after litigants have spent a lot of money and lower court judges have worked hard, the Supreme Court's usual inclination is not to reverse unless it can explain the mistake that the lower court made. The tendency is therefore to write as if the criteria of decision are roughly the same at all levels of the system.

Many commentators write (accurately, in my view) as if constitutional adjudication lies somewhere between statutory interpretation (of mostly modern, mostly detailed statutes) and common law development. The lapse of time from the adoption of most constitutional provisions, with the diminishing authority of the adopters (who were not representative of large portions of the population) is important, but the generality of the relevant constitutional language matters still more.

Smith's version of constitutionality is at a strange remove from some of his values of constitutionalism. He says, among other things, that

> by making rapid change more difficult, constitutionalism can promote stability, which makes it easier for people to plan their lives securely. By establishing stable patterns of decision making that grow venerable with time, constitutionalism can also foster a sense of common memory and common cooperative endeavor among a political people that may promote both unity and belief in the system's legitimacy.[18]

These values would hardly be served if vast bodies of law shifted with each new understanding of original intention. Rather, the values are assured more by faithfulness to earlier judicial decisions than by an unending search for the best recent surmise about original intent.

Realistic attention to earlier judicial decisions would muddy Smith's handy dichotomy. Insofar as constitutional decision at its best resembles common law development, the line between legality and goodness blurs.

VI. CONCLUSION AND SUGGESTION

Smith's claim that social science should attend to differences between constitutionality and assessments of overall good is indeed the beginning of one part of wisdom. His concerns about judicial self-consciousness and judicial candor are certainly well grounded. However, anyone who seeks to find out where constitutionality ends and judgments of goodness begin and anyone who seeks to justify decisions at odds with constitutionality on the grounds that they promote good must strive for a deeper account of what constitutionality involves in our legal system.

A reader might suppose that all I have said up to now is essentially destructive of Smith's enterprise. When everything runs together, how can we draw distinctions? If the core of Smith's thesis is sound, as I have granted, maybe it is preferable to work with a somewhat controversial, overly simple version of constitutionality than to introduce complexities that will defeat the project. This indeed was part of Smith's response when I commented on his paper at the society's meeting in December 1995. This response is understandable, but my negative remarks can be converted into a positive program in either of two ways.

Before I perform the conversion, I want to show from a somewhat different angle why Smith's categorization will not do the job he wants. Imagine four justices. Justice A slavishly adheres to constitutional precedents as he understands them, believing that continuity is the essence of law. Justice B is an extreme believer in judicial restraint. She recognizes that the framers meant to give judges considerable powers, but she is so troubled by the counter-majoritarian nature of judicial review and by the difficulty of drawing lines that she defers to legislative choice even when she both believes the framers would have wished otherwise and dislikes the legislative choice. Justice C is a genuine originalist. Justice D often decides in accord with what she thinks are good results for society, even when these are at odds with the original understanding, legislative choice, and precedent.

Smith seems mainly interested in Justice D: she decides in accord with her evaluation of the overall good, not in accord with legal standards of constitutionality. But Smith's version of constitutionality ends up placing A and B in the same box as D; all choose overall good (in some sense) over constitutionality. It is just this categorization that is so unrevealing, linking the activist Justice D with her legalistic colleagues, Justices A and B, who practice forms of judicial restraint. This is not a welcome payoff for someone who aims to develop a realistic appraisal that justices rely on their views of goodness.

There are at least two better ways to proceed. One would be to offer a single version of constitutionality, as Smith does, recognizing that other scholars will give different accounts. We could then determine when justices depart from this as an exclusive guide—almost always may be the answer. But we would need also to find out how they depart. Do the justices blindly follow precedent, exercise severe restraint in the face of legislative choice, rely on their ideas of social good, or what? And are they self-conscious and candid about whatever they do? We could then, with some difficulty, look at the questions that concern Smith, without putting apples and baseball bats in single box of nonvegetables.

I believe that Smith's version—as well as any single-factor version—of constitutionality is a misguided description of, or prescription for, our legal system. Accordingly, I prefer a second approach in which scholars would identify the considerations that matter to the justices in constitutional cases. These considerations would include (1) original understanding (in the sense of "adopter intent" or "reasonable reader" or both) of particular practices, (2) original understanding of more abstract ideas (such as of the basic relation of religion to government, (3) ideas about deference to legislative and executive judgment (insofar as these do not follow from original understandings), (4) consistency with results in prior authoritative cases, (5) consistency with prior judicial doctrines, (6) developments in other parts of the legal system, (7) modern community notions of (nonlegal) justice and welfare, and (8) the justices' own assessments of (nonlegal) justice and welfare. This list is rough and not meant to be complete.

For any one consideration to matter, it is not necessary that justices self-consciously give it relevance, much less discuss it in their opinions. All that is required is that a scholar see that the justices are moved by that consideration and that it might justify a result. (I add this last caveat so as not to include the various biases and prejudices that also influence people but cannot be said to justify a result.)

Scholars would do the best job they could to discover why justices decide in the way that they do and whether their announced reasons carry the force that they claim. The scholars could then determine whether judicial and community notions of justice and welfare are playing a greater role than is acknowledged, perhaps asking whether a form of opinion writing that downplays these factors is justifiable. Scholars might also ask whether these factors rightly underlie results when more "legal" factors point in contrary directions.

This approach, which requires a sensitive understanding of how justices conceive their responsibilities, would explore all the questions that concern Smith. It would not yield a neat dichotomy between "constitutionality" and "goodness" decisions, but no scholar interested in truth should welcome a Procrustean framework that yields tidy categorization at the cost of distorting existing practices and defensible outlooks.

NOTES

1. Rogers M. Smith, "The Inherent Deceptiveness of Constitutional Discourse: A Diagnosis and Prescription," this volume, 231.

2. I touch on these issues in "Truth or Consequences," in Ian Shapiro and Judith Wagner DeCew, eds., *Theory and Practice*, NOMOS XXXVII (New York: New York University Press, 1995), 386–99.

3. Smith, "The Inherent Deceptiveness of Constitutional Discourse," 249.

4. For this purpose, I count as desirable consequences the satisfaction of nonlegal deontological norms, as well as the production of desirable states of affairs.

5. *Brown v. Board of Education*, 347 U.S. 483 (1954).

6. This strategy could be a variation of the second if all deontological reasons to adhere to constitutionality counted as part of overall goodness.

7. Smith, "The Inherent Deceptiveness of Constitutional Discourse," 232.

8. Of course, he might argue that judges acting in this manner produce corrosive long-term consequences for the system of law.

9. Federal courts follow state decisions on common law except for limited areas, such as admiralty, in which a kind of federal common law prevails.

10. Melvin Eisenberg, in *The Nature of the Common Law* (Cambridge, Mass.: Harvard University Press, 1988), explains this and argues that the courts should rely only on community morality. I suggest that such reliance alone cannot be sufficient, in my *Law and Objectivity* (New York: Oxford University Press, 1992), 217–18.

11. Smith, "The Inherent Deceptiveness of Constitutional Discourse," 241, 229.

12. See, for example, Ronald Dworkin, *Law's Empire* (Cambridge, Mass.: Harvard University Press, 1986).

13. *Roe v. Wade*, 410 U.S. 113 (1973).

14. *Reynolds v. Sims*, 377 U.S. 533 (1964).

15. *Miranda v. Arizona*, 384 U.S. 436 (1966).

16. A lawyer's judgment often is that a claim is not worth pushing.

17. See *Agostini v. Felton*, S.Ct. (1997) (1997 WL 338583).

18. Smith, "The Inherent Deceptiveness of Constitutional Discourse," 233.

12

PRAGMATISM, HONESTY, AND INTEGRITY

CATHARINE PIERCE WELLS

INTRODUCTION

In this chapter, I respond to the chapter by Rogers Smith criticizing constitutional discourse for its "inherent deceptiveness." Smith's complaint is that constitutional argumentation and commentary tend to confuse two different concepts. The first is the rightness of a decision in terms of its conformity to constitutional texts, and the second is the goodness of a decision as an instance of government policy. By "conformity to constitutional texts," Smith means "adherence to what seems most likely to have been the meaning or meanings of a provision originally accepted by those who ratified it, stated at the highest level of generality they would have recognized." By the "goodness" of a decision, he means that it is genuinely the best outcome, all things considered.[1]

Smith's definition of *constitutional*—adherence to the original meaning of the constitutional text—seems, at least on the surface, to entail a kind of originalism. Thus Smith shares with writers such as Antonin Scalia and Robert Bork an understanding of the Constitution as a historical document whose meaning can be determined primarily by examining the linguistic intent of its original proponents. A closer reading of Smith's chapter, however, indicates that he is seeking to locate himself in a more moderate position, somewhere between the conservatism of Bork and Scalia and the liberalism of Ronald Dworkin. For example, he denies that the courts are always bound by the historical meaning of the Constitution. They are sometimes free, he argues, to rule in favor of sound policy and fundamental justice.[2] His concern, he explains, is not with how judges decide cases but, rather, with how legal scholars and writers analyze constitutional decision making. In this context, Smith believes that the distinction between the original meaning of the Constitution and what is good as a matter of contemporary policy serves to promote clarity, honesty, and integrity in constitutional analysis.

It is not hard to get an intuitive grasp of the distinction that Smith is endorsing. In his chapter, Smith illustrated this distinction by describing students' confusion when they begin to talk about constitutional decision making:

> They come in knowing little about the Constitution's text, its origins, or its previous interpretations. Yet when they read a constitutional provision, many instantly assume that it must have been intended to mean what they think it would be good for it to mean. Conversely, when they read about a constitutional controversy, they intuit the result that seems good to them, and they assume that it is not only appropriate but also constitutionally necessary to reach that result.[3]

Indeed, as someone who has taught constitutional cases (though not constitutional law), I have encountered such confusion and addressed it by asking students to consider whether goodness and constitutionality are always the same thing. The intuitive appeal of Smith's distinction is that it purports to unscramble these two overlapping concepts. In addition, it is intended to clarify the dilemma posed by some of the most difficult constitutional cases—cases in which what is "good" and what is "constitutional" do not coincide.[4]

Despite the intuitive appeal of Smith's distinction, I believe that it does little to illuminate the complex process of constitutional decision making. One problem is that Smith's distinction lacks the precision and clarity that would make it genuinely useful.[5] A second and more serious problem is that his account of the distinction overstates its mark. Although I agree that "What does the text say?" is a different question from "What is the best thing to do?" I disagree with the notion that the first question can be correctly settled without serious consideration of the second. By overlooking the mutual dependence of interpretive and normative questions, Smith erects a wall that is much too thick between constitutionality and goodness—two norms that are importantly and interestingly related.

My plan in this chapter is to talk about Smith's distinction in three different contexts. First, I consider his proposal as an endorsement of a semantic distinction to be carefully observed in constitutional analysis.[6] Since the distinction draws heavily on original intent as the source of constitutional meaning, I begin by examining the standard objections to originalism and by determining whether and how they apply to Smith's more limited proposal. I then argue that his overly simple reliance on a bright-line distinction between "good" and "constitutional" obscures an important aspect of constitutional decision making and should therefore be avoided.

Second, I look at Smith's distinction in a more practical context—what we should say to students who persist in making no distinction between the meaning of the Constitution as a historical document and the desirability of certain constitutional outcomes. Smith's view is that we should train students to observe a rigorous distinction between the two. If I am right that emphasizing this distinction obscures important aspects of constitutional decision making, then it is necessary to deal with this pedagogical problem in a different way.

In the third and final section, I return to jurisprudential considerations and look at Smith's underlying theory of constitutional adjudication. This theory might be summarized as follows:

> In most cases, judges ought to do what is good under all the circumstances, weighing heavily the damage to constitutionalism that results from decisions that are not based on the historical meaning of the Constitution. In an exceptional case such as *Brown v. Board of Education,* the court may exercise a sovereign's limited prerogative to reach a good result that is at odds with the best constitutional interpretation.

Even though this jurisprudential theory is not Smith's main focus, the clear implication of his argument is that such a theory would have the virtue of eliminating dishonesty and confusion in judicial interpretations of constitutional texts.

In making this argument, Smith follows the lead of many legal theorists and assumes that legal decision making has integrity if, and only if, it is governed by principles that are accurately and fully disclosed (see section III). To the contrary, I argue that Smith's distinction promotes integrity only in the context of a particular conception of integrity. This conception is antipragmatic in that it favors "principled decision making" over what it dismisses as "ad hoc decision making." In short, by defining integrity in terms of adherence to principle, it inevitably entails the conclusion that those who advocate more pragmatic theories have less integrity. As an alternative, I offer a pragmatic concept of integrity that is not based on adherence to principle but nevertheless captures our intuition that judges must follow "the law."

I. ANALYZING CONSTITUTIONAL LAW: THE PITFALLS OF ORIGINALISM

Smith's analysis has two components—a semantic one requiring that we use the word *constitutional* only in its historical sense[7] and a jurisprudential component that assigns to the historical notion of constitutionality a somewhat limited role in the practice of constitutional adjudication.[8] Thus on one hand, Smith shares with originalists such as Scalia and Bork the claim that questions of constitutionality are normally factual questions requiring an empirical analysis of historical information. On the other hand, he differs from them by recognizing that historical considerations cannot always be decisive in the context of constitutional decision making. In this section, I survey the standard objections to originalism and consider their salience as applied to Smith's more moderate version.

Originalism is subject to a number of familiar criticisms. One set of criticisms stems from the general ambiguity of the historical information.[9] The adoption of a constitution requires participation and debate in a variety of public and private forums, and so the resulting historical record is often complex and ambiguous. Furthermore, even if the historical ambiguities could be clarified, the standard problems of interpretation would remain. That is, how can we determine an individual speaker's intent when we suspect that at least some of the speaker's statements are made for strategic reasons? How do we understand a person's meaning when his or her words express strong but vague aspirations? And even if we ascertain individual intent, the familiar problems regarding group intent would remain. Originalism requires that we look to the intent of the framers or the ratifiers, but if we make the natural assumption that not all of them have the same intent, whose intent is to count? Is it majority rule? Or should we simply register the intent of the most vocal and articulate? And as a final problem, there are the doubts suggested by the philosopher W. V. O. Quine, who reminds us that even under the best of circumstances, semantic interpretations are always underdetermined by the linguistic data.[10]

A second criticism is more substantive and political. Every historical tale is told from a distinctive point of view. Many things happen in the course of adopting a constitution. Inevitably, what we understand about these things is only a partial story—a story that requires us to recreate continuity and detail. As a result, the historical record often lends credibility to several competing constitutional interpretations. Choosing among them requires not only historical expertise but also a "sense" of which facts are salient and which are not, a sense that is importantly related to a network of other normative judgments.

Consider, for example, two historians. Historian A identifies with the founding fathers and admires both their devotion to public service and the depth of their vision. Thus, for Historian A, the Constitution represents a just and timeless foundation for political life. Historian B is less admiring. The founding fathers, she believes, were holders of privilege in a patriarchal, white supremacist society. In accordance with this view, Historian B thinks of the Constitution not as a source of justice but as a political settlement that divides and preserves the spoils of an initially unjust distribution of power and property. Given the breadth and complexity of the historical record, the views of neither historian can be easily dismissed. Nevertheless, the two different mind-sets provide different frameworks for questions of constitutional interpretation. For Historian A, the forward-looking aspirations of the most progressive members of the Constitutional Conventions are entitled to have great interpretive weight. Historian B, on the other hand, understands constitutional provisions in the context of the bargains they represent; their inherent fairness or wisdom is not an issue. Thus the two historians have a different "sense" of what facts are important, and these two different senses are related to other evaluative judgments. Ultimately, these differences have their origin in a distinctly personal context—a context in which an individual's underlying attitudes, temperament, and purpose play an important role.

In addition to these problems of interpretation and viewpoint, the theories of Bork and Scalia represent an extreme form of political conservatism. For instance, they are frequently criticized for rejecting the idea that the Constitution should be interpreted in the light of progressive notions of freedom and fairness.[11] Instead, they refer fundamental questions about human rights to the customs and practices of those who lived hundreds of years ago. Furthermore, to the extent that the Constitution "constitutes" the national government, the originalist approach commits them to antiquated forms of self-rule.[12]

When applying these criticisms to Smith, it is important to note that his liberal originalism differs from the more conservative versions in a number of ways. For example, unlike the conservatives, Smith believes that in some cases, it may be appropriate for a court to exercise its "prerogative power"[13] by deciding a case in accordance with the public good, even in the face of countervailing constitutional (historical) considerations. And even though Smith thinks that a sovereign prerogative can be utilized only in exceptional cases, there are many other situations, he believes, in which it is appropriate for the Court to be swayed by considerations of public policy.

For example, in many cases, several different outcomes may be equally plausible from a constitutional (historical) point of view. In this situation, Smith argues, the Court is free to decide the case in accordance with its own sense of what is right and to describe its decision as based on a constitutional (historical) interpretation.[14] And just as there may be too many plausible historical interpretations, there may also be too few. Suppose a case presents a question for which there is little persuasive evidence of what the ratifiers intended. What, for example, would be the ratifier's view of free speech and the Internet? Because there is no historical evidence, conservative originalists may urge the Court to abstain from an activist position, but Smith, with his more liberal instincts, seems to suggest that the Court should rule with a view toward promoting the public good. In short, the Court should "do the right thing" even as the lack of a constitutional (historical) basis renders it more cautious.

At first glance, many of the objections to originalism that I discussed at the beginning of this section seem less forceful when applied to Smith's more limited proposal. For example, the frequency with which the historical record fails to make an unambiguous endorsement of a single interpretation does not refute the proposal that we use the word *constitutional* to refer to such interpretations. Indeed, as we have seen, Smith acknowledges that there may be constitutional (historical) considerations that support both sides of a given issue. Similarly, the fact that historical interpretations are heavily influenced by individual perspective and viewpoint is an objection only to those forms of originalism that assume that historical considerations must be decisive with respect to questions of adjudication.

Even though Smith's more moderate approach avoids the specific objections that weigh heavily against other forms of originalism, it remains vulnerable to a more general problem—an overdependence on too strict a distinction between questions of fact and questions of value. This problem leads him to overlook the profound interdependence between them and, as a result, to give an impoverished account of constitutional debate. In the next two sections, I analyze this interdependence at greater length; in the remainder of this section, I focus on the way in which Smith's proposal narrowly circumscribes the analysis of constitutional discourse.

Smith's approach relies on a supposed distinction between factual questions (historical intent) and value questions (good policy). By insisting on a firm distinction between these two concepts, he believes that he is purchasing honesty and clarity for constitutional discourse. Beginning with these two conceptions as the basic elements of constitutional decision making, the task then is to describe the procedure by which these elements are combined into a correct constitutional decision. As a constitutional theorist, Smith must tell us which facts matter, which values must be consulted, and in what order and proportion. Although this procedure may seem to give an orderly account of constitutional decision making, as a prescription for court action, it fails to achieve its stated objectives of honesty and clarity.

To see why, suppose that the Supreme Court has a staff of expert historians and also a staff of moral theorists. Each time the Court decides a case, the historical experts are asked to develop a full historical account of the constitutional provision in question and to generate information that would help determine how the framers or ratifiers would have felt about the issue before the Court. When the historians are finished, the moral philosophers are dispatched to analyze the issue in terms of competing values. The Court, for example, might want to know which values would be promoted by each of several possible outcomes. It might also seek the philosophers' advice about which values its decision should seek to implement. Finally, the Court would decide in accordance with Smith's protocol:

1. When the historical record is clear that the framers intended one result or the other, the Court would follow their intent in most cases and would listen to the historians.

2. In rare cases, the Court would rule contrary to the framers' intent because of an overriding public good, and as a matter of sovereign prerogative, the Court would listen to the moral philosophers.

3. In cases in which the historical evidence was inconclusive, the Court could rule on the basis of the public good but could characterize its decisions as based on constitutional (historical) meanings. In such cases, it would follow the advice of the moral philosophers but selectively use the historians' research to justify its ruling.

According to Smith, the Court should evaluate the historical evidence in each case and decide which of the preceding three categories is applicable. This theory of constitutional decision making is predicated on what Smith calls the "conclusiveness" of the historical argument.

A good example of Smith's idea of historical debate is contained in his discussion of *Brown v. Board of Education*.[15] In disputing the constitutionality (historical) of the result reached in *Brown*,[16] Smith examines the historical arguments put forward by Michael McConnell.[17] While not disputing the accuracy of McConnell's facts, he does disagree with McConnell's interpretations of them. Thus the recognition that certain congressmen believed the Fourteenth Amendment prohibited school segregation is followed by Smith's argument: "But McConnell supplies no evidence that any of these legislators explicitly contended that by itself, the Fourteenth Amendment empowered the *courts* to overturn state school segregation."[18] This quotation is instructive. It does not matter whether Smith is right or wrong about the Fourteenth Amendment; rather, what is notable is his argument and the way he draws conclusions from the historical record: McConnell found it significant that certain congressmen thought the amendment outlawed segregated schools, but Smith does not. The dispute here is not about historical fact but about the interpretation of historical fact and what it tells us about an important contemporary controversy.

Certainly, it is not surprising that historical arguments are primarily about interpretation rather than the accuracy of historical facts.[19] Smith, no doubt, would recognize that this is so. But unfortunately, recognition of this fact poses certain difficulties for the "clarifying" strategy that Smith is pursuing. To avoid the standard objections to originalism, Smith must make constitutional (historical) arguments decisive only in those cases in which the historical facts are unequivocal. Nevertheless, in *Brown*—the case he uses as an example of a clear case—the historical record appears unequivocal to him only because he weighs the facts in a particular way; that is, he considers some to be decisive while dismissing others as unimportant. The arguments are therefore not about facts but about the relative importance of facts, and such arguments are inevitably affected by normative considerations.

In short, Smith is between a rock and a hard place. On one hand, if the term *constitutional (historical)* refers only to the unequivocal endorsement of a case outcome by the historical data, it will be an extremely rare (or nonexistent) case that belongs in one of the first two categories. Indeed, most (or all) the cases will be decided in accordance with the third: the historical evidence is inconclusive, thereby leaving the Court to decide on policy grounds and to make strategic use of the historical evidence to justify its conclusions.

On the other hand, if constitutional (historical) arguments require evaluation and interpretation of the data, then Smith will have the same problem as the strict originalists do. Under this alternative, there will be plenty of cases in the first category, but they will be in the first category precisely because Smith is giving the historians—historians with their own normative understanding of constitutional history—an opportunity to interpret the data. As we have seen, these opportunities are inherently deceptive in that they hide substantive value choices under the guise of an objective examination of the historical record.[20] Thus, whether Smith construes the notion of historical evidence broadly or narrowly, his moderate version of originalism does not vindicate his conception of integrity, because it fails to provide for full disclosure of the reasons that are truly operative in judicial decision making.

The problem is that Smith's proposal shares the central weakness of the originalist position. The fundamental problem with originalism is that it attempts to convert a normative inquiry into an empirical historical inquiry. Values are made to disappear as the question "What should the courts do?" becomes "What would certain historical figures want the courts to do?" The supposed advantage of this conversion is a kind of philosophical alchemy in which the courts transform themselves from instruments of naked political power to legitimate representatives of the founding fathers. Nevertheless, as the preceding criticisms demonstrate, the value questions underlying every constitutional inquiry do not simply disappear. Instead, they are hidden in suppressed premises and covertly expressed in supposedly factual interpretations of the historical record. Smith seems to avoid this difficulty by restoring value questions to the center of constitutional adjudication. He believes that the courts should decide cases in accordance with the public good, and he assigns to historical considerations a certain value that should be considered in determining the best result. Smith's proposal appears modest: honesty and clarity will be served by a clear distinction between historical and policy considerations. The problem with the proposal, however, is that it ignores the inherently normative character of historical analysis and therefore promotes apparent clarity at the expense of a realistic understanding of constitutional decision making.

II. Teaching Constitutional Law: The Inherent Complexity of Normative Discourse

Constitutional reasoning is both subtle and complex. Describing it, we are often lost in a tangle of abstract terms and competing considerations. Consequently, most of us who teach constitutional cases rely on some form of learning by doing: students argue for a given result; they reflect on the persuasiveness of their arguments; and they contemplate the consequences of their arguments for other cases. In this context, students frequently confuse constitutionality and goodness by making arguments about goodness when arguments about interpretation would be more appropriate. In this section, I consider the question of what we should tell students about the concept of constitutionality and its relationship to notions of goodness. The reason for doing this is not so much to deal with the pedagogical problems that arise in teaching constitutional law but, rather, to explore the complex nature of the relationship between goodness and constitutionality in a simple and straightforward way.

Smith urges us to respond to students who use "good" and "constitutional" interchangeably by pointing out the confusion and insisting that they use the terms more precisely. On one level, I agree with Smith: "What does the constitution mean?" is not the same question as "What does the public good require?" On a deeper level, however, Smith seems to oversimplify the problem by treating the distinction as merely a matter of semantic clarification. Because I am concerned about oversimplification, I tend to explore the problem more extensively, trying to be more specific about the nature of the distinction and the reason that it is a central dilemma in constitutional law.

One thing I avoid in discussing the distinction between goodness and constitutionality is the temptation to align it with the more general distinction between facts and values. The concepts of both constitutionality and goodness are inherently normative: goodness is a matter of applying a relevant set of values to a particular set of circumstances, and constitutionality is a matter of determining how a particular constitutive text should be interpreted.

When talking about this distinction, the first thing to stress is that interpretive questions can never be fully answered by references to historical facts. With respect to the Constitution, students do not need any complicated postmodern arguments to see that this is true. For example, those who think that historical interpretations are possible frequently argue that the phrase "cruel and unusual punishment" should be understood in terms of whatever punishments were permitted at the time the Constitution was enacted.[21] This, they claim, is a "factual" interpretation because the meaning of the phrase "cruel and unusual" is determined solely by reference to the historical facts.

Much is assumed in this interpretation that is normative rather than factual. For example, the interpretation presumes that those who drafted, debated, and supported the Constitution meant to immunize all existing punitive practices from claims that they were cruel and unusual. But how could such an overstated assumption be supported by factual evidence? The problem is that interpreting abstract statements requires particularly complex forms of reasoning. "Stop where you are!" yelled by a police officer to a lone runner on an otherwise empty street has a relatively clear meaning. The more abstract prohibition "Never run from police" has a higher degree of ambiguity; it takes a more complex pattern of reasoning to apply it to particular cases. Likewise, we cannot decide what the Constitution means until we have evaluated the relative merits of different interpretive strategies. Nor can we choose one interpretation over another without deciding what kinds of arguments are relevant (and/or decisive) to making the choice. Thus, interpreting the Constitution requires a commitment to specific interpretive practices, and choosing these practices is inevitably a normative choice.

In addition to emphasizing the normative nature of interpretive problems, I also stress the interdependence of questions about constitutional interpretation and questions about the requirements of justice and goodness. Generally, students have no problem understanding and using these two terms. Indeed, the difficult thing for them is not so much to distinguish these concepts as it is to explain why, given the obviousness of the distinction, the two concepts become so easily confused. It therefore is important to address not only the students' confusion but also the reason for it. I think that Smith is partially correct in stating that the reason is a kind of wishful thinking: students hope and believe that there is some relationship between the Constitution and the public good but are unable to define it precisely. To help students see this, I ask a series of questions: Why is it tempting to use these terms interchangeably? What issues are suppressed when we do this? What are the consequences of this confusion? Answering these questions requires us to explore what the world of constitutional government would look like if the notions of constitutionality and goodness were entirely distinct. Notwithstanding our hopes to the contrary, suppose that we were forced to conclude that the founding fathers' historical intent was to perpetuate fundamental injustice and make irrational arrangements of human affairs. If true, this conclusion would force us to confront a series of difficult questions: What is the basis of constitutional authority? Why should we tolerate injustice and inefficiency to comply with the directives of men who lived more than two hundred years ago? Is there any compelling reason to follow the Constitution after we have recognized its limitations as a governing document? These questions illustrate the problem with a complete separation between constitutionality and goodness. Severing the Constitution from its moral aspirations reduces its moral authority. When we focus too exclusively on its historical/factual elements, we limit the justification for its continuing power over human affairs to certain kinds of positivistic considerations, considerations that do not provide a very strong justification for maintaining an unjust and inefficient political order. It is only when we suppose that the dictates of the Constitution are rooted in our sense of justice that the reason to limit political choices becomes compelling.

Similar considerations apply to thinking of constitutionality solely in terms of its substantive goodness. Suppose that calling an outcome "constitutional" means nothing more than that the outcome conforms to our best aspirations toward justice. If this were all that constitutional meant, the Constitution would lose its power to define the substantive moral commitments that form the foundation of our national life. Indeed, the document itself would seem to be nothing more than a political relic that reminds us of our aspirations for justice but does little to help us determine what the substantive content of those aspirations should be.

The American constitutional tradition requires that we understand the concept of constitutionality in terms of both its historical elements and its attempts to define the substantive terms of beneficial human interaction. This is the reason that there is so much confusion between constitutionality and goodness; it is not entirely the result of wishful thinking. The so-called confusion actually reflects a reality at the heart of constitutional debate — the reality that the Constitution's continuing authority depends on the inseparability of normative and traditional elements in determining what is constitutional and what is not. We could say, "So much the worse for the Constitution!" but for me at least, this would be too high a price to pay for semantic rigor.

In the end, it comes down to choice: do we insist on a rigorous distinction between "good" and "constitutional," or do we accept the reality that constitutional government depends on an equivocation between these two terms. For a number of reasons, I embrace the second alternative. First, I believe that the Constitution's reliance on the equivocation between good and constitutional is an important fact about our political system and that denying this fact is its own kind of wishful thinking. Second, I believe that recognizing the close connection between questions of constitutionality and questions of morality is essential to realistic political debate. Smith's distinction permits us to talk about values as long as we understand that such talk must stand on its own two feet.[22] The distinction thus isolates conversations about values from their constitutional context. Third, our continuing commitment to constitutional government can be justified, I think, only in terms of its underlying claims to justice and goodness. Indeed, if we ignore these claims, we will not be able to explain the continuing relevance of constitutional questions. And even more important, we will not recognize the need to listen carefully to those who are alienated from the Constitution and the values it represents.

III. Deciding Constitutional Law: Pragmatism, Honesty, and Integrity in Legal Decision Making

The first two sections focused on the distinction between goodness and constitutionality; this last section centers on the related notion of judicial integrity. Smith argues that the distinction promotes integrity by providing two contrasting terms that can be used to analyze the justification for judicial action in particular cases. I disagreed by contending that the distinction is based on a deceptively simple description of the decision-making process and that it is therefore counterproductive in the pursuit of judicial integrity. The requirement of judicial integrity, however, merits a closer examination. What do we expect honest judges to do? How do we understand the word *integrity* in this context? It is clear that judicial integrity amounts to more than the mere avoidance of bribery and partiality. When we say that we want judges with integrity, we do not simply mean that we want them to tell the truth. We also are saying that we want them to be faithful to the task of legal decision making. Judges should apply "the law"—whatever "the law" is—rather than simply follow their own personal inclinations. Thus, we cannot be precise about the concept of judicial integrity without some prior notions about the nature of the decision-making process.

I begin with a discussion of two different theories of legal decision making. The first is the originalist theory proposed by Justice Antonin Scalia for adjudicating constitutional cases. His theory describes legal decision making as a process of historical exegesis by which the judge is able to interpret the Constitution in accordance with the best estimate of the framers' original intent. The second theory is that proposed by Justice Benjamin Cardozo in *The Nature of the Judicial Process* (1921). This theory is not exclusively—or even primarily—concerned with constitutional decision making. Instead, Cardozo treats constitutional decision making as a special case of a more general theory of legal adjudication.[23] This theory is pragmatic in that it describes the process of legal decision making as a multilayered, multifaceted activity that is at least partly intuitive. Thus, for Cardozo, judges may "follow the law," even though they do not follow a reasoning process that can be fully characterized as the result of a single strand of argumentation.

Cardozo's theory differs strongly from the general theory underlying Scalia's originalism. Scalia's theory suggests that legal decisions are the result of applying a single set of considerations—in the case of constitutional law, historical considerations—to reach a conclusion. Cardozo's theory, in contrast, sees legal decision making as the result of many different strands of legally acceptable argument. Thus, these two theories of judicial decision making result in two different conceptions of judicial integrity. Although both theories require that judges follow the law, they envision this requirement in very different terms. The first concept of integrity is a formal notion underlying Scalia's originalism and many other "single-strand" theories of legal decision making. The second is a more procedural notion that requires giving due weight to justifiable legal reasons.

A. *Scalia's Account of Constitutional Decision Making*

The substance of Scalia's originalism is well known, and I will not belabor it here. I will focus instead on what he identified as the strengths and weaknesses of his position, in his essay entitled "Originalism: The Lesser Evil."[24] Scalia argues for originalism by balancing its defects against what he sees as the more serious difficulties encountered by nonoriginalist positions. In this argument, the concept of integrity plays an important role.

Scalia concedes two defects in the theory of originalism. One is that the theory sometimes endorses extremely unpalatable constitutional decisions. What if historical research suggests that an important and long-standing line of cases should be overruled? What if a state adopts a criminal sanction—flogging, for example—that is undeniably cruel by today's standards but was nevertheless permitted when the Constitution was enacted? Could originalism be the correct theory, Scalia asks, if it entails constitutional decisions that are repugnant to contemporary standards? And even though he assures the reader that repugnant decisions are unlikely, his own attitude toward this reality seems somewhat ambivalent. On the one hand, he insists that such compromises involve a true retreat from originalist principles. Yet on the other hand, he seems relieved that the inevitability of such compromises ensures that we do not always have to swallow the "strong medicine"[25] of the originalist approach.

Scalia also recognizes that the originalist position is weakened by the real difficulties it encounters in practical application:

> [I]t is often exceedingly difficult to plumb the original understanding of an ancient text. Properly done, the task requires the consideration of an enormous mass of material. . . . Even beyond that, it requires an evaluation of the reliability of that material— many of the reports of the ratifying debates, for example, are thought to be quite unreliable. And further still, it requires immersing oneself in the political and intellectual atmosphere of the time—somehow placing out of mind knowledge that we have which an earlier age did not, and putting on beliefs, attitudes, philosophies, prejudices and loyalties that are not those of our day.[26]

Scalia illustrates his point with an analysis of Taft's opinion in *Myers*.[27] One issue in *Myers* was whether the president's executive power included the power to dismiss executive officers. Writing for the Court, Chief Justice William Howard Taft concluded that it did, based on an assumption that the president's power had been modeled on the British system. Scalia quotes Taft's brief argument and then proceeds to describe half a dozen "gaps" in his reasoning. Scalia then assembles bits and pieces of historical evidence that could be used to fill them. But some of these bits and pieces are from historical research that was not available at the time of Taft's opinion.[28] The point of this analysis is to demonstrate the practical difficulties with historical interpretation, and it is these difficulties that he considers to be the second defect of originalism—the complexity of historical analysis and the court's resulting inability to do it with substantial accuracy.

As a counterweight to the defects of originalism, Scalia describes what he sees as the chief weakness of nonoriginalist positions.[29] The weakness in such positions, he argues, is that they are inconsistent with what, to him, is the strongest justification for judicial review of constitutional questions. Citing Chief Justice John Marshall's argument in *Marbury v. Madison*,[30] Scalia contends that the Supreme Court's jurisdiction over constitutional questions stems from its expertise in reconciling the conflicting claims of various authoritative legal texts and not from some presumed ability to resolve important political controversies by applying contemporary social values. If the Constitution really were an invitation to subsequent generations to apply their own social values, Scalia argues, then surely the invitation would have been addressed to the legislature rather than to the judiciary.

The point of Scalia's discussion is to contrast the practical difficulties of originalism with the more fundamental problems of a nonoriginalist position. Although Scalia recognizes that neither approach is perfect, he suggests that we choose the approach that has "defects most appropriate for the task at hand—that is less likely to aggravate the most significant weakness of the system of judicial review."

> Now the main danger in judicial interpretation of the Constitu-
> tion . . . is that the judges will mistake their own predilections for
> the law. Avoiding this error is the hardest part of being a conscien-
> tious judge. Non-originalism (by invoking fundamental values)
> plays precisely to this weakness. It is very difficult for a person to
> discern a difference between those political values that he person-
> ally thinks most important, and those political values that are "fun-
> damental to our society." Thus, by the adoption of such a criterion
> judicial personalization of the law is enormously facilitated. . . .
> [But] originalism does not aggravate the principle weakness of the
> system, for it establishes a historical criterion that is conceptually
> quite separate from the preferences of the judge himself.[31]

Note that Scalia's argument appeals to an ideal of conscien-
tious judging that, like the concept of judicial integrity, is based on the requirement that judges "follow the law" rather than their own inclinations. For Scalia, it is the relative importance of this requirement that establishes the ultimate authority of originalism. Whatever its practical difficulties, they are outweighed by the role of rule following in facilitating judicial integrity. But even if we agree in principle that integrity is more important than practical problems, Scalia's argument overlooks a serious objection. The problem is that what he identifies as the practical defects of originalism undermine its claim of promoting integrity. For example, the fact that the Supreme Court lacks the personnel and the expertise to do authoritative historical research suggests that it has no more competence in this area than it does in that of

identifying contemporary values. Furthermore, Scalia's concession that originalism is unrealistic in its pure form (i.e., some cases require us to allow contemporary values to trump historical interpretation) means that judges must always consider contemporary values, if only to reject them. Thus, originalism does not follow a clear path to judicial integrity.

B. Cardozo's Theory of Legal Adjudication

Scalia's originalism presupposes a general view of legal decision making that characterizes the process as a rigorous application of a single principle to particular circumstances.[32] By contrast, Cardozo views legal decision making as a process that is appropriately influenced by a number of competing considerations. When describing the process, he asks:

> What is it that I do when I decide a case? To what sources of information do I appeal for guidance? In what proportions do I permit them to contribute to the result? In what proportions ought they to contribute? If no precedent is applicable, how do I reach the rule that will make precedent for the future? If I am seeking logical consistency, the symmetry of the legal structure, how far shall I seek it? At what point shall the quest be halted by some discrepant custom, by some consideration of the social welfare, by my own or the common standards of justice and morals?[33]

For Cardozo, legal decisions are intuitive judgments influenced by a number of legally relevant considerations. That such decisions are "judge-made" law rather than the product of applying a single theory troubles him not at all:

> Into that strange compound which is brewed daily in the caldron of the courts, all these ingredients [described earlier] enter in varying proportions. I am not concerned to inquire whether judges ought to be allowed to brew such a compound at all. I take judge-made law as one of the existing realities of life.[34]

Whereas Scalia begins with the principle that judge-made law is to be avoided at all costs, Cardozo begins by acknowledging the reality that judge-made law is a fact of life.

I have used a word that Cardozo does not use—the word *intuitive*—to describe the type of judgment that judges must make. I use this word to suggest that Cardozo thinks of legal judgments as personal in the sense that they are not always replicated from person to person.[35] Judges—even judges with similar theories of judging—sometimes disagree about legal outcomes because the decision-making process is not mechanical.[36] Rather, good legal decisions require wisdom, insight, and something appropriately called "good judgment." That is, judges "follow the law" in the sense that they are moved by legal reasons but not in the sense that legal outcomes are dictated by a particular legal theory or doctrine. What it means to be "moved by legal reasons" can be discerned from what Cardozo says about the "methods" of judging.

In describing the judicial process, Cardozo identifies four different methods:

> The directive force of a principle may be exerted along the line of logical progression; this I will call the rule of analogy or the method of philosophy; along the line of historical development; this I will call the method of evolution; along the line of the customs of the community; this I will call the method of tradition; and along the lines of justice, morals and social welfare, the *mores* of the day; and this I will call the method of sociology.[37]

Each of these methods is a way of thinking about a legal problem. For example, "the method of philosophy" is a form of deliberation that we now describe as legal reasoning. Cardozo, like Oliver Wendell Holmes,[38] did not think of legal reasoning as the application of an immutable set of abstract principles. Instead, he embraced a more experimental view: "The common law does not work from preestablished truths of universal and inflexible validity to conclusions derived from them deductively. Its method is inductive, and it draws its generalizations from particulars."[39] Thus, the method of philosophy is a method of, first, attempting to generalize principles from particular cases and, second, applying the principle to new cases to determine whether they can be appropriately decided by the same principle.[40]

One justification for the method of philosophy is that it rationalizes and explains large numbers of individual results: "Given a mass of particulars, [a group] of judgments on related topics, the principle that unifies and rationalizes them has a tendency, and a legitimate one, to project and extend itself to new cases within the limits of its capacity to unify and rationalize."[41] A second justification of this method is that its use—especially combined with the other three methods—tends toward satisfactory resolutions of legal disputes. A third justification is that legal reasoning—like the other three methods—is recognized in the legal community as an appropriate way to think about legal cases.

For Cardozo, judging is a specialized form of normative decision making. It is "legal" in the sense that it proceeds by describing and redescribing a particular case in the languages of various legally justifiable doctrines and theories;[42] it is "intuitive" in the sense that it requires a uniquely personal act of judgment; and finally, it is "situated"[43] in the sense that despite the decision maker's consideration of abstract legal reasons, it is influenced by his or her preexisting worldview.[44]

C. Two Concepts of Judicial Integrity

I began this section with two observations: first, that one element of judicial integrity is the notion that judges should follow the law rather than their own personal inclinations, and second, that this element of judicial integrity requires some preexisting notion of what it means for a judge to "follow the law." Thus, answering "What should judges do when they decide a case?" is an important prerequisite for deciding whether a particular judge has integrity. If, for example, we thought that judges should consult the *I Ching* before they reached a decision, then judicial integrity would require strict adherence to this procedure.

Thus far, most of this section has been taken up with sketching two different types of theories about how judges ought to decide cases. The purpose of this was to provide two different theoretical contexts in which we could consider the issue of judicial integrity. On the one hand, if Scalia is right that constitutional decision making requires a rigorous pursuit of historical truth, then the good-faith rigor of that pursuit will be the measure of judicial integrity. On the other hand, if Cardozo is right that legal decisions are ultimately based on intuitive and situated judgments, then integrity will relate to the way in which such judgments are made.[45] In what follows, I describe the two concepts of integrity and give examples of each.

The first concept of integrity—the one I associate with Scalia—focuses on the arguments that judges offer as justification for their decisions. It presupposes that a case is correctly decided if, and only if, the judge reaches a decision by applying approved forms of reasoning to an approved set of legal assumptions. Stated in the most general terms, the first conception characterizes judges as "following the law" if, and only if, they (1) confine themselves to assumptions that are recognized as true in the legal culture, (2) employ only those types of arguments recognized as appropriate, and (3) limit their conclusions to those that can be fairly drawn by an approved form of reasoning from the stated assumptions. Note that this picture of legal decision making is limited to a single set of legal considerations. This is because several sets of admittedly relevant considerations would force judges to do something intuitive in order to reach a decision; that is, they must weigh competing considerations to determine—on balance—the best outcome. Thus, the first concept of integrity is a matter of habitually deciding cases according to a single, dominant set of legal considerations.

Many legal theories rely on this notion of judicial integrity. Perhaps the most obvious is Langdell's formalism,[46] according to which judges decide with integrity only if their premises are recognizable as common law principles, their method is deductive, and their arguments are valid. The first concept of integrity does not require that legal decisions be based on deductive reasoning. There is nothing deductive, for example, in the kind of reasoning that Scalia requires in constitutional cases. And indeed, other nondeductive examples abound. For Wechsler, judges deciding constitutional cases demonstrate integrity when they decline to act except when their action is supported by neutral principles.[47] Even some nonoriginalists invoke this concept of integrity. Dworkin, for example, includes current norms and practices among the permissible assumptions and suggests that the correct form of legal reasoning is one that interprets contemporary standards.[48]

The second concept of integrity relies on a notion of legal decision making that stems not so much from a single strand of reasoning as from a process of deliberation. The goal of this process is to make a bottom-line assessment of what the law requires in particular cases. Under the second conception, we must do more than look at the validity and sincerity of certain arguments; we must make a far more subtle evaluation of judges' decision-making process. Were they open to all forms of evidence and legal authority? Did they examine the case from every viewpoint? Did they consider all the legally relevant aspects of the case? Were they able to close their mind to influences that were real but forbidden in a legal context?

Cardozo's description of judicial decision making allows room for individual judgment. This does not mean that judges should do "their own thing." Cardozo's theory requires, for example, that judges conscientiously consider precedent, custom, sociology, and prevailing notions of justice and fairness. But it does not mean that judges must count these factors in calculable ways. Rather, their decisions involve weighing these factors in a good-faith effort to make a fair and balanced decision. What distinguishes the second concept of integrity from the first is that it does not presume that judges will limit their decision making to a single strand of argumentation. Instead, the second concept requires that judges take responsibility for making an inherently personal judgment that accords with legal standards.

The first concept of integrity appears to raise issues that are easily judged: Are assumptions true? Are methods of reasoning valid? By contrast, the second concept of integrity appears to raise issues that are far more subtle and complex. Instead of evaluating the arguments directly, the second concept requires us to venture into the realm of assessing good-faith deliberation and character. Despite the subtlety of these assessments, they are not impossible to make. They are similar to judgments that we make all the time. For example, we must often decide whether people are fair-minded; whether they have a judicious temperament; and whether, when analyzing a problem, they normally get to the heart of the matter. Indeed, we think of good judgment not just in terms of sound reasoning but also in terms of wisdom, temperance, and discernment.

There are many writers besides Cardozo whose views of legal decision making are incompatible with the first concept of integ-

rity. For example, the pragmatists and the moderate realists—
men such as Holmes,[49] Hutcheson,[50] and Radin[51]—seem to follow the second concept, and it is certainly the second concept I
would be thinking about in my own work on pragmatic theories
of adjudication.[52] In addition, this approach makes sense to other
writers—writers who are not normally described as pragmatic or
realistic. Cover, for example, portrays the dilemma of the fugitive-
slave judges in exactly these terms; he sees them as confronting a
multilayered dilemma to which a wide array of considerations are
undeniably relevant.[53] Even Aristotle—the originator of the idea
that we can determine which forms of reasoning are valid—does
not think of judicial decision making as following prescribed
forms of argument: "When disputes occur, people have recourse
to a judge; and, to do this, is to have recourse to justice, because
the object of the judge is to be a sort of personified Justice."[54]
Thus, for Aristotle, judges do not simply calculate a result. Rather,
as justice personified, they are responsible for making their decisions with mind, heart, and soul attuned to the dictates of law and
justice.

CONCLUSION

This chapter examined the distinction between goodness and
constitutionality in a number of different contexts. It also considered the concept of judicial integrity and its relationship to various theories of judicial decision making. Before closing, I would
like to put the question directly: Does Smith's proposal enhance
the prospects of judicial integrity?

In the last section I sketched two different notions of judicial
integrity. Obviously, these sketches were not intended as full accounts, but I hope they are sufficient to demonstrate that the
notion of integrity is a contested notion. Too often, a vague appeal
to integrity is offered as the final endorsement of some normative
theory about how common law or constitutional cases ought to be
decided. The form of these appeals is something like this:

> Judges should decide cases by carefully examining a particular set
> of considerations. If they also consider other factors, they will
> increase their own discretion. But greater discretion is suspect
> because it permits judges to consult their own subjective prefer-

ences in deciding legal cases. This should not be allowed, since "subjective decision making" violates the judicial role and therefore compromises integrity.

I have used Scalia's argument for originalism as an example; others are cited in the notes. The conclusion in such cases is that theorists use the concept of integrity to trump objections to their theories. They term these objections "merely practical" when they are compared with the more fundamental requirements of integrity.

It is possible to see Smith's chapter as yet one more example of this type of argument. Smith insists that we should make a precise verbal distinction between "good" and "constitutional." To support this distinction, he shows, first, how it can be understood and, second, how these two distinct concepts are fused in a variety of contexts. But with just these arguments, Smith is in no better position to claim that his distinction promotes integrity than is someone who claims that we can improve judicial decision making by clarifying the procedures for consulting the *I Ching*. For the latter argument to work, its proponent must also make a case that consulting the *I Ching* is an essential part of good legal decision making.

Similarly, if Smith wants to prove that distinguishing between goodness and constitutionality promotes integrity, he must show that the correct normative theory of legal decision making ultimately depends on the clarity of this distinction. My criticism of Smith's argument applies equally to the pragmatist position outlined in the last section of this chapter. The pragmatic concept of integrity can stand on no firmer footing than the substantive theory of legal decision making that supports it. In this chapter, it was not my aim to develop such a theory. Rather, my goal was to clear space for a pragmatic theory by undermining the notion that *by definition,* such theories lack integrity.

NOTES

1. Rogers M. Smith, "The Inherent Deceptiveness of Constitutional Discourse: A Diagnosis and Prescription," this volume, 219, 220.

2. Smith uses *Brown v. Board of Education*, 347 U.S. 483 (1954) (holding that "separate but equal" public schools are inherently unconstitutional) as an example of a case in which the Court was justified in reaching a result that was contrary to the weight of historical evidence.

3. Smith, "The Inherent Deceptiveness of Constitutional Discourse," 225.

4. Smith cites such cases as *Brown v. Board of Education* and *Minor v. Happersett*, 21 Wall. 162 (1875) (holding that the post–Civil War amendments did not give women the right to vote), which some contend is a "bad" policy result that is nevertheless correct as a matter of historical interpretation.

5. While insisting that the distinction between "good" and "constitutional" be precisely observed, he uses both terms in a number of different ways throughout the article. For example, "good" sometimes means "good as a matter of social policy"; it also sometimes means "good in terms of achieving a correct balance between social policy concerns and historical considerations." The problem, of course, is that "good" and "constitutional" are not precise terms; rather, they are evaluative terms that gather much of their meaning from the context in which they are used.

6. As noted earlier, this is the particular context with which Smith is primarily occupied.

7. Smith's use of the term *constitutional* most often means "conforming to the intentions of the ratifiers." Throughout this chapter when I use the term *constitutional* in Smith's sense, I will so indicate by saying "constitutional (historical)."

8. Although Smith describes constitutional decision making as most often controlled by constitutional (historical) considerations, his jurisprudence recognizes a number of specific circumstances in which historical interpretation is not the most important factor.

9. For an extended discussion of this issue, see Peter Novick, *That Noble Dream* (Cambridge: Cambridge University Press, 1988).

10. This is the point of much of Willard V. O. Quine's argument in *Word and Object* (Cambridge, Mass.: Technology Press of the Massachusetts Institute of Technology, 1960).

11. A short but effective statement of this criticism is made by Justice Thurgood Marshall in "Reflections on the Bicentennial of the United States Constitution," *Harvard Law Review* 101 (1987): 1–5. See also Ronald Dworkin, *Taking Rights Seriously* (Cambridge, Mass.: Harvard University Press, 1977), 132–36.

12. If the procedure for amending the Constitution were less difficult—if for example, the national Constitution could be amended in the

way that a number of state constitutions can be amended, by a simple vote of the citizenry—then originalism might not be such a conservative position. Although there are excellent reasons for making the process of adopting an amendment difficult, one consequence of this difficulty is that originalist arguments do not necessarily represent contemporary or majoritarian ideals.

13. Smith, "The Inherent Deceptiveness of Constitutional Discourse," 222.

14. Ibid., 240.

15. *Brown v. Board of Education*, 347 U.S. 483 (1954).

16. Of course, the opinion in *Brown* does not rely on historical argument. For example, Chief Justice Earl Warren characterized the historical evidence as "inconclusive" and maintained that "we cannot turn the clock back to 1868 when the Amendment was adopted, or even to 1896 when *Plessy v. Ferguson* was written. We must consider public education in the light of its full development and its present place in American life" (ibid., 492).

17. Michael W. McConnell,, "Originalism and the Desegregation Decisions," *Virginia Law Review* 81 (1995): 947–1140.

18. Smith, "The Inherent Deceptiveness of Constitutional Discourse," 244 (italics in original).

19. As a pragmatist, I am unhappy with the distinction between *facts* and *interpretations of facts* because it suggests that some aspects of experience cannot be challenged and that they cannot be interpreted in other than the most obvious ways. Such a distinction, however, is necessary to make sense of Smith's analysis of *Brown*.

20. For example, our judgment about the relative importance of certain facts is likely to be affected by our overall theory of constitutional meaning, and this theory, in turn, is strongly influenced by our political commitments.

21. This is clearly the assumption behind Scalia's argument in his "Originalism: The Lesser Evil," *University of Cincinnati Law Review* 57 (1921): 849–65, 861.

22. It must stand on its own two feet in the sense that arguments for normative conclusions must be made independently of appeals to the constitutional text.

23. Benjamin Cardozo, *The Nature of the Judicial Process* (New Haven, Conn.: Yale University Press, 1921), 17.

24. Scalia, "Originalism."

25. Ibid., 861–62.

26. Ibid., 857.

27. *Myers v. United States*, 272 U.S. 52 (1926).

28. He concludes his analysis with "Well, I leave it to the listener's imagination how many pages would have had to have been added to Taft's seventy page opinion, and how many months to his almost three years of intermittent labor, to flesh out this relatively minor point in a fashion that a serious historian would consider minimally adequate" (Scalia, "Originalism," 860). After reading this, one wonders whether the Court is ever able to decide a case in accordance with Scalia's demanding conception of the historical method.

29. Scalia's characterization of a second so-called defect seems somewhat less plausible: "If the law is to make any attempt at consistency and predictability, surely there must be general agreement not only that judges reject one exegetical approach [originalism], but that they adopt another. And it is hard to discern any emerging consensus among the nonoriginalists as to what this might be" (ibid., 855). The difficulty with this argument is that if it is a valid argument against the nonoriginalists, it is also a valid argument against any legal theory, including originalism, that has more than one version or more than one alternative.

30. 5 U.S. (1 Cranch.) 137 (1803).

31. Scalia, "Originalism," 863.

32. In constitutional cases, for example, he argues that the principle should be fidelity to the original meaning of the constitutional text.

33. Cardozo, *The Nature of the Judicial Process*, 2.

34. Ibid.

35. In some contexts, however, the word *intuitive* is used to describe decisions that are impulsive and irrational. Certainly Cardozo would not think of legal judgments as "intuitive" in this sense.

36. As every student of logic knows, even logical judgments are not "mechanical" in that they require an act of choice that must be made independently of logical constraint. Lewis Carroll illustrated this point with a pointed story about Achilles and the Tortoise that is widely reprinted in Carroll anthologies and logic textbooks under the name "What the Tortoise Said to Achilles."

37. Cardozo, *The Nature of the Judicial Process*, 30–31. Unfortunately, this terminology does not quite mirror modern usage. By "the method of philosophy," Cardozo means something like legal reasoning; by "the method of evolution," he means assessing the impact of changing social conditions on the wisdom of certain legal practices; by including "the method of tradition," he recognizes that social customs should play a role in determining legal outcomes; and, similarly, by including "the method of sociology," he means to acknowledge the relevance of contemporary norms of justice and goodness.

38. I give an extended description of the experimental method of

legal reasoning in my "Holmes on Legal Method: The Predictive Theory of Law as an Instance of Scientific Method," *Southern Illinois University Law Journal* 18 (1994): 329–45.

39. Cardozo, *The Nature of the Judicial Process*, 22–23: "The rules and principles of case law have never been treated as final truths, but as working hypotheses, continually retested in those great laboratories of the law, the courts of justice."

40. As Cardozo describes it, "Every new case is an experiment; and if the accepted rule which seems applicable yields a result which is felt to be unjust, the rule is reconsidered. It may not be modified at once . . . but if a rule continues to work injustice, it will eventually be reformulated" (ibid., 23).

41. Ibid., 31.

42. I use the term "legally justifiable doctrines and theories" to refer to theories that are justified by some or all of the three types of justification described in the preceding paragraph.

43. I developed the notion of situated decision making at greater length in my "Situated Decisionmaking," *Southern California Law Review* 63 (1990): 1727–46, and "Improving One's Situation: Some Pragmatic Reflections on the Art of Judging," *Washington and Lee Law Review* 49 (1992): 323–38.

44. As Cardozo put it, "There is in each of us a stream of tendency, whether you choose to call it philosophy or not, which gives coherence and direction to thought and action. Judges cannot escape that current any more than other mortals. . . . In this mental background every problem finds its setting. We may try to see things as objectively as we please. None the less, we can never see them with any eyes except our own" (*The Nature of the Judicial Process*, 12–13).

45. Given the polarities that have traditionally defined American jurisprudence, it is tempting to describe one theory as formalist and the other as realist. But this, I think, would be a mistake. The terms *formalism* and *realism* have become markers for ideological arguments, and their use generally obscures rather than clarifies discussions about judicial decision making.

46. Christopher Columbus Langdell, "Preface to the First Edition," *Selection of Cases on the Law of Contracts* (Boston: Little, Brown, 1871).

47. Herbert Wechsler, "Toward Neutral Principles of Constitutional Law," *Harvard Law Review* 73 (1959): 1–35.

48. Dworkin, *Taking Rights Seriously*.

49. Oliver W. Holmes, Review of Langdell, *Summary of Contracts*, *American Law Review* 13 (1880): 233–34.

50. William C. Hutcheson, "The Judgment Intuitive: The Function

of the Hunch in Judicial Decision," *Cornell Law Quarterly* 14 (1929): 274–88.

51. Max Radin, "The Theory of Judicial Decision: Or, How Judges Think," *American Bar Association Journal* 11 (1925): 357–62.

52. Wells, "Situated Decisionmaking" and "Improving One's Situation."

53. Robert M. Cover, *Justice Accused: Antislavery and the Judicial Process* (New Haven, Conn.: Yale University Press, 1975).

54. Aristotle, *Nicomachean Ethics,* book V, 1132A. I discuss Aristotle's pragmatism at greater length in my "Tort Law as Corrective Justice: A Pragmatic Justification for Jury Adjudication," *Michigan Law Review* 88 (1990): 2348–2413.

13

THE ASYMMETRICALITY OF CONSTITUTIONAL DISCOURSE

MICHAEL W. MCCONNELL

Rogers Smith describes American judges as "almost irresistibly impelled to justify their results publicly as mandates of authoritative legal sources, especially the Constitution, rather than as products of a calculus of overall benefit." He also argues that "if we are to say that it is the Constitution that constrains judicial results, . . . it is logical to contend that those ascertainable, enduring limits must in some fairly determinate way trace back to what was meant by those who authorized the Constitution." This creates "pressures for judges . . . to produce interpretations that treat the Constitution's meaning as bounded and properly interpretable through some form of 'originalism.'"[1] On the other hand, he says that judges, like all constitutional interpreters, are committed to substantive ideas of the good, which sometimes diverge from the norms of constitutionality (understood in this originalist way). The resulting tension between goodness and constitutionality,[2] according to Smith, gives rise to constitutional discourse that is "deceptive" and "confusing."

I would have thought this, on balance, a good system. All judges, whatever their political or jurisprudential stripe, would strive to advance their understanding of the good (which varies from judge to judge), and all would be constrained by the need to justify their conclusions by reference to the original understanding (which, in principle, does not vary from judge to judge). The need to justify outcomes by reference to a fixed, shared meaning rooted in history would give judges significant but not unbounded flexibility. Many desired outcomes would be fair game under such a system, but many more would be excluded.

Moreover, since all the participants in this system would be playing by the same rules and all would be both defending their own outcomes and criticizing others, professional norms regarding the criteria for acceptable justification would likely emerge. Shame places a certain limit on hypocrisy, and judges would be under some (admittedly imperfect) obligation to abide by the same norms of justification that they demand of their ideological opponents. In this way, a tolerably objective system of law is created. Even though there is more "deceptiveness" in such a system than there would be if judges were not bound by any external constraints, a degree of "deceptiveness" is preferable to a system in which judges are free to overturn the decisions of representative institutions purely on the basis of their notions of "goodness," unchecked by any norms of "constitutionality."

More troubling is a feature of modern constitutional discourse that Smith appears to have overlooked: that the norms of perceived legitimacy in constitutional argument are not evenly distributed across the ideological spectrum. If advocates of activism and restraint, originalism and nonoriginalism, strict and loose theories of stare decisis, and so forth were found in roughly equal numbers among judges and commentators of conservative, libertarian, liberal, and left-wing orientation, an equilibrium might yet emerge from the methodological dissonance. But in fact, for complex reasons, adherence to Smith's originalist conception of legitimacy is confined almost exclusively to scholars and judges on the conservative side of the ideological spectrum. Those on the left–liberal side of the spectrum have generally abandoned fealty to original understanding—or to any other "formalistic" constraint—as the touchstone of legitimacy. The predominant view among liberal and left-wing judges and academics is some version of Dworkinism, in which, as Smith points out, the constraints of "fit" quickly give way to the decision maker's view of goodness or to the view of Critical Legal Studies, in which law is seen as indistinguishable from politics and the very idea of "constitutionality" (as Smith understands it) is derided as a smoke screen for power.

The effect is an asymmetrical, and therefore unstable, system in which one side is self-constrained by articulable professional norms and the other side is not. It does not take a sophisticated game theorist to predict the effects. On one side, the asymmetricality creates an incentive to obfuscate and stretch the truth. (If *they* can write their political preferences into law, why can't *we?*) On the other side, it removes the constraint of knowing that one's opponents have the same weapons. (We can be as activist as we wish, without any serious concern that the other side will do likewise.) If "constitutional discourse is unusually deceptive and confusing," as Smith says, the reason is that the very norms of legitimacy and professionalism that we must use to evaluate the discourse are up for grabs, with different rules for different players.

The mere fact that positive and normative modes of reasoning ("constitutionality" and "goodness," to use Smith's terminology) are jumbled together in legal argument does not account for the sad state of the discourse, as he seems to think. That jumble could even be a strength. Knowledge of historical practice and experience influences lawyers' understanding of the good, and their understanding of the good influences their perception of historical practice and experience. The former engrafts a solid, cautious empiricism onto the process of theorizing about "goodness" and thus serves as an antidote to rationalistic abstraction and utopianism. The latter gives an ameliorative and reformative flavor to the process of discovering "the law." Indeed, some of the best legal theorizing consists of a reflective description of our legal tradition, an enterprise that is normative at the same time that it is descriptive. There is nothing new in this.

The novel feature in current constitutional discourse is the erosion, on one side of the ideological spectrum, of the very norm of "constitutionality." The consensus among constitutional law scholars of this generation is that an originalist approach to the Constitution cannot account for much of modern constitutional law, including much that is best (on normative grounds). They conclude that "constitutionality" (as Smith defines it) should be jettisoned (or at least radically reduced in importance) and that some version of normative theory or common law constitutionalism should be substituted, because this would lead to better results and would more accurately describe constitutional practice.

A great deal of this is attributable to the myth of *Brown*. In what I consider to have been both a historical and a rhetorical mistake, Chief Justice Earl Warren's unanimous opinion in *Brown* expressly abjured reliance on the historical meaning of the Fourteenth Amendment.[3] In the immediate aftermath of the decision, two scholars sympathetic to the result (historian Alfred Kelly, who worked with the plaintiffs, and Alexander Bickel, who was a law clerk to Justice Felix Frankfurter during deliberations on the case) wrote important essays in which they conceded that the evidence did not support the conclusion that the framers and ratifiers of the Fourteenth Amendment believed the amendment made school segregation unconstitutional.[4]

As I will explain later, I think those essays were flawed in that they failed to take into account constitutional argument in the half decade after ratification—the period in which the segregation issue came to the forefront—and relied almost entirely on the ratification period, when segregation was barely discussed. Since Kelly and Bickel, little work has been done on the historical question, although two of the most prominent historians of the period, Charles Lofgren and William Nelson, concluded (without detailed analysis) that the historical evidence on the segregation question was mixed,[5] which should have been a signal that the complacent consensus was in need of reevaluation.

But constitutional scholars in the forty years since *Brown* have delighted in repeating, with increasing certitude, the conclusion that the decision cannot be supported by the historical understanding. This has been said to be "obvious," "[un]ambiguous," "inevitable," and "inescapable." "Virtually nothing" supports the opposite claim, which is said to be "fanciful."[6] Rogers Smith now joins the parade, charging, if I read him correctly, that any scholar who purports to conclude the opposite must not have sufficient "integrity" or "fidelity to truth."

It is possible that this chorus of scholarly judgment is based on a dispassionate look at the historical facts. But it should not escape notice that the conclusion that *Brown* cannot be supported on the basis of the original understanding has proved to be of great value in the ideological campaign to discredit originalism as a method of constitutional interpretation and to legitimate freewheeling judicial review in the service of social change. Stephen Carter has detailed the part that the *Brown* issue played in the defeat of Robert Bork,[7] but the *Brown* issue goes far beyond the unseemly Bork affair.

Brown is indispensable to the case for modern judicial activism because there are surprisingly few Supreme Court decisions that are (1) important, (2) widely agreed to be correct from a moral point of view, and (3) clearly insupportable as a matter of history.[8] If a decision is widely agreed to be correct from a moral point of view, it almost necessarily accords with the predominant opinion, which means that judicial intervention was unnecessary, that at most, judicial intervention hastened a process of change that would have come about anyway.

Such opinions seem important because the issues they address are important, but when predominant opinion is on the side of the Court, it is likely that political decision making would eventually have reached the same conclusion. Examples include decisions on the right of married couples to use birth control (already achieved in all but one state at the time of *Griswold*) and decisions striking down discrimination against women on the basis of empirically flawed stereotypes (achieved just as feminism became a powerful political force). Nobody complains about these decisions (as a matter of policy) because they did no more than anticipate what the democratic processes were already doing.

In other cases, the Court defies the majority sentiment but does so in the service of constitutional principles that can be traced to the constitutional text and history. These cases may be controversial politically, but jurisprudentially they are unexceptional. Many free speech cases fall into this category (think of the flag-burning and hate speech cases). So do the school prayer cases, some separation-of-powers cases (such as the legislative veto decision), and (more controversially) the recent federalism decisions. In my judgment, this category of cases is much larger than is commonly thought. It is these cases that show the value of an independent judiciary, not as social engineers or philosopher kings, but as comparatively dispassionate enforcers of constitutional norms, even in the face of political pressure to violate them.

The most problematic cases, jurisprudentially speaking, are those in which the Court strikes down legislation that commands majority support, on the basis of "constitutional" principles nowhere evident in the text of the Constitution, as understood by its framers and ratifiers. *Roe v. Wade*[9] is the most prominent case in this category, but there are many others, old as well as new. Recent examples include the term limits case, the gay rights case, and the lower courts' "right-to-die" cases. It is in these cases that judicial discretion matters, because it produces a different result than would come about through either democratic or strictly "constitutional" processes. Unfortunately for advocates of judicial activism, it is also this class of cases that arouses controversy and popular opposition.

Theoretically, this form of judicial review (i.e., judicial review based on neither the historic constitution nor widespread moral consensus) could be desirable if we had reason to believe that on the whole, judicial moral decision makers were superior to those in the other branches of government (putting aside the noninstrumental value of representative government). This seems to be Ronald Dworkin's implicit assumption. Experience, however, suggests that this is not so clear.

History has not been kind to the notion that in conflicts between courts and legislatures, the courts are usually right. As recently as 1941, Attorney General Robert Jackson (later to be one of our greatest Supreme Court justices) made the remarkable statement that "in no major conflict with the representative branches on any question of social or economic policy has time vindicated the Court."[10] Jackson's summary of the Court's history is worth remembering:

> In spite of its apparently vulnerable position, this Court has repeatedly overruled and thwarted both the Congress and the Executive. It has been in angry collision with the most dynamic and popular Presidents in our history. Jefferson retaliated with impeachment; Jackson denied its authority; Lincoln disobeyed a writ of the Chief Justice; Theodore Roosevelt, after his Presidency, proposed recall of judicial decisions; Wilson tried to liberalize its membership; and Franklin D. Roosevelt proposed to "reorganize." It is surprising that

it should not only survive but, with no might except the moral force of its judgments, should attain actual supremacy as a source of constitutional dogma.

Surprise turns to amazement when we reflect that time has proved that its judgment was wrong on the most outstanding issues upon which it has chosen to challenge the popular branches. Its judgment in the *Dred Scott* case was overruled by war. Its judgment that the currency that preserved the Union could not be made legal tender was overruled by Grant's selection of an additional Justice. Its judgment invalidating the income tax was overruled by the Sixteenth Amendment. Its judgments repressing labor and social legislation are now abandoned. Many of the judgments against New Deal legislation are rectified by confession of error. In no major conflict with the representative branches on any question of social or economic policy has time vindicated the Court.[11]

We are too close to the events in question to know whether "time" will "vindicate" many of the Court's more recent ventures in what Smith calls the "prerogative power." But the Court has been forced to retreat (at least partially) on a number of these issues, including capital punishment, obscenity/pornography, religion, statistical "discrimination," welfare rights, and criminal procedures. On other issues "resolved" by the Court, the nation remains divided, and the "rightness" of the Court's resolution is open to question. Today, even commentators of the left and moderate left, who are generally sympathetic to many of the Court's more controversial rulings, have questioned whether activist judicial review is a legitimate, desirable, or even effective means of achieving social change.[12] If the Supreme Court becomes less timid in its rulings on property rights, affirmative action, and federalism and especially if a new Republican president appoints more conservative justices, it is a fair bet that calls for judicial restraint in the legal academy would quickly swell.

Rogers Smith admits that he is more enthusiastic about the "prerogative power" in the hands of the "wise and good" Warren Court than in those of the current Rehnquist Court. The difficulty is that in a pluralistic nation, we all cannot agree on what is wise and good. From the point of view of those vulnerable to crime, for example, much of what the Warren Court accomplished looks naive, even irresponsible.[13] I therefore hope that Smith and others of his ideological persuasion keep the unpleasant vision of the

Rehnquist Court before their eyes whenever they try to prescribe the extent of judicial power. When contemplating vesting power (particularly "prerogative power," or power uncontrolled by law) in human beings, it is better to imagine this power being wielded by our ideological opponents than by those whom we deem "wise and good." As Jefferson observed, "Free government is founded in jealousy, and not in confidence; it is jealousy, and not confidence, which prescribes limited constitutions to bind down those whom we are obliged to trust with power." [14] That warning applies no less to the courts than to Congress, the president, or the states. [15]

But as long as adherence to Smith's norms of "constitutionality" is largely confined to one end of the ideological spectrum, it is doubtful that we will achieve anything like a consensus on legitimate interpretive methodology. Asymmetrical constraint is too good a deal. And if (through continued Democratic control of the presidency) the danger of conservative judicial activism fades, it is likely that the legal academy will return to its traditional practice of justifying judicial activism to achieve what cannot be achieved through politically accountable institutions, whether or not the Constitution (originally conceived) has anything to say about the issue.

This desire to justify expansive and uncabined judicial review, I suspect, has something to do with the remarkably uninquisitive attitude of most scholars toward *Brown v. Board of Education* and their surprising acceptance of the weak historical arguments the defenders of Jim Crow put forward in defense of segregation. The unhistorical *Brown* is needed because it proves the necessity of an activist judiciary.

So let us turn now, therefore, to the historical question. Did the Fourteenth Amendment, as it was understood by those responsible for framing and ratifying it, permit the de jure segregation of public schools?

I have advanced the thesis that the Fourteenth Amendment was understood by many of its prominent supporters to outlaw de jure school segregation; more tentatively, I have suggested that this appears to have been the predominant view among Republicans during Reconstruction. [16] Rogers Smith has said that the evidence on this point, viewed in the most "charitable" light, is "inconclusive." In the rest of his chapter, which is less charitable, he calls my argument "self-deceptive." Unfortunately, his summary of that argument is so incomplete that readers of his chapter have no basis for judgment. The following may help.

Deliberations on section 1 of the Fourteenth Amendment were remarkably nonsubstantive. Whether they were pressed for time, whether they had the votes and therefore did not need to engage in deliberation, whether they wished to stress the uncontroversial aspects of the amendment, or whether they were intentionally being evasive, the amendment's supporters were almost silent about what section 1 would mean—beyond constitutionalizing the Civil Rights Act of 1866, which was its central purpose. When he was arguing the case for segregation before the Supreme Court in 1952, the great appellate lawyer John W. Davis admitted to the Court that "perhaps there has never been a Congress in which the debates furnished less real pablum on which history might feed."[17]

After the amendment was passed, Congress set about enforcing it (and the Fifteenth Amendment) through a series of enforcement acts. It is plain that Congress viewed itself as the principal enforcer of the amendments and also that in enforcing the amendments, the congressmen were engaged in constitutional interpretation. It was during the debates regarding these acts that the various theories about the meaning of the new amendments were thoroughly discussed for the first time. Congress first turned its attention to the problem of Black Codes, then to suffrage, then to violence against the freedmen, and finally to segregation. For three and a half years, segregation in schools and common carriers was the leading subject of debate in the two houses of Congress. Even critics of the originalist argument for *Brown* concede that the "congressional support for school desegregation" shown in these debates "should be understood not merely as a policy preference, but also as probative of constitutional interpretation."[18]

Smith notes that "majorities in each house voted for banning school segregation at various preliminary points," but he passes by this evidence as if it meant nothing. The sole source of authority to enact this measure, as acknowledged on both sides of the aisle, was Congress's power to enforce the provisions of section 1. That they voted to ban segregation meant either that they thought segregation violated section 1 or that they were deliberately violating the Constitution.[19]

After extensive debate on the constitutional question, the Senate voted for the school segregation bill on four separate occasions, by margins as high as 29 to 13. In the House, majorities voted in favor of the bill on countless procedural votes (with margins as high as 141 to 72) but never could achieve the two-thirds vote needed to break a Democratic filibuster. To be sure, the bill did not ultimately pass in this form. But viewing these events as evidence of interpretation, it surely is significant that almost two-thirds of the Congress—and more than 90 percent of the Republicans—took the position that the amendment did not allow de jure school segregation. (Party affiliation is significant because it was an almost perfect proxy for support for or opposition to the amendment.)[20]

Moreover, proposals to allow separate but equal facilities were rejected three times in the Senate and once in the House, by substantial margins. Prominent supporters of civil rights explained at length why they deemed separate but equal a counterfeit to equality. Smith says that the "evidence better supports . . . the conclusion that 'separate but equal' segregation was generally expected to be permitted" and that "many Republicans . . . saw no harm in segregation so long as the schools were equal." But more than three-quarters of the Senate Republicans and 90 percent of the House Republicans voted against allowing separate but equal schools. And Smith neglects to mention that in the end, Congress enacted legislation prohibiting segregation in common carriers—thus showing that *Plessy v. Ferguson*[21] was inconsistent with its understanding of the amendment.[22] The supporters of the Fourteenth Amendment in Congress in 1870–75 believed that the amendment forbade segregation of public schools as well as common carriers, but when they did not have the votes, their second choice was to have no legislation on schools at all and to turn to the courts. The idea of separate but equal was anathema.

Almost as significant as the votes were the arguments. Proponents of the bill argued persuasively that school segregation was a violation of constitutional principles, interpreted in accordance with the legal canons of the day. To dismiss those arguments, it is necessary to do more than invoke generalities about the racism of the period; it is necessary to address the Republicans' constitutional arguments on their own terms and show why they were wrong. Significantly, opponents of the bill relied on inconsistent arguments (some arguing that the amendment did not cover education and others conceding that it did cover education but contending that separate schools were equal) as well as open opposition to the amendment and blatant appeals to prejudice. If it was so plain that the Fourteenth Amendment did not forbid school segregation, one would expect to see more cogent arguments than these.

Taken as a whole, I believe this historical account is powerful evidence that Reconstruction-era Republicans understood school segregation to be unconstitutional. I think the historical argument at the time of the *Brown* litigation appeared inconclusive (or even contrary to this) because the participants conceived of "legislative history" too narrowly, citing only materials prior to ratification and overlooking the principal debates on segregation, which occurred a few years later.

Smith offers several arguments in response. First, he refers to two appropriations bills for the segregated schools of the District of Columbia, which he apparently takes as an authoritative construction of the amendment, even though these bills were not debated and the Fourteenth Amendment did not apply to these schools. In any case, he neglects to give the whole story. The same congressional forces that fought for school desegregation through the civil rights bill also came close to requiring desegregation in the District (winning in the Senate by a margin of 35 to 20 on a procedural vote[23] and losing in the House by 71 to 88).[24] Their tactical judgment to devote their political energies after 1871 to nationwide reform, which appeared to be within their reach, should not be mistaken for a considered constitutional judgment that segregation was permissible, in the District or elsewhere.[25]

Second, Smith points out—correctly—that most Republicans were unwilling to accept "social equality" for the races. But under the legal categories of the day, that did not resolve the issue. Much of the constitutional debate over the school desegregation bill centered on whether the right to attend school without distinction on the basis of race was, in fact, a "social right" (as the Democrats maintained) or a "civil right" (as the Republicans argued). The Republicans believed that racial equality was required in all institutions in which all citizens had a legally enforceable right to receive service without discrimination. Thus, no one had an obligation to serve blacks at their own dinner table, but an innkeeper—who had a legally enforceable common law obligation to serve all comers—could not lawfully discriminate against blacks or isolate them from the table at which he served the other travelers. A Louisiana Republican quoted Confederate General P. G. T. Beauregard:

> It would not be denied that in traveling and at places of public resort we often share these privileges in common with thieves, prostitutes, gamblers, and others who have worse sins to answer for than the accident of color; but no one ever supposed that we thereby assented to the social equality of these people with ourselves. I therefore say that participation in these public privileges involves no question of social equality.[26]

Perhaps more important, Smith points out that my historical defense of *Brown* "relies almost exclusively on what congressmen said *after 1870* in pushing for forerunners of what became the 1875 Civil Rights Act." Fair enough. If there were significant evidence from the framing and ratification processes, I would agree that it would, in principle, carry more weight. But there is no such evidence.[27] Moreover, despite what Smith says, it is not unusual to examine the early acts of Congress as evidence of constitutional meaning. Much of our understanding of the original meaning of the Constitution of 1787 is informed by the debates and acts of the early Congresses, whose task was to implement it. No one thinks it is illegitimate to cite the early acts of Congress (and even the letters and private memoranda of Jefferson and Madison written decades after the fact) to illuminate the meaning of the establishment clause. The debates over the Alien and Sedition Acts, which took place ten years after Congress passed the First Amendment, are among the most important sources of insight into the original understanding of freedom of speech. I fail to see why evidence from the Congresses that set out to enforce the Fourteenth Amendment between 1870 and 1875 is any less probative.

Finally, Smith observes that the debates did not center on whether the courts could overturn school segregation but, rather, on whether Congress could do so. This is beside the point. The debates pertained to what the amendment meant, and there is no evidence that members of Congress thought that the amendment's meaning varied according to the identity of the enforcer.

This is not to say that my thesis has been conclusively established. As with most interesting issues, there are plausible arguments on both sides.[28] But I think that enough has been said to show that the historical case for *Brown* is based on more than "wishful" thinking or "self-deception."

It will be interesting to see the reaction to this opening of the debate on the historical basis of *Brown*. For years, most people have assumed that *Brown* is historically indefensible, a view that has been an important ingredient in the defense of nonoriginalist judicial activism—the swift and sure answer to anyone who dared to question the nonoriginalist orthodoxy. Now that we know that this answer is not so sure, will serious—and not one-sided— reflection on the norms of constitutional justification again be possible?

NOTES

1. Rogers M. Smith, "The Inherent Deceptiveness of Constitutional Discourse: A Diagnosis and Prescription," this volume, 227–28.

2. Smith's analysis is flawed because he uses the terms *goodness* and *constitutionality* inconsistently. When in a descriptive mode, he uses the term *overall goodness* to refer to norms' constitutionality as well as normative preference. But when Smith is in a critical mode, he uses the term *goodness* to mean something like normative desirability. Of course, it is not "deceptive" to "confuse" goodness and constitutionality if goodness is defined as adherence to norms of constitutionality.

Similarly, whereas Smith defines *constitutionality* in terms of original meaning, he apparently employs a broader definition (including decisions that are not "in any defensible sense . . . constitutionally authorized") when attempting to demonstrate that scholars do not adequately distinguish between the constitutional and the good. If they used Smith's narrow definition of constitutional, there would be numerous positions that constitutional commentators would label "constitutional" but "bad."

3. *Brown v. Board of Education,* 347 U.S. 483, 492 (1954).

4. Alfred H. Kelly, "The Fourteenth Amendment Reconsidered: The Segregation Question," *Michigan Law Review* 54 (1956): 1049–86; and Alexander Bickel, "The Original Understanding and the Segregation Decision," *Harvard Law Review* 69 (1955): 1–65.

5. Charles Lofgren, *The Plessy Case: A Legal–Historical Interpretation* (New York: Oxford University Press, 1987), 65 (concluding that for school segregation, the evidence of historical meaning "points both ways"); William E. Nelson, *The Fourteenth Amendment: From Political Principle to Legal Doctrine* (Cambridge, Mass.: Harvard University Press, 1988), 134–35.

6. For citations to this literature, see Michael W. McConnell, "Originalism and the Desegregation Decisions," *Virginia Law Review* 81 (1995): 947–1140, 950–52.

7. Stephen L. Carter, "Bork Redux, or How the Tempting of America Led the People to Rise and Battle for Justice," *Texas Law Review* 69 (1991): 759–93, 777–78.

8. In addition to *Brown,* the only other great exception is the reapportionment decisions, which, insofar as they rest on the equal protection clause, are historically indefensible (although we could argue that reapportionment so egregious that it entrenches minority control of the legislature—which was true of most of the early reapportionment cases—violates the guarantee clause) but which are generally regarded as "good" decisions. One of the most important modern interpretive theories, John Hart Ely's "representation reinforcement," is essentially based on the logic of these decisions. See John Hart Ely, *Democracy and Distrust: A Theory of Judicial Review* (Cambridge, Mass.: Harvard University Press, 1980).

9. 410 U.S. 113 (1973).

10. Robert H. Jackson, *The Struggle for Judicial Supremacy: A Study of a Crisis in American Power Politics* (New York: Knopf, 1941), x.

11. Ibid., ix–x.

12. See, for example, Cass R. Sunstein, *The Partial Constitution* (Cambridge, Mass.: Harvard University Press, 1993), 145–53; and Robin West, *Progressive Constitutionalism: Reconstructing the Fourteenth Amendment* (Durham, N.C.: Duke University Press, 1994).

13. See, for example, Paul Cassell, "All Benefits, No Costs: The Grand Illusion of *Miranda*'s Defenders," *Northwestern University Law Review* 90 (1996): 1084–1124; Dallin Oaks, "Studying the Exclusionary Rule in Search and Seizure," *University of Chicago Law Review* 37 (1970): 665–757; and Robert Ellickson, "Controlling Chronic Misconduct in City Spaces:

Of Panhandlers, Skid Rows, and Public-Space Zoning," *Yale Law Journal* 105 (1996): 1165–1248.

14. Thomas Jefferson, Kentucky Resolutions (November 14, 1799), reprinted in Philip B. Kurland and Ralph Lerner, eds., *The Founders' Constitution* (Chicago: University of Chicago Press, 1987), vol. 5, 131, 135.

15. Smith assures us that his proposed legitimation of a judicial "prerogative power" to make decisions "according to discretion, for the public good, without the precept of the law, and sometimes even against it" (quoting Locke) "is not meant to encourage unbridled judicial activism." The question, however, is whether it would have that effect. Why would it not?

16. McConnell, "Originalism and the Desegregation Decisions," 947.

17. Argument of John W. Davis, Esq., in Philip B. Kurland and Gerhard Casper, eds., *Landmark Briefs and Arguments of the Supreme Court of the United States: Constitutional Law* (Frederick, Md.: University Publications of America, 1975), vol. 49A, 481.

18. Michael J. Klarman, "*Brown*, Originalism, and Constitutional Theory: A Response to Professor McConnell," *Virginia Law Review* 81 (1995): 1881–1936, 1882.

19. It is also logically possible they believed that the reach of their power under section 5 went beyond the practices prohibited by section 1. But the debates provide no evidence that any member of Congress entertained this position, and much evidence against it. See McConnell, "Originalism and the Desegregation Decisions," 1110–17.

20. All these votes are documented and presented in tabular form in ibid., 1093–1100.

21. 163 U.S. 537 (1896).

22. In fact, *Plessy* was more extreme than the position of the Democratic opponents of the Civil Rights Act in 1870–75. See McConnell, "Originalism and the Desegregation Decisions," 1128–31.

23. *Congressional Globe,* 42d Cong., 2d sess. 3124 (May 7, 1872).

24. *Congressional Globe,* 41st Cong., 3d sess. 1367 (February 17, 1871).

25. For a fuller treatment of this issue, see McConnell, "Originalism and the Desegregation Decisions," 977–80.

26. This and other similar quotations explaining the Republicans' understanding of social equality can be found in ibid., 1021–23.

27. Smith makes much of the single comment by the floor leader of the 1866 act that the act would not forbid school segregation, and of the early state court rulings in favor of school segregation. I refer readers to my detailed responses to these points in McConnell, "Originalism and the Desegregation Decisions," 957–62, 971–75. Smith appears to have missed the point regarding the state court decisions. It is true that the

courts that struck down segregation during this period did so on state law grounds and that those that upheld segregation did so on federal constitutional grounds. But this is attributable to the fact that courts considered the state law arguments first. Only those courts that interpreted the state law as allowing segregation would reach the federal issue. To treat this as evidence that the courts were unanimous on the federal issue is to confuse procedure with substance.

28. Those interested in the debate since the publication of my article should read the exchange between Michael Klarman and myself in the *Virginia Law Review* 81 (1995): 1881–1955; and that among Earl Maltz, John Harrison, and myself in *Constitutional Commentary* 13 (1996): 223–31, 233–41, 243–55.

14

CONSCIENCE, CONSTITUTIONALISM, AND CONSENSUS: A COMMENT ON CONSTITUTIONAL STUPIDITIES AND EVILS

MARK A. GRABER

Henry David Thoreau condemned both "the sanction which the Constitution gives to slavery" and judges who based decisions on constitutionality instead of justice.[1] "What is wanted," he insisted, "is men, not of policy, but of probity—who recognize a higher law than the Constitution, or the decision of the majority."[2] From these premises, Thoreau concluded that no person of integrity or conscience could remain loyal to a society whose constitution tolerated human bondage. He "[could] not for an instant recognize that political organization as *my* government which is the *slave's* government also."[3] The "only government [Thoreau] recognize[d] . . . is that power that establishes justice in the land, never that which establishes injustice."[4]

The majority of Thoreau's fellow abolitionists rejected this disjunction between justice and constitutionality. Lysander Spooner spoke for many Northern radicals when he insisted that "the constitution will not sanction slavery," that "slavery neither has, *nor ever had* any constitutional existence in this country."[5] Many sophisticated late-twentieth-century constitutional commentators have similarly interpreted the antebellum Constitution as imposing no obligation on abolitionists to choose between their conscience and the law. Sotirios Barber, for example, maintains that "judges with a constitutional attitude would have viewed the practice of slavery as inconsistent with the Constitution's broader purposes [and] would have considered the fugitive slave clause and other parts of the Constitution that recognized slavery as constitutional contradictions."[6] Indeed, most contemporary commentators (and citizens) perceive no serious divergences between their perception of justice and their perception of constitutionality. As Louis Seidman and Mark Tushnet observed, "Many participants in constitutional debate seem unwilling to live with an approach that generates *any* result they find unattractive."[7] The Constitution, most citizens believe, protects their most cherished values directly in the text and indirectly through a nearly perfect structuring of governing institutions.[8] Americans may debate what the Constitution means, but they apparently agree "that the Constitution embodies a public morality" that is "rich and inspiring,"[9] whatever that morality may be.

A number of academic commentators have questioned this consensual identification of constitutional with just or good. In 1988 Sanford Levinson insisted that citizens of the United States must consider "the possibility that life under even the American Constitution may be a tragedy, presenting irresolvable conflicts between the realms of law and morality."[10] Seven years later, Levinson helped organize a symposium, Constitutional Stupidities, in which twenty prominent legal commentators briefly discussed what each believed to be "the primary imperfections of our current constitutional scheme."[11] In this volume of *NOMOS*, Rogers Smith not only criticizes the American tendency to blur the distinction between constitutionality and goodness but also reaches the remarkable conclusion that *Brown v. Board of Education*[12] is a clear example of a good legal decision that lacked adequate constitutional foundations.[13]

Smith's analysis of the inherent deceptiveness of constitutional discourse promises both integrity and conscience. Intellectual integrity is maintained because scholars can state freely the real philosophical justifications for controversial judicial decisions and no longer rely on constitutional rationalizations that few sophisti cates take seriously. Judicial conscience is maintained because judges retain a prerogative power to dispense justice in cases in which the constitutionally mandated result is clearly stupid or evil. This power, Smith emphasizes, ought to be used sparingly. Significant costs to constitutionalism occur whenever justices base their rulings on grounds other than the framers' specific intent. Still, if *Brown* is an example of a case in which conscience appropriately trumped constitutionality, Thoreau could rest assured that Judge Rogers Smith would free fugitive slaves in those cases in which the Constitution required rendition.[14]

Smith's interpretation of *Brown* will not satisfy scholars who claim that the framers of the Fourteenth Amendment intended to mandate desegregated education,[15] although for reasons that Smith and others point out, this claim seems dubious.[16] Other commentators will criticize Smith's judicial originalism for unduly narrowing the scope of legitimate judicial argument. In their view, a constitutional modality other than originalism does provide a more than adequate justification for the *Brown* decision.[17] This critique has much merit, but such analyses evade Smith's central challenge. *Brown* may have been a constitutional exercise of judicial power, but all methods of constitutional interpretation that admit a gap between constitutionality and justice are vulnerable to unjust outcomes (think of slavery cases). The question remains what justices and other constitutional authorities should do when the Constitution requires a political wrong. Should they enforce the Constitution, resign, or misinterpret the Constitution in the interests of justice?

This brief commentary suggests that the central problem with Smith's chapter and other recent efforts to explore the gap between constitutionality and justice lies less in their failure to treat questions concerning the Constitution as difficult than in their failure to treat questions concerning justice as difficult. Either through the examples they choose (slavery or Jim Crow segregation) or their reference to "stupidities," modern constitutional critics imply a consensus among intelligent people on contemporary constitutional imperfections. In practice, however, alleged constitutional stupidities or evils exist only when a substantial part of the population regards those very practices as wise or good.

Particular gaps between constitutionality and justice, in other words, exist only from particular, contestable political perspectives. Given the disagreements that exist in any heterogenous society over what policies are wise and just, a constitutional union can be maintained only if most citizens are sometimes willing to sacrifice both integrity and conscience to accommodate persons who have a different vision of the best society. Thus, analyses of the amendment power, a judicial prerogative power or other means of responding to constitutional imperfections that fail to recognize that so-called constitutional stupidities or evils are rooted in honest disagreements over fundamental values may inadvertently encourage the abandonment of those crucial constitutional compromises that make constitutional governance possible.

Recognizing that constitutions are in part compromises among people with different notions of the good life cannot fully close the gap between constitutionality and justice. Just as constitutions may not embody the best political principles, so constitutions may inhibit necessary political compromises. Still, ongoing constitutional enterprises must be at least as concerned with reaching reasonable accommodations between citizens who disagree on fundamental values as with realizing those national aspirations that may exist. For this reason, contemporary constitutional critics and citizens can better conceptualize and respond to possible gaps between constitutional law and political morality by using rhetoric and examples that highlight the mediating role that constitutions and constitutional adjudication do and should play in societies that lack consensus on broad political principles.

Bridging the Gap

It is easier to identify the gap between constitutionality and justice in theory than in practice. Constitutions can obviously contain provisions that are venal, inefficient, or just plain stupid. The difficulty is determining just which provisions of a functioning constitution meet this description. Possible gaps between constitutionality and justice are difficult to identify in part because constitutional judgments can be contested. Whether the constitutional guarantee of free speech is indefensible, for example, depends on how the phrase "Congress shall make no law . . . abridging the freedom of speech" is best interpreted. If those words, properly interpreted, forbid only prior restraints, one set of Americans will find a constitutional error; if the First Amendment, properly interpreted, forbids the regulation of hate speech, another set of Americans will become constitutional critics.[18] Still, to the extent that constitutional reasoning is at all different from moral reasoning, most theorists should recognize some difference between constitutional governance and ideal governance.

The more fundamental problem in identifying possible gaps between constitutionality and justice is that judgments concerning political morality can be contested. For obvious reasons, living constitutions rarely contain uncontroversially indefensible provisions. Constitutional provisions that everyone agrees are stupid or evil are rejected by constitutional framers, formally abandoned by an article 5–style amendment, or informally abandoned by some practice that may or may not constitute an amendment, depending on one's idea of what constitutes an amendment.[19] In practice, therefore, alleged constitutional imperfections are ratified and maintained only when many intelligent people favor the particular constitutional provision under attack. Contemporary constitutional critics, unfortunately, write in ways that obscure these live controversies regarding constitutional justice. Some critics use phrases that seem to deny the possibility of serious political debate on the virtues of a particular constitutional provision, whereas others provide little help to the living by choosing dead controversies as their example of the gap between constitutionality and justice.

The titles of two works edited by Sanford Levinson illustrate how misleading language may inhibit sincere efforts to explore the gap between constitutionality and justice. The first work, "Constitutional Stupidities," highlights what each contributor believes to be "the stupidest, most mistaken, most deleterious, or their least favorite clause of the current Constitution."[20] The second, *Responding to Imperfection: The Theory and Practice of Constitutional Amendment,* is devoted to the nature and limits of legitimate constitutional change in the United States.[21] Together, the two works raise a troubling question. Why have Americans not amended their national Constitution to rid themselves of its constitutional stupidities? If the title "Constitutional Stupidities" is taken seriously, the best answer must be that Americans are too dumb to recognize or too lazy to remedy their constitutional foibles.

In fact, intellectual dullness explains few if any of the possible defects in our constitutional order noted in the symposium on constitutional stupidities. Consider Suzanna Sherry's reasonable claim that the Senate "is in conflict with the most basic principles of democracy underlying our Constitution and the form of government it establishes."[22] Sherry may well be correct that the United States would be more justly governed if the Senate as presently constituted were abandoned. Still, Wyoming citizens hardly seem "stupid" for supporting a constitutional institution that gives them more political power than would be warranted under the rule of one person, one vote. Moreover, many leading jurists believe that federalism and the Senate serve important values.[23] Justice Sandra Day O'Connor and others may be mistaken in their devotion to the states,[24] but judicial opinions and scholarly articles defending federalism and the Senate do not seem stupid by any conventional measure of stupidity.

To their credit, no participant in the symposium on constitutional stupidities actually charged the proponents of the offending provisions with possessing mental deficiencies. Still, even if the title "Constitutional Stupidities" is a rhetorical flourish, the term *stupidities* conceals how the amendment process actually functions in societies whose members disagree about the merits of various constitutional clauses.

In some cases, alleged constitutional imperfections cannot be amended because too many people have good reasons for supporting the practice under political attack. Even when proponents of constitutional change enjoy the support necessary to pass an amendment (however amendment is defined), they must still consider the theoretical problem that those persons raise who do not consent to the amendment (or the process of amendment) and the practical problems that nonconsenters may raise if they refuse to adhere to the new constitutional regime. The passage of a "no-slavery" amendment in 1850, for example, would have provoked a civil war.[25] Thus, given the potential costs of amendments that alter or undo vital constitutional compromises, the best response to some perceived constitutional imperfection may often be to do nothing. This political alternative, however, is likely to be overlooked by persons who think of offending provisions as "stupid" and not as expressions of different political visions that must be accommodated to some degree if Americans are to continue sharing the same civic space.

Smith finesses the constitutional gap between constitutionality and justice by defending the constitutional legitimacy of a now uncontroversially evil policy, Jim Crow education. His chapter does not criticize on constitutional grounds the specific result in *Brown*. Because Jim Crow education was part of the government's policies designed to maintain white supremacy, Smith correctly notes that the separate-school policies struck down by the Court violated the original and plain meaning of the Fourteenth Amendment.[26] The constitutional problem with *Brown*, in his view, lies in that decision's core holding that separate schools are "inherently and always unconstitutional."[27] Although Smith proclaims the goodness of that ruling, he maintains that the Warren Court's decision is not supported by the Fourteenth Amendment, whose framers tolerated separate racial institutions.[28]

The rhetorical power of *Brown* as an illustration of the gap between constitutionality and justice, however, may depend on an important ambiguity in Chief Justice Earl Warren's opinion. In one reading, the Court's holding in *Brown* was more historically specific than the word *inherently* might suggest. In this view, the justices were not concerned with the constitutional status of separate schools in all possible worlds. Rather, they believed that given the specific history of racial hierarchy in the United States and the specific place of segregated public education as a means of maintaining that hierarchy, no American locality in the foreseeable future could possibly institute a dual school system that provided white and black children with a truly equal education.

In a second reading, the justices gave *inherently* a much stronger meaning, that any racially segregated school system must be unequal. That is, *Brown* was about what Charles Black derisively called "the metaphysics of sociology: 'Must Segregation Amount to Discrimination?'"[29] If astronauts reported that on Mars little green children go to one school and little purple children go to another, constitutionalists who know no other facts about Martian society and history could nevertheless, according to this interpretation of *Brown*, confidently proclaim that Martian schools do not satisfy American equal protection standards.

The two possible meanings of *inherently* in the *Brown* opinion present Smith with a dilemma. If the Court was using inherently in the first, weaker sense, *Brown* may not illustrate the gap between constitutionality and justice for the reason Smith gives as justifying the specific result in that case. As a matter of historical fact, in 1954, "separate" could not be constitutionally equal. Hence, both justice and the Constitution supported the Court's ruling. If, however, the Court was using *inherently* in the stronger sense, then Smith does present a strong case that the Constitution as originally understood provides insufficient support for the basic principle articulated in *Brown*. Still, the gap between constitutionality and justice may not exist because separate but truly equal schooling is not an obvious evil. Many prominent persons of color now support resegregation because they believe that doing so will improve black education.[30] Perhaps they are wrong (as I think they are), but proposed black schools for black male teenagers do not present the clear injustice that might justify exercising a judicial prerogative power.

Even if aspects of Jim Crow were both evil and constitutional,[31] the strength of the ethical argument for *Brown* would still weaken it as a practical illustration of the gap between constitutionality and justice. *Brown* is a powerful example because that decision is so universally acclaimed that Americans will accept no theory of the judicial function that does not yield the result of that case.[32] In a political universe in which all citizens regard *Brown* as a great judicial decision, however, politicians do not attempt to reinstitute Jim Crow practices, at least in ways universally acknowledged to be inconsistent with *Brown*. Instead, American communities are reinstituting freedom-of-choice plans, challenging school busing, and asking the courts to declare past racial practices to be fully remedied. Unfortunately, by relying exclusively on court decisions striking down de jure segregation as his example of a good judicial ruling that nevertheless lacked sufficient constitutional support, Smith provides few guidelines that might help justices and citizens determine when and whether a prerogative power should be used to resolve those racial questions that currently divide Americans citizens.

A greater emphasis on live political controversies would also raise important concerns about possible judicial responses to perceived gaps between constitutionality and justice. *Brown* is too easy an example for any theory of the judicial function because, forty years after this decision was handed down, a strong consensus exists that the decision was substantively good and had good consequences.[33] No present exercise of the judicial power comes with the same guarantees. Instead, contemporary judicial uses of a prerogative power to resolve race and other issues will typically rely, perhaps implicitly, on a very contestable theory of justice.[34] As a result, no social consensus will exist when the Court's decision is substantively good. Such a consensus may never form or, as in the case *Dred Scott v. Sandford*,[35] the consensus that does form may regard the judicial decision as a moral outrage.

Moreover, because judicial prerogative powers almost always are based on contestable theories of justice, such rulings are likely to divide the body politic in ways that have harmful social consequences. A court too bent on achieving justice may undermine vital compromises that maintain national unity. When too few citizens actively support a judicial decision, even one that is substantively good, the decision may not be enforced or be enforced by unacceptably coercive measures. Citizens who feel betrayed by the judiciary may seek to regain control of public policy by promoting single-issue electoral politics or by engaging in terrorism. Thus, even though Americans may agree that the social consequences of *Brown* are, on balance, good, they have no reason that to assume future uses of the judicial prerogative power will have the same happy ending.[36]

CONSENSUS AND CONSTITUTIONALISM

At bottom, the central problem with both recent constitutional criticism and celebration lies in the dubious claim, explicit or implicit in too much constitutional theory, that Americans agree on certain political fundamentals. Those who celebrate the Constitution (or suggest that the Constitution may be worthy of celebration) typically maintain that the Constitution, properly interpreted, embodies a philosophically attractive consensus on sound rules and principles of governance. Publius, Barber claims, "supposes that the people of his generation are united in one coherent set of fundamental political values," and he adds, "those who believe that Publius's argument remains a good argument suppose that Americans are still more or less united in those values."[37] Contemporary constitutional critics similarly assume a philosophically attractive consensus among intelligent people on fundamental principles or ideal governmental structures. They maintain, however, that the Constitution does not fully embody this consensus. The point of the amendment process and a judicial prerogative power is to bring, formally or informally, American constitutional practice more in line with American political morality.

In fact, the best explanation for most gaps between constitutionality and justice is that at present we have no politically useful consensus on the best rules and principles of governance. Constitutional stupidities and evils exist in this political universe because, as Justice Oliver Wendell Holmes Jr. noted in *Lochner v. New York,*[38] constitutions are made for "people of fundamentally differing views."[39] Maintaining a diverse society in which "one person's notion of justice is often perceived as manifest injustice by someone else"[40] requires that citizens, out of deference to others, accept that their mutual constitution will not sanction what every party to the constitutional bargain regards as the true, the good, and the beautiful. Instead, from the perspective of each member of the constitutional community, the national Constitution is likely to include both unjust and inefficient provisions.

Government is likely to be given too much power to abridge some rights and too little power to protect others. Some fundamental rights may be missing altogether from the national charter, and other enumerated rights may license socially reprehensible behavior. Government may lack the power necessary to achieve certain vital national ends while being vested with too much authority over other matters. All parties to the constitutional bargain are also likely to believe that the structure of constitutional institutions contains certain design flaws, flaws that would have been avoided had they been the sole constitutional architect. One branch of government may have too many members, another too few. Electoral institutions may insufficiently reflect public opinion or tether elected officials too closely to popular sentiment. The different branches of government may be too prone to conspiracy or too prone to stalemate.[41] Providing uncontroversial examples of these constitutional infirmities is, unfortunately, impossible, because what some citizens perceive as unjust practices and principles, others will regard as necessary evils or positive goods. Pacifists, for example, may detest warmaking powers that militarists celebrate (or regard as too weak).

That constitutions are almost always compromises does not mean that no social unity exists on some deeper level. All Americans may believe in popular sovereignty, human dignity, or the value of autonomy. The problem is in the significant differences among specific applications of these general values and in the fact that members of a political order are likely to insist that their particular conceptions be constitutionally recognized to some degree. A constitution also might contain such provisions as a guarantee of free speech that will enable members of the constitutional community to reach a broader consensus in the future on fundamental values.[42] Even those provisions, however, are subject to compromise. Persons may disagree over the best institutional means for reaching that broader consensus on fundamental values. Other persons may believe that the best means for reaching this broader consensus threaten other legitimate interests and values. Allowing advocacy of race and gender inequality may increase violence against women and persons of color,[43] and allowing advocacy of racial equality may increase slave revolts.[44]

Of course, some persons take a purely instrumental stance toward various constitutional compromises, seeing them as pragmatic accommodations to be disregarded as soon as the forces of good can safely do so.[45] Any sincere attachment to the constitutional order, however, requires some respect for the unjust practices and unjust aspirations of the other. This is not to say that persons should sacrifice their most sacred principles to form a more perfect union but only that some relatively permanent sacrifice of principle typically is necessary if any human relationship is to endure for a long time. As Henry Clay pointed out, "the spirit of compromise . . . is occasionally necessary to the existence of all societies."[46] Hence, the first question one must ask in deciding whether to participate voluntarily in a constitutional order is not whether that order is nearly perfect but whether when compared with constitutional alternatives, it is sufficiently just to justify one's allegiance. "It is not necessary that the [Constitution] should be perfect," Madison observed. "It is sufficient that the [Articles of Confederation were] more imperfect."[47]

Citizens who recognize that constitutions are in part compromises would rather adjust than abandon their constitutional criticisms and calls for constitutional change. Persons responding to perceived constitutional evils, for example, realize that they must either persuade or coerce their political opponents, activities rarely discussed by contemporary constitutional critics. This greater emphasis on persuasion and coercion treats constitutional change as a political process, one with significant political costs and limits. In some cases, persuasion or coercion may be impossible. In other cases, the expenses associated with persuasion or coercion may outweigh the benefits of the desired political change. When these unfavorable conditions seem to prevail, members of a constitutional community must consider abandoning possible constitutional improvements and tolerating what they perceive to be an imperfect constitutional order.

In other circumstances, however, constitutional commentators concerned with promoting compromise might advocate constitutional change. Citizens might sometimes respond to a perceived constitutional perfection by proposing a less perfect constitutional amendment when doing so promises to reduce divisive social conflicts. Justices might exercise a prerogative power to settle fierce political debates in ways acceptable to most people. The *Bakke* case may be one instance when this prerogative power was used. Justice Lewis F. Powell's distinction between quotas and pluses in affirmative action programs[48] probably has little foundation in the Constitution.[49] Nevertheless, his *Bakke* opinion may have been a reasonable, though failed, effort to defuse the sort of racial politics that can seriously damage national unity.

Compromise is not the only constitutional or political virtue. Some persons, in their eagerness to please everyone, commit too many injustices. Other persons, unwilling to accept any compromise, consistently sacrifice attainable goods on the altar of an unattainable perfection. Thus, while assertions of constitutional aspirations remain central to constitutionalism, compromise must also play some role in theories of constitutional creation, maintenance, and change. For this reason, no discussion of possible gaps between constitutionality and justice that ignores the honest political disagreements among Americans over fundamental values can adequately conceptualize and respond to the numerous perceived flaws in the United States' republican order.

At the very least, constitutional critics must recognize that most constitutional stupidities and evils cannot be excised without any adverse impact on the health of the body politic. More often than not, public toleration of and support for such constitutional evils as slavery and racism plays a vital role in the creation and maintenance of a constitutional order.[50] Hence, the decision to limit or eliminate a constitutional stupidity or evil may entail the dramatic alteration, if not destruction, of the existing political order and all the virtues that made that order desirable to morally decent persons. When we cheer Thoreau for demanding that judges ignore the fugitive slave law, we should remember that the election of a regime that might have appointed such jurists resulted in a civil war that killed 620,000 young men.

NOTES

1. Henry David Thoreau, *The Portable Thoreau*, ed. Carl Bode (New York: Viking, 1964), 134.

2. Henry David Thoreau, *Reform Papers*, ed. Wendell Glick (Princeton, N.J.: Princeton University Press, 1973), 104. Also see pp. 98, 102–3, and, in addition: "In important moral and vital questions like this, it is just as impertinent to ask whether a law is constitutional or not, as to ask whether it is profitable or not. . . . The question is not whether you or your grandfather, seventy years ago, did not enter into an agreement to serve the devil, and the service is not accordingly now due; but whether you will not now, for once and at last, serve God,—in spite of your own past recreancy, or that of your ancestor,—by obeying that eternal and only just CONSTITUTION, which He, and not any Jefferson or Adams, has written in your being" (136–37).

3. Thoreau, *The Portable Thoreau*, 113 (italics in original).

4. Thoreau, *Reform Papers*, 129.

5. Lysander Spooner, *The Unconstitutionality of Slavery* (New York: Burt Franklin, 1860), 74, 20 (italics in original). Also see pp., 55–57, 89, and, in addition: "There is, in the whole instrument, no such word as slave or slavery; nor any language that can legally be made to assert or

imply the existence of slavery" (107, 114). For a thorough discussion of the many variations of abolitionist constitutional thought, see William M. Wiecek, *The Sources of Antislavery Constitutionalism in America, 1760–1848* (Ithaca, N.Y.: Cornell University Press, 1977).

6. Sotirios A. Barber, *On What the Constitution Means* (Baltimore: Johns Hopkins University Press, 1984), 200. See Sanford Levinson, *Constitutional Faith* (Princeton, N.J.: Princeton University Press, 1988), 192, 76–77; and Christopher L. Eisgruber, "Justice Story, Slavery, and the Natural Law Foundations of American Constitutionalism," *University of Chicago Law Review* 55 (1988): 273 (treating the fugitive slave clause as part of a constitutional effort to eradicate slavery). See also Mark E. Brandon, "The 'Original' Thirteenth Amendment and the Limits to Formal Constitutional Change," in Sanford Levinson, ed., *Responding to Imperfection: The Theory and Practice of Constitutional Amendment* (Princeton, N.J.: Princeton University Press, 1995), 219–28 (giving reasons why several prominent constitutional theorists would regard as unconstitutional a constitutional amendment entrenching constitutional protections for slavery).

7. Louis Michael Seidman and Mark V. Tushnet, *Remnants of Belief: Contemporary Constitutional Issues* (New York: Oxford University Press, 1996), 22 (italics in original).

8. Rogers Smith notes that students in introductory constitutional law classes automatically assume that the Constitution protects those rights they hold most dear. Rogers M. Smith, "The Inherent Deceptiveness of Constitutional Discourse: A Diagnosis and Prescription," this volume, 225–26. I have similarly discovered that students are loath to amend even relatively trivial constitutional clauses. Despite numerous European counterexamples, my students fervently believe that such constitutional features as bicameralism and an independent executive are vital to good government.

9. Owen M. Fiss, "Objectivity and Interpretation," *Stanford Law Review* 34 (1982): 739, 763. See Ronald Dworkin, *Freedom's Law: The Moral Reading of the Constitution* (Cambridge, Mass.: Harvard University Press, 1996), 38, 73, 104, 110 (describing "the Bill of Rights" as "a commitment to an ideal of just government"); Sotirios A. Barber, *The Constitution of Judicial Power* (Baltimore: Johns Hopkins University Press, 1993), 223; and Christopher L. Eisgruber, "Justice and the Text: Rethinking the Constitutional Relation between Principle and Prudence," *Duke Law Journal* 43 (1993): 1, 2 ("trac[ing] constitutional authority to the substantive goodness of constitutional norms"). For more general discussions of the tendency in contemporary scholarship to conflate constitutionality and justice, see Mark A. Graber, "Our (Im)Perfect Constitution," *The Review*

of Politics 51 (1989): 86, 87–92; and Smith, "The Inherent Deceptiveness of Constitutional Discourse," 231–42.

10. Levinson, *Constitutional Faith,* 59.

11. Sanford Levinson and William N. Eskridge Jr., "Introduction: Constitutional Stupidities: A Symposium," *Constitutional Commentary* 12 (1995): 139.

12. 347 U.S. 483 (1954).

13. Smith, "The Inherent Deceptiveness of Constitutional Discourse," 222, 242–46. For another stimulating work of contemporary constitutional criticism, see H. Jefferson Powell, *The Moral Tradition of American Constitutionalism: A Theological Interpretation* (Durham, N.C.: Duke University Press, 1993), esp. 277 ("Christians cannot adopt the language of [American] constitutionalism and remain faithful to their own social vision").

14. Smith, "The Inherent Deceptiveness of Constitutional Discourse," 247–49.

15. See especially Michael W. McConnell, "Originalism and the Desegregation Decisions," *Virginia Law Review* 81 (1995): 947.

16. See Smith, "The Inherent Deceptiveness of Constitutional Discourse," 242–46; and Michael J. Klarman, "*Brown,* Originalism, and Constitutional Theory: A Response to Professor McConnell," *Virginia Law Review* 81 (1995): 1881. For McConnell's defense of his original article, see Michael W. McConnell, "The Originalist Justification for *Brown:* A Reply to Professor Klarman," *Virginia Law Review* 81 (1995): 1937.

17. See Kent Greenawalt, "Constitutional Discourse and the Deceptive Attractiveness of Sharp Dichotomies," this volume, 255–69.

18. One reason that virtually all the contributors to the symposium on constitutional stupidities selected provisions concerning the structure of government may be that the clauses in articles 1, 2, and 3 are, with many exceptions, more specific and historically less subject to differing interpretations than are the clauses in the Bill of Rights and the post–Civil War amendments, which are almost universally interpreted as protecting the rights that a given interpreter believes any decent society would remove from majoritarian politics. One suspects, for example, that the reason that no participants selected as their "stupidity" the Constitution's failure to prohibit gender discrimination is the widespread belief among even weak feminists that, history to the contrary, most of the failed equal rights amendment is somehow implicit in Fourteenth Amendment.

19. For debates over what constitutes an amendment, see Levinson, *Responding to Imperfection.*

20. Levinson and Eskridge, "Introduction," 140.

21. See Sanford Levinson, "Introduction: Imperfection and Amendability," in Levinson, ed., *Responding to Imperfection*, 7.

22. Suzanna Sherry, "Our Unconstitutional Senate," *Constitutional Commentary* 12 (1995): 213.

23. See, for example, Deborah Jones Merritt, "The Guarantee Clause and State Autonomy: Federalism for a Third Century," *Columbia Law Review* 88 (1988): 1; and Michael W. McConnell, "Federalism: Evaluating the Founders' Design," *University of Chicago Law Review* 54 (1987): 1484.

24. See, for example, *New York v. United States*, 505 U.S. 144 (1992).

25. Significantly, perhaps, the Confederacy might have had a better chance of winning a civil war during the 1850s because of the lower level of industrialization in the North.

26. Smith, "The Inherent Deceptiveness of Constitutional Discourse," 242.

27. Ibid., 222. See *Brown*, at 495 ("separate educational facilities are inherently unequal").

28. Smith, "The Inherent Deceptiveness of Constitutional Discourse," 222, 242–46.

29. Charles L. Black Jr., "The Lawfulness of the Segregation Decisions," *Yale Law Journal* 69 (1960): 421, 427.

30. For a good survey of some issues that school resegregation presents, see Derrick Bell, *And We Are Not Saved: The Elusive Quest for Racial Justice* (New York: Basic Books, 1987), 102–22.

31. The law banning interracial marriage declared unconstitutional in *Loving v. Virginia*, 388 U.S. 1 (1967), may be a better example than *Brown* of an evil that was not unconstitutional.

32. See Klarman, "*Brown*," 1928–29 and n. 125 (citing sources making the same claim).

33. For a notable dissent on the latter point, see Gerald N. Rosenberg, *The Hollow Hope: Can Courts Bring about Social Change?* (Chicago: University of Chicago Press, 1991).

34. The only exception to this claim is when the judiciary voids such unenforced statutory relics as the Connecticut ban on the use of birth control that was declared unconstitutional in *Griswold v. Connecticut*, 381 U.S. 479 (1965).

35. 60 U.S. (19 How.) 393 (1857).

36. To be fair, Smith recognizes that *Brown* was extremely controversial in 1954 and that opponents of the Court's decision significantly limited the good that the justices could do. Smith, "The Inherent Deceptiveness of Constitutional Discourse," 248. Still, I think the exclusive

emphasis on *Brown* may help explain why Smith does not ask his readers to consider whether the judicial uses of a prerogative power are more likely to be substantively bad than substantively good, or if substantively good, destructive of important constitutional accommodations.

37. Barber, *The Constitution of Judicial Power,* 213. See Ronald Dworkin, *Law's Empire* (Cambridge, Mass.: Harvard University Press, 1986), 211.

38. 198 U.S. 45 (1905).

39. *Lochner,* at 76 (Holmes, J., dissenting).

40. Levinson, *Constitutional Faith,* 72.

41. As the debates over the Constitution indicate, virtually all the Constitution's *supporters* believed that the final product was marred by at least one of the defects described in the preceding paragraph. Madison, for example, favored proportional representation in both houses of Congress and thought that the final Constitution did not adequately limit the states' power to violate individual rights. See Max Farrand, ed., *The Records of the Federal Convention of 1787,* vol. 1 (New Haven, Conn.: Yale University Press, 1937), 36–37, 164 ("an indefinite power to negative legislative acts of the States [is] absolutely necessary to a perfect system"). See Helen E. Veit, Kenneth R. Bowling, and Charlene Bangs Bickford, eds., "Madison Resolution: June 8, 1789," in *Creating the Bill of Rights: The Documentary Record from the First Federal Congress* (Baltimore: Johns Hopkins University Press, 1991), 11 (proposing constitutional amendments that would limit the states' power to violate individual rights). Near the end of the Constitutional Convention, Hamilton asserted that "he had restrained from entering into the discussion by his dislike of the Scheme of Govt in General" and that he "meant to support the plan to be recommended [only] as better than nothing." See Max Farrand, ed., *The Records of the Federal Convention of 1787,* vol. 2 (New Haven, Conn.: Yale University Press, 1937), 524.

42. See Barber, *On What the Constitution Means,* 149–50; and Barber, *The Constitution of Judicial Power,* 191–92.

43. See Mari J. Matsuda, Charles R. Lawrence III, Richard Delgado, and Kimberle Williams Crenshaw, *Words That Wound: Critical Race Theory, Assaultive Speech, and the First Amendment* (Boulder, Colo.: Westview Press, 1993).

44. Michael Kent Curtis, "The Curious History of Attempts to Suppress Antislavery Speech, Press, and Petition in 1835–37," *Northwestern Law Review* 89 (1995): 785; Michael Kent Curtis, "The 1859 Crisis over Hinton Helper's Book, *The Impending Crisis:* Free Speech, Slavery, and Some Light on the Meaning of the First Section of the Fourteenth Amendment," *Chicago–Kent Law Review* 68 (1993): 1113.

45. See the sources cited in note 6, which claim that appearances to the contrary, slavery was really unconstitutional.

46. 16 Cong. 2d sess., 1094. Good marriages and good friendships also require persons to accept and accommodate some undesirable features of the other.

47. Alexander Hamilton, James Madison, and John Jay, *The Federalist Papers* (New York: New American Library, 1961), 237, 224–31 (discussing the Constitution as compromise); Philip Bobbitt, *Constitutional Interpretation* (Oxford: Blackwell, 1991), 170 ("it is not enough . . . for the critic to describe a possible world in which there is less injustice than in the present. He must also show that it is possible to actualize such a world"); Mark A. Graber, "Why Interpret? Political Justification and American Constitutionalism," *The Review of Politics* 56 (1994): 415, 434–40; Graber, "Our (Im)Perfect Constitution," 99–102.

48. *Regents of the University of California v. Bakke,* 438 U.S. 265, 315–20 (1978).

49. At least nothing in the text or history of the equal protection clause suggests that the distinction between quotas and pluses is of any constitutional significance. See generally Eric Schnapper, "Affirmative Action and the Legislative History of the Fourteenth Amendment," *Virginia Law Review* 71 (1985): 253 (discussing the many varieties of race-conscious measures passed by the Reconstruction Congress).

50. Edmund Morgan and others suggest, for example, that "racism made it possible for white Virginians to develop a devotion to the equality that English republicans had declared to be the soul of liberty," that "American economic opportunity and political freedom rest[ed] on Virginia's slaves." Edmund S. Morgan, *American Slavery—American Freedom: The Ordeal of Colonial Virginia* (New York: Norton, 1975), 386. See Bell, *And We Are Not Saved,* 26–50; and Donald L. Robinson, *Slavery in the Structure of American Politics 1765–1820* (New York: Harcourt Brace Jovanovich, 1971), 430–34 (discussing the "positive contributions" of slavery "to the founding of the country"). For a discussion of the centrality of this theme in southern proslavery thought, see Eugene D. Genovese, *The Slaveholders' Dilemma: Freedom and Progress in Southern Conservative Thought, 1820–1860* (Columbia: University of South Carolina Press, 1992), 18, 26.

INDEX